G000280248

201272911

ROGER WATERS
THE MAN BEHIND THE WALL

ROGER WATERS
THE MAN BEHIND THE WALL

DAVE THOMPSON

Backbeat
Books

AN IMPRINT OF HAL LEONARD CORPORATION

Published in 2013 by Backbeat Books
An Imprint of Hal Leonard Corporation
7777 West Bluemound Road
Milwaukee, WI 53213

Trade Book Division Editorial Offices
33 Plymouth St., Montclair, NJ 07042

Book design by Mark Lerner

Printed in the United States of America

Library of Congress Cataloging-in-Publication Data is available upon request.

ISBN 978-1-61713-564-4

www.backbeatbooks.com

Contents

ROGER WATERS
THE MAN BEHIND THE WALL

PART 1

The tradition of all dead generations weighs
like a nightmare on the brains of the living.

—Karl Marx, *The Eighteenth Brumaire of Louis Bonaparte*, 1852

1

Learning to Fly

The Wall was Roger Waters's first solo album.

He never told the band, such as it was, because there were times when it felt as though there wasn't really a band left to tell. Pink Floyd's last tour, shipping *Animals* across Europe and the United States, had ended fractiously to say the least, with a final night in Montreal, Canada, that saw guitarist David Gilmour absent the stage before the encore, keyboard player Richard Wright admit that the album was decidedly not one of his favorites, and drummer Nick Mason effectively sidelined from any part in the decision-making process whatsoever.

Waters himself was utterly conflicted, on the one side relishing the lifestyle that Pink Floyd's success allowed him to live so lavishly, but on the other hand resenting the compromises that the success demanded from him—the kowtowing to the industry, to the expectations of the audience, and to his audience itself.

Maybe he regretted the flash point that had already become a legend of sorts, when he spat full in the face of one especially enthusiastic fan on that final night of the tour. But not as much as he regretted the accumulation of all the personal triggers that provoked him to do such a thing in the first place.

Neither did his bandmates seem at all put out by the absence of Pink Floyd from their lives. Gilmour and Wright were both working on and promoting solo albums that presumably allowed them to exorcise whatever musical demons had been caged by Waters's increasingly firm hand on the Floydian tiller, and Mason was off producing the latest LP by Steve Hillage, *Green*, not to mention the second album by the Damned, one of the more ambitious bands hawked up by the British punk rock movement. Rumor insisted that the punks had actually asked their record label to procure them the services of Syd Barrett, Floyd's long-since-absent founder-member. He was unavailable, so they were offered Mason instead.

So, did Pink Floyd still exist? As a legal entity, yes. As a permanent fixture in the record racks, yes. But did Pink Floyd need to exist? That was another question entirely. So Waters proceeded as though they didn't.

Which turned out to be a lot easier than a lot of people might have expected. As far back as *Wish You Were Here*, in 1975, Waters had complained that the traditional sounds of Pink Floyd frustrated him, that he was limited by the need to shoehorn his increasingly personal, and increasingly bitter, lyrical worldview into the soporific free fall of the "typical" Pink Floyd epic.

He was tired of endless guitar solos, sick of keyboard extravaganzas that went on forever. He was fed up with his music being tagged as "space rock," and he hated the idea that his listeners got stoned and blissed out to the atmospheres when they should have been rising up to ride his lyrics and raze society to the ground.

That was what "Sheep," on *Animals*, was about: the fans who read in magazines, or were told by their friends, how to behave in Floyd's presence, and who didn't even consider the possibility that there might be a more enlightened alternative. For those people, the band's music was nothing more than a succession of sweet sounds and sweeping stereo effects with which to illuminate and enliven another night spent huddled around the bong.

Fans turned up at shows dressed more like the merchandising table than the merchandising table itself, as though fines would be levied on anybody who wasn't clad in full Floyd couture—a memory so ironically revived thirty-some years later, when seventies-style silken scarves were among the goodies tucked away inside Pink Floyd's Immersion box sets.

It was a problem Waters had always wrestled with. Ten years before, in the very infancy of Pink Floyd's career, Waters railed, "I've got nothing against the people who come [to our concerts] and I'm not putting down our audiences. But they have to compare everybody. So-and-so's group is better than everybody else. It's like marking exercise books."

Try telling that to the rest of the band, though. Gilmour enjoyed letting rip with his extended guitar solos; Wright was never happier than when expanding a keyboard motif to kingdom come. And Nick Mason, who had once been Waters's closest friend in the band (and was godfather to Waters's son, Harry) didn't really seem to care either way.

It was time, Waters decided, to go back to basics, and the two hours of demo snippets that Waters included on the Immersion edition of *The Wall*'s 2011 remaster, while scarcely a satisfying listening experience, indicate just how far from the Floydian norm those basics had shifted. Talking of his eponymous first solo album in 1978, David Gilmour remarked that he had been trying to escape the cult of musical perfection that had built up around the Floyd. That, presumably, was before he heard Waters's demos.

There was nothing here that spoke to Pink Floyd's core audience, nothing that touched upon the pastoral dreams or extended jams of old. Half of the "songs" weren't even songs; they were simply lyrics expelled at the speed of frustration, while sounds that may or may not have resolved themselves into a tune were strummed, thumped, or thundered out beneath them. It was as if Waters was creating an entirely new form of music, one in which the words themselves became the music, syllables as synthesizers, consonants as conga drums, glancing affectionately back at the rhythms that the young Bob Dylan discovered in his machine-gun poetics, and presciently forward to the raw vocal insistence of rap.

Waters had always written from the heart; now he spat from the soul. His words had always been personal. Now they were private, too. In demo form, *The Wall* was not a new Pink Floyd album. It was a first vicious volume of excoriated autobiography that twisted halfway through into the demolition of the very lifestyle that Floyd's success and popularity had made possible. Originally, the principle figure in the tale was even named Roger—Waters later changed it to Pink, reigniting still-bitter memories of the record company execs who somehow expected one of the band members personally to be named Pink Floyd—and you could trace his early life through the unfolding narrative.

In the years that followed *The Wall* and, thereafter, Waters's acrimonious departure from the band, it would become very fashionable to describe him as a dictator, furiously insisting that only his path was the right path. But friends agree, and history would ultimately accede as well, there was more to it than that.

Waters was not asking people to do what was best for him. He was asking that they do their best for the music. He loathed laziness; he despised the "this will do" attitude that so many people fall into once they have grown accustomed to success. His own personal standards were set so high that even the suggestion of a shortcut felt like a direct and deliberate insult. Was it really too much to expect other people to place their own endeavors on the same lofty pinnacle?

"We all had the opportunity to write as much as we wanted," Waters explained. "There was never any question of me saying 'don't write. I don't want your stuff.' I was desperately keen for everybody in the band to contribute as much as possible. But Nick doesn't write at all, and Dave and Rick are not prolific writers. So . . . it fell to me as a more prolific writer to fill in the gaps, to actually produce the material, which I have done and continued to do, clearly, since."

⁓

George Roger Waters was the youngest of two sons, following brother John. Born on September 6, 1943, he first opened his eyes in Great Bookham, a picturesque village in the south-of-London commuter belt of the Mole Valley, smack between the towns of Leatherhead and Guildford. Though there was not much commuting going on at the time. Britain was at war—had been for almost exactly four years (World War II broke out on September 3, 1939)—and Great Bookham, a mere twenty-three miles from London, was gripped by the same fears and restrictions that benighted the capital itself.

With good reason. Nobody, the parental Waterses among them, had forgotten the nights earlier in the conflict when terror rained down all round them—the long nights in September and November 1940, when Guildford was itself a target for the raiders, bombs blitzing down upon streets and stores that were as familiar to the family as those of Great Bookham.

There were targets in the village. Eastwick Park, a gorgeous manor house whose grounds contained Great Bookham Commons, was occupied by the Canadian artillery throughout the war, and the Germans probably knew it. They knew, too, of Polesden Lacey, the stately home where King George VI honeymooned.

The Waterses attempted to keep the war at bay. Both of young Roger's parents, his Scottish mother Mary (née Whyte) and his father Eric Fletcher Waters, were schoolteachers; Eric taught physical education and religious education at a time when the two were frequently twinned in the minds of British educators—robust young men in the service of the Lord were the backbone of society, it was believed, and the backbone, too, of such institutions as the Boy Scouts and the Boys' Brigade. Eric exemplified those virtues both through his bearing and his background.

He was a northerner; he grew up in County Durham, perched on the upper eastern shores of the island, a land where the coal mines were the inexorable fate awaiting any youngster whom destiny did not single out for a career in politics or sport, and even they generally put in an apprentice-ship beneath ground before going on to "greater things."

Eric was one of those who did escape, but his own father was a miner, at least until a fiery temperament, a powerful presence, and a gift for soul-soaring oratory saw him elected the Labour Party's agent for the city of Bradford, an assignment that staggered even a man who had grown up accustomed to the poverty and hardship that was a miner's life. Bradford had no mines; it was an industrial city, but only if the word "city" became a euphemism for "giant slum," where children barely even knew what shoes were, let alone had such things of their own, and home was whatever half-adequate shelter that despairing parents could fashion around themselves.

It was in Bradford, and so many other similarly appointed cities, that British Communism, and other forms of political radicalism too, took root, not as the intellectual playthings of the moneyed classes in the south, but as a utopian vision that perceived the most basic human needs—shelter, medical care, food, and a living wage—as the most basic human rights, rights that any incumbent government should supply to its people without a second thought.

If a man wanted to go into business for himself, manufacturing goods and trinkets that people wanted, then let him. But the things that people needed, the essential requirements of life, they should be a person's birthright. "Communism," in the hands of both intellectuals and fearful authorities, would become a byword for oppression, suffering, and worse. But to men like Granddad Waters and his son Eric, it was less a way of life than an indisputable right.

It was Eric's politics that kept him out of the war. Communist Russia's role in the forthcoming conflict was still unknown in 1939, but it was generally assumed to be hostile to the Allies. Treaties between Soviet leader Stalin and his opposite number in Nazi Germany, Hitler, bound the two nations together politically, while Russia's own territorial ambitions seemed no less ambiguous than the Nazis'. Two months after Germany (and, with far fewer headlines, Russia) invaded Poland, the Soviets made their move against Finland. It would be June 1941 before Hitler's invasion of the Soviet Union bound Russia together with the rest of the Allies; until then (and even after), Communist sympathizers in the UK were regarded with suspicion at best, hostility at worst. Many were interned, others kept under watch, and others still kept as far from the war effort as possible.

A declared pacifist, and registered as a conscientious objector, Eric Waters was enlisted as an ambulance driver, itself a profession that could scarcely be regarded as one of the war's safest. The ambulances were among the first vehicles to venture out once the bombs started falling, making their way into the heart of the resultant inferno to pluck as much life from the fires as the falling masonry, roaring flames, and choking fumes would allow. Only the fire brigade placed themselves so close to the frontline as the ambulance men, and even they knew when a building should be declared a loss and it was time to pull back. For the ambulance crews, as long as the possibility of life still existed, they were there.

Maybe it was the carnage that he witnessed on the streets of civilian England that drew Eric away from his early pacifism. Maybe it was the newly consummated marriage of Communism and Democracy against the common Nazi foe. Either way, Eric volunteered for the army.

He enlisted as a second lieutenant with the Eighth Battalion of the Royal Fusiliers (City of London Regiment), a regiment that grew out of the Tower of London's guard in 1648, and on January 22, 1944, his unit was among those that were first to land on Peter Beach, six miles north of Anzio, as part of Operation Shingle.

A massive operation built around the Allied advance on Rome and intended to outflank the German forces waiting on the Winter Line, the Battle of Anzio was destined to become one of the war's most bloody stalemates, as the German Fourteenth Army raced to counter the invasion, pinning down the Allied troops, flooding the marshes on which they were stationed, and allowing constant shelling and disease to do the rest. It would be May before the Allies finally broke through, by which time it was already too late for Eric Waters, service number 292975. He was reported killed on February 18, 1944.

His youngest son would not even have memories of his father. But he would have memories of his absence.

As the Allies moved up the boot of Italy and now gathered on the French coast too, a pincer movement directed at the heart of the German fatherland, the Nazis responded with a wave of unprecedented terror, pilotless V1 flying bombs that simply flew until they ran out of fuel (which was generally just enough to get them to London) and then fell to the ground and exploded.

Great Bookham lay directly beneath one of the chosen flight paths, not only for the V1 but also for their silent, rocket-propelled V2 successors, which meant that any miscalculation in the fueling, any problem with the motor, or simply any lucky strike from the ground and air defenses could send a bomb hurtling down upon them. Neither had the conventional air offensive ended.

Just a week after Eric Waters was killed, a German Dornier bomber was shot down over the nearby market town of Dorking. Two weeks later, another bomber, a JU88, came down close by. A V2 rocket hit Guildford in January 1945; another hit Leatherhead the following month.

Like so many children born while the war was still waging, young Roger would have few, if any, tangible memories of the war itself. But the fear that was every family's most constant companion, the mournful wail of the air-raid sirens that signaled another night cowering in the bomb shelter, the way his mother would clutch her children to her body, tight and tearful through the nights that never seemed to end—these things became a part of who he was, a part of his emotional DNA, and all the more powerful because of his youth.

Older children, brother John for instance, could chase away the fears of the night with the bravado of daylight, talking with their friends, discussing the sights they'd seen and the aircraft that had flown overhead—plane spotting was a hobby for almost every youth in the land through the war. There were bomb sites to explore, shrapnel to collect, and one another's bravery (or lack of) to draw from, a carapace of courage that transformed the most terrifying night into some kind of adventure.

A baby did not have those distractions. A baby simply lay in its crib, absorbing the sound, the fear, and the terror, wordlessly accepting that this was what life was. A succession of sirens, explosions, and screams, and the somber voices that floated out of the adult world, discussing the latest war news.

Finally Mary could take it no more. She applied for a new teaching post, scooped up her two sons, and fled to the relative quiet of Cambridge, one of England's great university cities, to a roomy, three-story terraced home at 42 Rock Road. The house itself was called Fleetwood, a pleasant name ideally in keeping with its surroundings; the River Cam meandered through Grantchester Meadows just a short bicycle ride away, and the pastoral tranquility of what remains one of the city's most beautiful areas would become her children's favorite playground.

The war was not wholly distant. East Anglia, the region over which Cambridge presides, lay at the operational heart of Bomber Command, the wing of the British Royal Air Force that oversaw the now-nightly raids on Germany. The Americans, too, were present in vast numbers—it was said you could not travel eight miles in any direction without encountering another US air force base, and when an operation was on, the skies overhead were literally blotted out by the silhouettes of the monster air fleets carrying the memory of the German bombing raids back to the embattled Reich. And so another sound embedded itself into the mind of the infant Waters, the deafening drone of hundreds of bombers flying overhead, and the sympathetic rattle of the very walls around him.

Then, when it was all over, when peace was declared and silence returned, the war hit home again, and this time harder than ever before. The fighting men were returning from the war, thousands upon thousands of conquering heroes coming home to reunite with the families they had left behind. Wave upon wave of them, released from service periodically so that the homecomings spread out across the next year or more, until Rock Road seemed to be in a constant state of celebration as father after father was reunited with his folks.

Except there were some families that did not have a hero to welcome. Some families that did not have a warrior to parade in front of their friends. Again, Roger would have been too young to be consciously aware of the fact. But the tears of his mother and brother were real enough, and so was the continuing fatherless silence of his house, compared to the bustle and noise of their neighbors and the street outside.

Later in his childhood, exploring his own home, he would discover the neatly folded and pressed uniform that his father once wore with such pride and distinction, and which his mother now kept in her bedroom. He would read the letter of condolence that she received when he died, signed by the King and thanking her for the sacrifice she'd made in the name of freedom. He would find photographs of his parents in happier times. He would question his mother and brother about his dad and treasure the memories that they were able to share.

And none of it was enough.

In September 1947, with his fourth birthday cake still a delicious, recent memory, Roger Waters enrolled at Morley Memorial Junior School on Blinco Road, just around the corner from his home. Mary taught there and would continue doing so after her son moved on to Cambridgeshire High

School for Boys, on Hills Road, seven years later. He attended Saturday morning art classes at Homerton College, and it was friendships (or at least acquaintances) that he developed this early in life that would come to shape his future, a decade and more later. Among his fellow students at both Morley and Homerton, albeit a couple of years his junior, was a pair of all-but-inseparable rebels named Roger Barrett and David Gilmour.

2

Raving and Drooling

In 1954, Waters arrived at Cambridgeshire High School, and anybody tracing his life through the music of *The Wall* has now arrived at the second brick. A half-century-old establishment operating beneath the firm grasp of the newly-installed headmaster Arthur William Eagling, the high school already had a prepossessing reputation. With the staff seemingly dedicated only to funneling their charges into the universities for which Cambridge is internationally renowned, discipline was drawn as much from the pages of *Tom Brown's Schooldays* and a firm military tradition as it was from any more modern curriculum. (Apropos of very little, Eagling's predecessor as head, a former MI5 officer named Brynley Newton-John, left the school in 1954 in order to emigrate to Australia with his family and six-year-old daughter Olivia.)

Students were expected to follow the Victorian dictate that children should be seen and not heard, and education was less a matter of being taught than being cowed into submission with sarcasm and blunt put-downs, which might have worked in whatever prewar golden age of unquestioned adult authority the various teachers held dearest to their own hearts. And it presumably was successful when one studied the roll call of old boys who went on to greater things—the Liberal member of Parliament Sidney Peters, philanthropist David Robinson, Nobel Prize–winner Clive Granger, botanist William T. Stearn, and William Tutte, one of the unsung heroes of the British war effort, a mathematician who cracked some of the most devilish codes the Germans had developed.

Among Waters's own contemporaries too, there were several who were destined for great things—or, at least, things that their teachers would consider great. Gerald Hayden Phillips, a high-flying civil servant of the 1970s and beyond (he was ultimately knighted for his services) was a year ahead of Waters at the high school; politician Kevin Tebbit was three years behind him.

Neither would go on to publicly describe the school's regime as anything but educational. The young Waters, however, had very different experiences.

The mid-1950s was an age of great social change. Short-lived though it was, the Labour government that swept to power at the end of World War II had initiated a raft of social reforms that could almost have stepped out of Eric Waters's private ambitions—a National Health Service that guaranteed free medical care to all who needed it, reforms throughout the welfare system, subsidized housing for those who required it, livable pensions for the elderly, and so much more.

The country was still struggling to get back on its feet following six years on the frontline of war, but the politicians who were aiding it seemed, for the first time, to have reached conclusions that idle dreamers and utopian planners of the prewar years had doubted would ever percolate into the halls of government: that a people who do not have to worry about the most basic human requirements will thus have the time, energy, and inclination to help the country improve its own position even further.

It was working, too, no matter that each of the reforms would eventually become a battleground on which the left-wing Labour and right-wing Conservatives would fight out their own beliefs for the next sixty-plus years. (The warring continues to this day.) For the people who actually stood to benefit from such programs—the sick, the elderly, the unemployed, the disabled—Britain's politicians had finally abandoned the selfish quest for personal gain that had hitherto been their most potent motivation and were actually thinking about the people they were supposed to be governing.

But it was a double-edged sword, at least so far as the authorities were concerned. With increased prosperity, there came increased leisure time. With fewer restrictions placed on people's lives, there came a demand for further rights. And by the mid-1950s, those demands, and that leisure time, had drip-fed down to, perhaps, the last people the older generation wanted to see start thinking for themselves: the young, the soon-to-be men and women who had once been encouraged to view their teenage years as just a necessary step toward responsible adulthood—and who now seemed to think of them as an excuse for unbridled bacchanalia.

Rising as one beneath the newly coined banner of "teenagers," quite possibly the most successful marketing term (for that is how it started) ever conceived, British youth began asserting the fact that kids had rights too.

Rock 'n' roll was born in 1955, and Waters, twelve years old and already looking for kicks, was drawn into its grasp. He built a crystal set radio (a popular project for boys in those days, with the instructions regularly published in every comic and magazine of the age), attached a pair of makeshift headphones, and spent his nights listening to Radio Luxembourg, beaming into Britain from across the North Sea and the duchy that gave the station its name with a musical diet that was far removed from the staid sounds that Britain's only broadcaster, the BBC, would give vent to.

The reception was appalling, a sea of static and hiss that rode weather patterns that regularly transformed the signal from inaudible to deafening in the space of mere seconds. But the music was magical anyway, a chance to hear the American rock hits as they were meant to be heard, as opposed to the safely sanitized homegrown cover versions that the state-run BBC made do with, linked by DJs who, if you didn't know better, sounded American as well.

Other nights, if "Luxy" was unlistenable, a twist of the tuning dial would pick up some real Americans, the American Armed Forces Network howling out of Frankfurt for the edification of all the American troops that were stationed in Germany, and offering them a taste of home as well.

Names like Elvis Presley, Little Richard, Gene Vincent, Jerry Lee Lewis sounded so different, so much more exotic, from anything that the homeland could conjure. And so did their music, raw and feral, exuberant and orgasmic. In Britain, radio was still dominated by the same novelty songs and neutered ballads that mom and dad had listened to (and grandmoms and dads as well). Now there was an alternative, and the kids wanted to live it. And yet people still asked why there was suddenly a generation gap forming.

Few of the traditional British chart toppers like Jimmy Young, Alma Cogan, and Dickie Valentine were older than the raucous Yanks whose sounds were deposing them. But the records they made sounded decades removed—grinning jingles about how she's a pink toothbrush and he's a blue toothbrush, gigglesome ditties to how he couldn't resist her once she got a transistor, stomach-curdling odes to pink cherry blossoms, Spanish eyes, and shifting, whispering sands. Cowboy ballads sung by soulless saps who had never been farther west than Acton.

And when Britain did have a stab at creating rockers of her own, the records were being made and played by the same old souls who had been running music into the ground for years already, old dance-band leaders and music-hall songsmiths who saw the demon beat as just one more fad to be milked for the month or two it lasted, then filed away in the novelty drawer. Even Tommy Steele, Britain's first true rocker, couldn't compete against their dictates. Compared to the monsters that America was spawning, there was no competition whatsoever. So Roger Waters grew into his teens riding the same waves of America-centric enthusiasm that consumed the rest of his cooler classmates.

Of course it couldn't last. The music industry will always win in the end, neutering the latest threat and returning pop to a softly spoken status quo of identikit heartthrobs and girls next door. By the very late 1950s and early 1960s, the initial flurry of rock 'n' rolling excitement had been almost completely replaced by callow youths with silly names (or, perhaps, sillier names), none of whom was guaranteed more than one or two hits before being airlifted to oblivion.

Jazz and folk were what the hip kids listened to now, especially well-bred cool kids like the Cambridge crowd. Serious music. Weekly dances at the Cambridge Corn Exchange, an echoing hall in the center of town, became the focal point of local activity. Coffee bars sprang up, where politics and poetry were downed with exotic cappuccinos, and record stores, where the demands of the now permanently fertile university-student populace guaranteed a constant supply of hot American imports.

Waters started collecting blues albums and never lost his love for them. Record labels with implausibly exotic names, hailing from impossibly distant American cities: Chess, Atlantic, Elektra, Vanguard, Memphis, Chicago, Detroit. Musicians whose careers reached back to the Great Depression, but whose lineage stretched back to the dark days of slavery: Howlin' Wolf, Willie Dixon, Big Bill Broonzy, Sonny Boy Williamson, Robert Johnson. Collecting their records was entertainment, but it was also an education. You learned about the world from the blues, a world outside the dreaming spires of Cambridge, a world beyond the monotone gray of Great Britain.

The first British blues bands were taking their initial baby steps. Mick Jagger and Keith Richards bonding over a Chuck Berry album on a suburban railroad station. John Lennon and Paul McCartney haunting Liverpool docks where returning seamen always had a few imported American records to sell. John Mayall, living in a tree house in a Manchester garden, playing along with the blues to which he would devote his entire life. Cyril Davies and Alexis Korner kicking their earlier careers in jazz to one side and adding electrifying rhythm to their acoustic blues. A musical revolution was under way, and a cultural one was to follow.

Suddenly, Waters's teachers were discovering that classes at the high school were no longer a matter of inculcating respect, restraint, and a love of the classics in the minds of their charges. Martin Amis, the future author, was gearing up for entry to the first form. Peter Fluck, a merciless caricaturist who would one day cocreate the satirical puppet show *Spitting Image*, was preparing to graduate. Another would-be artist, Storm Thorgerson, was there, and so was Roger Barrett, disheveled and disobedient, and not only far more interested in girls than his studies but happy to acknowledge that too. Overnight, the high school had stopped turning out future politicians and academics; it was a breeding ground for delinquency. Which, needless to say, was to be savagely suppressed with every weapon at the staff's disposal.

One of the most memorable scenes in *The Wall* finds our hero composing poetry in class, poetry that is snatched from his grasp and then read scornfully aloud by a master who is clearly unimpressed by his charge's efforts. In *The Wall*, the offending verse turns out to be the lyrics to "Money," which of course sets up one of the first (and only) laughs in the entire song cycle, as the audience smugly murmurs "shows how much he knows."

The reality of that particular situation, of course, was very different, although Waters's meaning remains the same. The art and writing being turned out by the students of the late 1950s was being created *for* the students too. Nobody dreamed of becoming the new Shakespeare or Dickens, Elgar or Holst, Constable or Waterhouse. Those names had their immortality, of course, but it was an immortality grounded in the time in which they worked. Which in turn was a long time ago.

The music of the day was what mattered; the literature and art, too. The first American beat poets were being fervently studied and imitated, just like the bluesmen of that same distant continent. And for some people, it was sufficient to simply reproduce their magic, to sound as authentic as the Americans themselves. For others, however, the brief was more complicated. They yearned to create a homegrown equivalent.

Author Colin MacInnes was in London, pounding out his fevered dissections of the city beat and emerging with *Absolute Beginners*, published in 1959 and destined to become the bible of the upcoming Mod generation. Harold Pinter was emerging as a playwright; theater critic and author Kenneth Tynan had not yet grasped infamy by becoming the first man to say "fuck" on British television (in November 1965), but he had already fucked the theater establishment with his condemnations of traditional thespian fare, then placed his money where his mouth was by championing, in 1956, the radical realism of John Osborne's *Look Back in Anger*.

Cliff Richard cut Britain's first true rock 'n' roll record, "Move It," in 1958, while his backing band, the Shadows, completely reinvented the electric guitar, gearing up for a sequence of inimitable instrumental-rock hit singles that would in turn inspire every key British guitarist of the next five years.

Everywhere, change was afoot, and the masters at the high school saw themselves as the last bastion of defense before the hordes of barbaric turpitude swept through the gates. Waters and his friends, on the other hand, welcomed the barbarians. Because only by scorching the tired old land would new growth be able to explode.

Yet the boy was not a total rebel. Not yet. Still growing gauntly into his lanky frame and the slim, equine face that Pete Townshend would one day describe as "strikingly handsome," Waters was, for now, more reliant upon the other quality that the Who guitarist would ascribe to him: his "incredible presence."

No matter that the weight of his personality was still comprised of a teen-age mash of bravado and belligerence, and the kind of unspoken toughness that dared the crueler kids to mock his bad skin. Still, he drew attention, and not always for what his teachers would describe as the right reasons.

Although he was also eminently capable of conforming. He played cricket for the school, a talented wicket keeper who was good enough to become a team regular, alongside Storm Thorgerson, whose mother was ranked among mother Mary's closest friends. The pair was on the rugby team too, alongside a couple of other friends, Bob Klose and Andrew Rawlinson. Beyond his propensity to mouth back at the occasional teacher, or question authority with a sneer on his lips, the young Waters's most rebellious act was to start smoking at age fourteen. (He quit in 1975 but vowed to resume again when he hits seventy-five.)

Mary, meanwhile, ensured that her youngest son balanced each of his personal interests with others drawn from her own experiences and beliefs. A Communist in her youth, she abandoned the creed in 1956, following the Soviet invasion of Hungary—an event that turned many party members away from what they had hitherto believed to be the purity of the Soviet system. Now she worked in local Labour Party politics, a fervent supporter of that administration's social policies, while also involving herself in other causes: the Anglo-Chinese Friendship Association, the Quakers, and more. Her son joined her in many of these.

But for several years, Waters's most consuming passion was the sea.

Aside from its obvious role, Britain's grammar school system was also very much seen as a recruiting ground for the military, with most educational institutions having their own army, naval, or air force cadet corps. Every boy in the school was expected to partake, unless they had a very good reason not to.

Tim Renwick, one of Waters's high school contemporaries, recalls, "I remember that Roger was permitted to not take part in the Combined Cadet Force because of the fact that his father had been killed in the war. I guess he must have been classified as a conscientious objector." Like his father, however, his exemption did not last long.

At age fourteen, he enlisted under his own volition and quickly found himself funneled toward a naval career, spending weekends at the HMS *Ganges* training school where youths aged fourteen and up were taught the art of sailoring. He surprised himself too, by actually enjoying the resultant lifestyle. He was taught to shoot, and would soon represent his school in small-bore rifle competitions. Only a seemingly incurable susceptibility to seasickness spoiled the time he spent with his fellow cadets at sea, aboard HMS *Vanguard*, but even that was not insurmountable. There are plenty of seamen who will argue that such an affliction is no barrier to a life at sea, and there were pills aplenty that could settle the stomach.

But he learned something else there: a capacity for becoming as demanding a taskmaster as the teachers he so hated at school. Given an inch of authority by the watching officers, he would try to take a mile, so much so that on one occasion, at least, the other cadets turned on him and gave him a sound beating.

In his defense, he argued that he rarely demanded any duty from his subordinates that he was not prepared to undertake himself. But that was no excuse for his behavior in the eyes of his victims. Just because he was devoted enough to want to wear himself to the bone doing something did not mean that they were as well.

Of course, Waters was never truly destined for a military career and tired of the discipline and orderliness. But his attempts to resign gracefully from the Combined Cadet Force instead brought him a dishonorable discharge, which itself was rewarded with untold admiration among the rest of the schoolkids. Without even intending to, he had shown himself to be a rebel. All he believed he wanted was the chance to be himself.

Aged fifteen, he joined, and quickly rose to chair, the Cambridge Young Socialists, and when the Campaign for Nuclear Disarmament (CND) raised its head, organizing vast marches and earnest seminars aimed at protesting the proliferation of what nobody had yet thought to christen "weapons of mass destruction," Waters threw himself into that, too.

The first truly youth-oriented political movement of the postwar era that actually threatened to make a difference to the world, it did not matter that even among CND's most devout adherents, the organization's social calendar was more an opportunity for typical teenage hijinks than a general political force. (More than one former member has acknowledged that CND rallies were a great place to get laid.)

Still there was a sense of involvement, of actually having a say in the future of the world, no matter how hard the authorities tried to dampen it down. Already resolute in his own feelings about the so-called nuclear deterrent, Waters began volunteering for the Cambridge branch of the Youth Campaign for Nuclear Disarmament, a branch of local CND groups established to address the concerns and interests of teens who were not studying at any of the city's universities. (Their concerns were handled by the Combined Universities CND.)

He was dating a girl. Judy Trim was not his first girlfriend, but she was his first serious one, the daughter of a research scientist at one of the universities, whose own inclinations took her into art. Born on October 11, 1943, making her just a month younger than Waters, she was aiming for (and succeeding in) A levels in art and natural sciences, while her politics already leaned so far to the left that Waters's own natural inclinations could not help but follow.

His mother disapproved of the girl from the outset: too smart, too respectable, too well-mannered. Mother Mary had wanted her boy to play the field, to sow all the wild oats he could before settling down with a "nice girl." Finding and falling in love with one while he was still in his teens, she was convinced, could only lead to problems later on, and so it turned out.

School, meanwhile, felt more and more irrelevant, especially as it became increasingly apparent that no ultimate career path had yet been carved out by his years in academia. His best subject, it seemed, was physics, but his failure to pass his A level in pure mathematics saw him forced to retake it twice. And when he did finally leave school in 1960, the idea of spending another three years in education mortified him.

Waters's initial intention was to study mechanical engineering at Manchester University. He opted, instead, to take a year off, a not too common practice in England at that time, and travel. With his friend Andrew Raw-linson ("Willa" in the song "Leaving Beirut"), and Mary Waters's car for company, the pair made their way across Europe to Istanbul, a three-month round-trip that they promptly followed up by hooking up with some more friends, and, all aboard an old ambulance that someone had christened *Brutus*, making their way back to the Middle East.

Brutus expired in Beirut, the victim of her occupants' ignorance about the needs of an engine. With her radiator bone dry, the noble beast went out with a bang, her engine exploding and stranding the friends with the not altogether unpleasant prospect of spending time in Beirut before hitchhiking home.

It was not an imposition. The city was just commencing its gallant forward thrust toward a Western idea of "civilized," at the same time retaining sufficient of its historical dynamic to offer a wholly new experience and, in the most exhilarating meaning of the word, education to impressionable young visitors.

Certainly Waters would never forget the absolute friendliness of the people he met there, Arabs and Westerners alike; nor could he help, in later life, to compare the wide open cheerfulness and magic of the city with the closeted paranoia that descended upon the entire region in later decades. Israel had yet to expand into territories beyond those it was initially granted by the United Nations; terrorism had yet to respond to that expansion by transforming Middle Eastern society into a battle zone. War had not visited Beirut, and neither had rabid politics. Seventeen years old, Waters had discovered an oasis that was as close to nirvana as he had ever seen.

But all too soon he was back in England, sitting through a series of aptitude tests devised by the National Institute of Industrial Psychology aimed at determining how his future should spool out. Back came the results—his greatest aptitude was for architecture, a subject he could not remember ever having considered for a career, and the necessary applications were made. He was bound for architect school.

Bidding farewell, or at least see you later, to girlfriend (and wife-to-be) Judy and friends Andrew Rawlinson, Tim Renwick, Roger Barrett, Bob Klose, David Gilmour, and Storm Thorgerson—and all the other people who had established Cambridge as the center of his universe—Waters moved to London in the summer of 1962 to study for his new career at the Regent Street Polytechnic. By the time he left, he had earned an intermediate diploma and become an associate of the Royal Institute of British Architects.

But he was already looking further afield, and far more important for his immediate plans was the cold-water flat he landed for himself, just off the Kings Road in Chelsea. He spent most of his student grant on music—a Spanish guitar and a couple of lessons—and most of his time with like-minded students, who, in that not quite organic but not especially premeditated way that so many teenage groups combine, would over time coalesce into a band. A band whose time, by the end of the 1970s, had finally run out. At college, he had been taught how to build a wall. Now it was time to tear it down.

3

Let There Be More Light

The Wall was not Roger Waters's only musical fascination as 1977 turned into 1978. He was also working on a second conceptual piece, one that was drawn at least in part from his experiences during his year hitchhiking around the Middle East and back across Europe, greedily absorbing whatever the outside world, and his internal imaginings, could offer him.

This second piece, which he had already titled *The Pros and Cons of Hitch Hiking*, concerned itself with dreams, and specifically with one single forty-two-minute sequence inside the mind of a sleeping narrator, himself perhaps, but just as likely not. Several sequences do ring true, however, not least of all the sexual encounter in an unnamed Middle Eastern locale that is interrupted rather brusquely by the arrival of some knife-toting locals.

Another encounter, fictional of course, was with Yoko Ono, and while some observers would shrug off great swaths of the story as the neurotic self-flagellation of a middle-class Englishman, pontificating on the state of the world without actually leaving his armchair, others saw in it that very same Englishman regretting the sad fate of the dreams he'd once enjoyed.

The enraged Arab gentlemen of the earlier song were no longer the aggressors, but a last line of decency against the tide of excessive permissiveness that masqueraded as popular entertainment. Yoko Ono was not the yowling, tuneless nemesis to John Lennon's life as a cuddly Beatle, but an artistic force that demanded only to be comprehended—a role that Waters certainly felt he could understand. And the domestic security to which the dreamer awakes, snug in his own bed with his wife asleep beside him, is not a cause for celebration nor a time to exhale, but a return to the humdrum where nothing ever changes because nobody can be bothered to get off their behind and make the first move.

The wife was Pink Floyd.

Two very different but in many ways conjoined projects, *The Wall* and *The Pros and Cons of Hitch Hiking* were remarkably vast in scope, even in rough demo form. What was perhaps most impressive, however, was that both were all but completed by July 1978, that is, within twelve months of the final concert on Pink Floyd's most recent tour.

—

Some two years earlier, Pink Floyd had joined the queue of showbiz and sporting personalities who sank their financial well-being into a newly formed investment company, the Norton Warburg Group, fronted by a very plausible, very convincing, twenty-nine-year-old accountant named Andrew Oscar Warburg.

With an apparently blemish-free couple of years already behind it, Norton Warburg offered Pink Floyd an excellent opportunity to put their earnings to work for them via a series of carefully selected investments that would also serve to shield the band's earnings from Britain's then-incumbent Labour government's rapacious 83 percent taxation demands.

It was a scenario that Waters both welcomed and disdained. His up-bringing as the son of two true-blue Labour diehards and the years he spent with his first wife Judy, still a committed left-wing activist and thinker, had long since inculcated him with the knowledge that it was through taxation that the social programs he had grown up alongside were financed. Neither of his parents had ever resisted paying "their fair dues" to the government, and neither, in the past, had he.

But there was a big difference between what had once been considered fair and what was now being demanded. A difference that was not being spent on the programs that required it, but was instead being frittered on . . . well, there was the monumental debt that the country now owed, as a result of too many years spent living beyond its means and too little attention being paid to finding self-sufficient alternatives to the country's actual needs. The health service was losing money; unemployment was skyrocketing; a front-line military force was being maintained, and actually expanded, even as the country's capabilities and requirements sank into a backwater. The government itself seemingly had lost faith in its ability to haul itself out of the mire.

So what did it do?

It increased taxation.

Norton Warburg offered a legal loophole through which a lot of people could save a lot of money, and Pink Floyd grasped it.

The band was, by any standards you care to name, rich. Not ostentatiously so—there were no color supplement spreads of their country homes or opulent motorcars, although that's not to say they didn't own them.

They were part of the blue-ribbon group that established the Hollywood eatery Le Dôme, among the most storied in mid-1970s America. Owner Eddie Kerkhof set about attracting investors by offering $5,000 in mealtime credit to anybody prepared to stump up $3,000 in start-up capital. Fellow investors included Rod Stewart, Elton John, Dudley Moore, and Olivia Newton-John, the now-grown-up daughter of a former Cambridge High School headmaster.

But Pink Floyd had never seriously thrown their capital to the wolves of high finance before, and, with hindsight, the prospectus they were now examining was chilling. It called for the investment of large amounts of money into a series of unspecified new businesses, in the hope that they would buck the prevalent trend of bankruptcies and closures and succeed in an economy that was being raped by inflation and debt. But Norton Warburg's pitch was convincing, and any spoken fears were swiftly reassured. The enterprises they would invest in were sound. And if they weren't, an unspoken subtext now seems to mumble, the band had enough money to keep them afloat until things turned around.

How much of Pink Floyd's money Norton Warburg actually invested is disputed. The financiers estimated a little over a million and a half pounds; Floyd's accountants would double that sum. Either way, some remarkable new businesses were launched on Pink Floyd's dime: £215,000 was spent on a 55 percent share in a skateboard importer and distributor called Benjyboards in the belief that the American craze for skateboarding was poised to make a major splash in Britain. (It wasn't.) Another £180,000 was sunk into a 60 percent share in the Willow Canal chain of floating restaurants, £450,000 bought a 20 percent share in their broker's own Norton Warburg Investments enterprise, a million and a half pounds purchased the band 100 percent ownership of a firm called Cossack Securities, and so on.

Few of which even remained afloat, let alone turned a profit.

In his defense, Warburg pointed to the investments that had worked: a real estate deal here, a carbon-fiber boat maker there, and a chain of what were laughably described as American-style pizza restaurants called My Kinda Town, best remembered for their dull decor and even duller menus. How they managed to prosper is a gastronomic mystery.

But the losses continued to grow, and as Pink Floyd's manager Steve O'Rourke, a bespectacled hipster who had worked alongside the band for a decade, looked deeper into the accounts, he came upon another disturbing development. The band's tax planning, too, had been mishandled, not only leaving them liable for taxes on the money they had lost, but also for cash they had never even received.

In September 1978, the band officially announced that they were severing all ties with the Norton Warburg Group and demanding the immediate return of the close to a million pounds that the company had on deposit but had not yet found a way of frittering away. They would also file a million-pound lawsuit alleging fraud and negligence. (Norton Warburg finally crashed in 1981 with multiple debts across the spectrum; Warburg fled to Spain but returned to the UK in 1987, when he was sentenced to three years' imprisonment for fraudulent trading and false accounting.) But all concerned knew that it would be years before they saw any redress. In the meantime, their battered finances needed a swift injection that would remedy the losses. And there was no point in even questioning what form it would have to take.

Within weeks of O'Rourke uncovering the catastrophe, Pink Floyd had reconvened at the Britannia Row studios the band had built three years earlier and let it be known that the complex was going to be in constant use for the next six months. At the same time, it was reported that EMI, Floyd's record label in the UK, and CBS in the USA, had between them stumped up almost five million pounds by way of an advance on a new Pink Floyd album—sums that were chicken feed when compared to the profits that a new album was undoubtedly destined to make, but it was a sizable figure regardless. All Floyd needed to do was repair the headache-sized breaches that had sundered them in the first place . . . and decide which of the two potential projects delivered up by Waters, *The Wall* or *The Pros and Cons of Hitch Hiking*, they wanted to turn their attention to.

It was not going to be an easy decision. Returning again to the demos that Waters has since aired in public, it is not hard to concur with David Gilmour's insistence that they were both unlistenable and largely incomprehensible.

A rough singer at the best of times, as too many of the band's live recordings glaringly reveal, Waters worked with whatever tools he had to hand and was far more concerned with getting his ideas down on tape than ensuring that the ideas actually translated into anything another set of ears might recognize.

Which could explain why his bandmates' original inclination was to work on *The Pros and Cons* and why the first few weeks in the studio were spent attempting to bring even a hint of Floydian grandeur to a work that might have been better addressed as a spoken-word project, or even a book of verse.

But ultimately they had no faith in it, nor interest, a state of affairs that made *The Wall* look more and more alluring, despite it suffering from many of the same drawbacks as its companion. At least the themes presented in *The Wall* were easily understood and related to by the average joe, within the world of Floyd's own past lyricism anyway, and the great swaths of autobiography that fed into them could likewise be scoured for some identifiable emotions. No matter that the most blatant aspect of *The Wall*, the whole story of a media messiah being shaped in part by an abusive childhood and the early death of his father in wartime, and wrestling his elevation to fame against a growing hatred of that fame, had already been told. The first half was basically the premise of the Who's *Tommy*, the second was a movie created by writer Ray Connolly back in 1974, the ultimate requiem for the star-crossed star, *Stardust*.

Sufficient personal detail drawn from Waters's own life allowed *The Wall* to quickly cloak in novelty the elements that might have otherwise seemed familiar, while the multimedia possibilities of the project—at Waters's dictate, both the stage show and the later movie were being constructed hand in hand with the album—likewise ensured *The Wall* would take on a life of its own.

With one final adjustment. They needed a referee.

Or maybe that is too strong a word for it. Rather, they needed an outside presence, somebody who would be sympathetic both to Waters's ambitions and his bandmates' concerns, but whose primary purpose lay in helping the band find the path that was best for the project as opposed to the individual egos. It would be too easy, left to their own devices, for the entire session to be devoured by arguments and criticism, a situation that had scarred so many of their past recording sessions in the years after they had dispensed with an outside producer. A temporary fifth set of ears in the studio would serve as a sounding board for both sides of any dispute, but would also be there to speak up for *The Wall* itself.

Waters knew who he wanted to recruit. Canadian producer Bob Ezrin had been a friend for some years, but more than that, he was one of the few producers around who might instinctively understand the sheer grandeur and scope of the slowly spooling project, because those were qualities that he brought to bear on every record he had ever been involved in.

Thrust to international attention as the producer behind Alice Cooper's 1971 to 1973 age of over-the-top rock 'n' roll, Ezrin had been Lou Reed's collaborator on the chilling *Berlin* album, the power behind Kiss's almighty *Destroyer*, and, just a year earlier, the master alchemist who gave Peter Gabriel's eponymous first album such vibrant life.

Ezrin was to the grandiosity of 1970s rock what Phil Spector was to the 1950s and Andrew Loog Oldham to the 1960s, the creator of a veritable wall (no pun intended) of sound that offered the listener the ultimate immersive experience. As Larry Fast, keyboard player on that Gabriel disc, explains, "Bob's instinct was to go bigger. Some tracks had orchestra overdubs done, even though the final releases did not."

He also had a reputation for thoroughness. Fast again: "Bob certainly let it be known when he had a specific idea that he wanted incorporated into the arrangement or overdubs. [He] set up the framework he wanted to hear, and would focus on some specific details that were pivotal. He did not micromanage every last thing. If he wasn't hearing what he wanted, though, things would be reworked until he got to his goal."

That was the approach he had always taken in the past, and it was that, Ezrin informed Waters when the invitation was extended, that hallmarked the approach he would take with Pink Floyd. Not only would he not take sides, he also intended to be merciless, even demanding absolute control over the proceedings, all the way down to rewriting lyrics or musical passages. Waters agreed but warned Ezrin not to expect to be given any credits.

Ezrin's first move was to sideline Waters altogether. He sat down instead with Gilmour to listen through the demos and to make the decision about what should be kept from a musical standpoint and what should either be rebuilt or rejected.

Waters, meanwhile, was taken back to the drawing board and talked through the entire concept, the entire story line, and told to either rewrite, or have rewritten, any elements that Ezrin disagreed with. One all-night session, the producer later said, was all it took him to completely redesign *The Wall*, rearranging both the mood and the running order of the songs, transplanting elements from one place to another, calling upon all his own training and experience as a writer to construct an album that flowed like a novel. A good novel.

New songs were written; old collaborations were revisited. While *The Wall* would remain Waters's baby from start to finish, Gilmour immediately grasped two cowriting credits, on the cock rocking "Young Lust" and the soaring finale of "Run Like Hell." Ezrin, too, was publicly acknowledged as the brains behind the music-hall interlude "The Trial," the kind of spoken-word-over-eerily-spiraling atmospherics that he had blueprinted on Alice Cooper's *Welcome to My Nightmare* in 1975. And when Ezrin found himself requiring one more song, for one specific moment in the cycle, he turned not to Waters but to Gilmour and wrung from him a song that the guitarist originally wrote for his *David Gilmour* solo album the previous year but didn't complete in time. It was called "Comfortably Numb," and in any worthwhile poll of the best songs on *The Wall*, it remains the undisputed king of the castle.

Even when the sessions were going well, however, outside pressures conspired to disrupt life. The fallout from the Norton Warburg saga had finally reached the ears of Britain's Inland Revenue, and officious beetle eyes were now being cast on the band's very whereabouts.

The tax structure of the time allowed breaks to be granted if a certain proportion of a taxpayer's income was derived from work undertaken overseas. That was why the Rolling Stones, and so many others, placed themselves into tax exile earlier in the decade; that was the cause of the "brain drain" that sucked so much talent and ability out of mid-1970s Britain. Roger Waters had always fiercely resisted his accountant's suggestions that he relocate overseas, establishing himself as just one of a handful of so-called superstars whose love of their homeland was greater than their love of money. But now he had no choice. Unless they wanted to be truly crippled by the tax man, Pink Floyd needed to vacate their homeland and finish the album overseas.

They traveled first to France, where Super Bear Studios in the southern idyll of Miravel had accommodated both Gilmour's and Wright's recent solo prolusions; later, they would move across the Atlantic and continue work in a string of American studios. And then, when it was time to return to everyday life, they traveled to the new lands that they now called home: Mason set up his personal tax exile in France, Gilmour and Wright on the Greek islands, and Waters in the rich rock 'n' roller's favorite haven of them all, Switzerland.

It is a fiction that bandmates are also often best mates. Richard Wright remarked on several occasions that he had never considered Roger Waters a friend, an observation that would be opened up for all the world to see before the sessions for *The Wall* were complete.

Degrees of friction and animosity will always exist; power plays will almost always take place. Generally, however, such disagreements are as much a part of the creative process as the moments when all are in agreement, and only at the beginning of a band's career does it become necessary for all concerned to develop any kind of bunker mentality, stuffed into the back of the van on a figurative survival course, learning to survive on the rock 'n' roll equivalent of roadkill and tree bark. When there are four of you, plus roadies, and just a single roll of toilet paper to see you through till the end of the tour, you learn to adapt.

Pink Floyd had been through that regime, but they had outgrown it quickly. Two hit singles straight out of the box and the knowledge that every new album was guaranteed a lofty chart position saw to that.

What the individual musicians did have was the ability to lock their music together—the consequence, perhaps, of the years they had spent as a proto–jam band in the late 1960s, improvising three or four songs to the length of their scheduled concert set. Now, under Waters's sharp instructions, but more importantly, Bob Ezrin's disciplined regimen, they found themselves going in the opposite direction entirely, reducing an idea that might once have lasted twenty minutes to barely one-tenth that length, while retaining all the focus they had once spread so far.

Pink Floyd had discovered brevity, and the short sharp shocks that Waters had long dreamed might someday deliver his lyrics were splashed across *The Wall* like spray-painted graffiti, sentiments punctuated by sudden exhalations of sound. And the longer the mixing process went on, the more abrupt the music became.

Tapes arriving from the UK delivered the sound effects that Ezrin deemed essential to the project, Britannia Row engineer Nick Griffiths working off a long list of desired noises, then making it his business to either arrange, construct, or discover them.

Included on the shopping list were the voices of a couple of schoolchildren singing a few lines from the song "Another Brick in the Wall (Part 2)"; it was Griffiths who decided that a whole class of kids would sound even better, so he popped round to Islington Green School, just a few blocks from the studio, and arranged to borrow the entire twenty-three-strong fourth form music class for an afternoon.

Orchestration was called for, but whereas Waters's instincts might once have led him back toward Ron Geesin, with whom he had constructed both Pink Floyd's *Atom Heart Mother* and the 1972 movie soundtrack *The Body*, now he acceded to Ezrin's edict and called in Michael Kamen, the brilliant New Yorker who had once been a part of the New York Rock

Ensemble, an ambitious if not exactly scintillating attempt to harness disciplines that would later be absorbed into progressive rock by playing the classics on conventional rock instruments, and rock on traditional classical tools.

Waters himself had not been a fan of the Ensemble. They sounded like "something Pete Townshend might have written when he was four" was his studied opinion of one of their records when a 1970 *Melody Maker* interview asked him to comment. But Kamen had redeemed himself, plunging into the worlds of ballet and Hollywood, and only occasionally dipping back into the world of rock. And when he mused on *The Wall* in an early 1990s interview, he recalled that even the perfectionist Waters left him alone with the music, sequestered away in New York City overdubbing scores that utilized up to fifty-five instruments onto tapes that were delivered from the studios in Miravel. Neither would he learn of any criticisms once the job was complete. "If there were any changes called for, I don't recall them. They would have been minor." Laughing, he said he didn't even get to meet his employers until the album was all but complete.

Which, by early November 1979, it was—but by then both band and record had changed significantly. The triple album that Waters originally envisioned had been carved down to a double; a sleeve design was commissioned from artist Gerald Scarfe, stepping in to replace the customary, and expected, services of old Cambridge friend Storm Thorgerson and his design company Hipgnosis. And keyboard player Richard Wright was bought out of the band's four way partnership, and then rehired as a session musician.

4

Another Hit in the Hall

The release of Pink Floyd's first British single in a decade—following ten years of steadfastly and purposefully snubbing the medium—was guaranteed a modicum of success whatever it might have sounded like. Mere curiosity would ensure that, at least, but the British media pushed it to the point of a national event. And once people actually heard the thing, there was no holding it back.

Back in the early 1970s, when Pink Floyd first enacted their injunction against 45 rpm tasters for new LPs in the UK, they were in fine company. Led Zeppelin had started the trend, but so many others were quick to follow, with both Yes and Emerson Lake & Palmer joining the Floyd in the exclusive no-singles club. Other bands—the likes of Black Sabbath, Genesis, and Deep Purple—were not quite so stringent, and all three would enjoy occasional hits. But they accepted 45s as a requirement of their contracts and made no effort whatsoever to promote them. They made it plain that singles were the record company's plaything and had nothing to do with the band—for they were all serious musicians, with no time for the frivolities of the weekly televisual antics of *Top of the Pops* and teenybop followings.

By the late 1970s, however, the worm had started to turn. ELP bounced back into action in 1977, after three years of hiatus, and promptly scored a massive UK hit with their rendition of Aaron Copland's "Fanfare for the

Common Man." Yes released their most rocking long-player yet, *Going for the One*, and racked up a brace of short, sharp hits. Genesis shed front man Peter Gabriel and celebrated when "Follow You Follow Me" made its way onto the British chart.

Suddenly a hit single was no longer something for musicians to feel ashamed of, and the spotlight now turned on making sure that a band's latest album had something that could be released as a single. ELP had to ruthlessly edit "Fanfare for the Common Man" down to fit onto a three-minute seven-inch, but even if Pink Floyd had been of a mind to join them, nothing on *Animals* could have been similarly sliced. *The Wall*, however, was a different proposition. Twenty-five tracks spread across four sides of vinyl wasn't simply the most generous offering the band had ever made, it was also their first to be positively bristling with potential hits, a point that Bob Ezrin took it upon himself to belabor in his conversations with the band.

He was a firm believer in the importance of singles, not necessarily for their "hit potential," but for the extra exposure they brought to a project, for the ease with which they could be picked up by DJs and spun into rotation without them having to first wade through an entire LP in order to find something suitable.

"Another Brick in the Wall (Part 2)" was the lucky, and exquisitely well-chosen, first choice.

Riding in, as do so many of Pink Floyd's signature numbers, on a distinctive Waters bass line (which in this case bore a striking resemblance to the super funk faux disco of the Climax Blues Band's 1976 hit "Couldn't Get It Right"), "Another Brick in the Wall (Part 2)" had everything a hit single could demand: an easily digestible message that was likewise easy to identify with, a chorus that was custom built for mass sing-alongs, and a mass sing-along of its own in the shape of the piping tones of the Islington Green School crowd.

And when more than one bemused listener described it as sounding like something from the soundtrack to Lionel Bart's *Oliver!* — that glorious *tout ensemble* chorale piece in which the titular hero's request for more food is greeted by a stomach-curdling litany of dire threats and punishments — maybe that opened another door through which a formative influence on *The Wall* could squeak. The schoolteacher who humiliates *The Wall*'s hero by reading aloud his poetry to the class is not at all far removed from the bullying beadle who makes the orphan Oliver Twist's life such a misery.

The sentiments of the song are reversed, however. In *Oliver!*, the song threatens dreadful consequences for the boy. In "Another Brick in the Wall (Part 2)," another in that glorious line of anti-school songs whose lineage stretched back to Alice Cooper's similarly schemed "School's Out" (which was also a Bob Ezrin production, of course), the boot is on the other foot. It is the teacher who is being answered back to.

So there was a lot to think about, and a lot to love. Released in the UK on November 16, 1979, "Another Brick in the Wall (Part 2)" sold 340,000 copies in its first week, steamrollering to the top of the chart within a week, and remaining there for the rest of the year. In America, it added another month at the top, and suddenly a band that had never cared two hoots for hit singles was closing out the decade with one of the biggest smashes of the age, and every other hit-hungry hopeful of the day, from Blondie to Paul McCartney, from Madness to Michael Jackson, saw their own latest offerings scattered in Floyd's wake.

All that before the main attraction had even hit the stores.

Riding the back of the hit single (but confident that it would have done so regardless), *The Wall* demolished all before it, its success not only vindicating Waters's decision to so radically alter the course of Pink Floyd, but also sowing the seeds for the events of the next few years.

His bandmates, Gilmour in particular, argued vehemently against the media's own suggestion that *The Wall* was essentially a Roger Waters solo album, rightfully pointing toward the countless hours that he, Gilmour, and Bob Ezrin had devoted to transforming the original concept into a listenable experience. He highlighted the contributions that both made to the songwriting, credited and uncredited; to the lead vocals he added throughout the two discs; and to the solos he laid down that, in sonic terms, were as self-defining as anything Waters brought to the show.

But it didn't matter. It may have been a Pink Floyd album, but it was one man's concept, and it also became swiftly apparent that there would have been no argument whatsoever had Waters himself decided to abandon *The Wall* at the outset of the sessions and suggest the band go back to the music they had built their last three albums around (not to mention their fame and fortune). In fact, if you want to get really down and dirty cynical, it could be argued that *The Wall* was only a Pink Floyd album because Pink Floyd needed the money. Without Andrew Warburg and his financial doings, Waters would probably have made it alone. He might even have used Bob Ezrin.

Nonetheless *The Wall* was released unequivocally as a Pink Floyd album, and so Pink Floyd set out to promote it, piecing together a tour that made past excursions into elaborate showmanship resemble a pub band with a half-cocked light show, and making plans, too, for the movie that had always been an integral part of Waters's vision.

In his studio in London's Fulham Road, cartoonist Gerald Scarfe was already at work on the animation, building from, and around, his designs for the album jacket to create the nightmarish world of grotesque caricatures and chilling symbolism that would bring the vision to life.

Seven years Waters's senior, Scarfe had been a constant presence on the British art scene since the early 1960s, when his already distinctive drawings were among the flagships of the then-newborn satirical magazine *Private Eye*. From there, he reached out to readers of *Punch*, the *Evening Standard*, the *Daily Sketch*, and the *Sunday Times*, and by the mid-1960s he was covering the Vietnam War for the *Daily Express*, filing a still horrifying series of on-the-spot impressions, a war artist who truly understood the nature of war.

Scarfe's critics compared his work, unfavorably as a rule, to that of Ralph Steadman, gonzo journalist Hunter Thompson's artist-in-residence. The two had studied together at East Ham Technical College in the 1950s, and there were certainly parallels to be drawn between the two artists' styles, even as both reached out for their own particular voice. Whether one chooses to acknowledge the similarities or not, however, Scarfe was truly a breath of fresh air on the English art scene of the early 1970s, and in 1974, he was commissioned to produce a comic strip for Pink Floyd's latest tour program after Waters and Mason saw a film he had produced for the BBC, *Long Drawn-Out Trip*.

Three years later, as Pink Floyd toured 1977's *Animals* album, Scarfe was back, this time creating the animations that would play behind the live performance of "Welcome to the Machine." Now he had reached the peak of that relationship, as Waters fell out with Storm Thorgerson over the sleeve for *Animals* (Waters, who conceived the design, believed Thorgerson was taking too much credit for it) and recruited Scarfe instead to transform his words into scratchy line art.

It was the right decision. One cannot, of course, say what Thorgerson and his Hipgnosis design team would have made of *The Wall* and its contents. But when they were given the opportunity to address the issue by offering up their own visualizations on *The Wall* DVD and sundry 1990s/2000s repackagings, it was in the knowledge that Scarfe's original artwork—the bricks of a blank, hand-drawn wall—had become as iconic as any of their own past creations.

Scarfe's contributions to *The Wall* movie would ultimately be restricted to just fifteen minutes of footage, but few would disagree that they remain among the most striking images in the entire production. Likewise, his work dominates memories of *The Wall*'s concert production, dwarfing even the return appearances of the flying pig and the crashing airplane, favorites drawn from an earlier age. Vast puppets cavorted, the schoolteacher, the wife, and the mother; and the animations that were projected onto the stage and the slowly rising wall at the front of the stage became the irresistible focal point for all but the most dedicated musician watchers.

Which was a thrill for everyone who wanted a show, but less so for those folk, critics among them, who wondered just how far beyond the realms of the traditional rock show a band could travel before they were no longer a rock band at all. Such complaints, of course, were music to Waters's ears, attuned as they had been to his dreams of presenting the ultimate theatrical extravaganza for so long; they appealed, too, to the sense of ruthless competition that had fired his onstage presentations since the days of *The Dark Side of the Moon*, when he heard the likes of David Bowie and Genesis speaking about (and attempting) theater of their own, but apparently running out of ideas once they were past the mask and costuming stage.

Perhaps Genesis had come closer than most; their *The Lamb Lies Down on Broadway* tour in 1975 and 1976 at least had unbridled ambition on its side, as the musicians were subsumed beneath the enormity of the associated concept album, and the story played out like a movie-in-miniature on the screens that towered above them. But even this extravaganza ultimately offered little more than pretty lights and arresting images, and the spectacle of Peter Gabriel disguised as a fat, warty blob whose vocals were lost within the manifold layers of his Slipperman costume.

The Wall would learn from those failings, and it would learn from past mistakes—Floyd's as well as Bowie's and Genesis's. Bowie's 1974 American tour, the one that first drew Michael Kamen into the mainstream rock consciousness, was likewise conceived as traveling theater, with a cityscape stage set that was so vast that many of the venues into which the tour was booked could not even house it.

Pink Floyd perceived problems of a similar nature and took steps to counter them; the group would tour, they declared, with their own portable concert hall, a cylindrical canvas beast the size of a medium sports arena, nicknamed "the slug."

But even as the gastropod slithered off the drawing board, it became apparent that it was not going to fly. Everything from fire regulations—which sometimes differ from town to town, let alone country to country—to finding a vacant lot large enough to set up on had to be absorbed into the slug's makeup. And for every obstruction that red tape might have thrown in its path, there was the saltshaker of the production's own logistics as well. The slug was laid to rest, and attention turned to venues, at home and abroad, that were already large enough, and experienced enough, to absorb a concert of this magnitude.

They found four.

The Wall opened at the Los Angeles Sports Arena on February 7, 1980, five nights that commenced with a near catastrophe that reinforced the wisdom of abandoning the original slug. Onstage fireworks set ablaze the drapes that were hanging over the stage and necessitated an unpredicted break in the show before it had even gotten started. The flames were easily extinguished on this occasion, but backstage, with the smoke drifting through the corridors, more than one murmur thanked the band's lucky stars that they were playing in a concrete block.

The end of the month brought five more nights at New York's Nassau Coliseum, and then there was a six-month break while the band waited out the end of the British tax year on April 5 and, correspondingly, the end of their personal tax exile. It would be early August 1980 before *The Wall* moved on to the cavernous Earls Court arena in west London where they would play six nights, and then a volley of more shows in Dortmund, Germany, in February 1981. There would be one final burst of five gigs, back at Earls Court in June, arranged wholly for the benefit of movie director Alan Parker's cameras, but that was all. With the exception of one song inserted into their Live 8 set thirty-four years later, *The Wall* and the four-man band that created it would never set foot on stage together again.

Richard Wright, at the time an employee of Pink Floyd as opposed to a member of it, would speak often of how *The Wall* concerts were simply a job, that he felt no emotional or physical part of the proceedings. He even eschewed the company of his former bandmates in favor of spending time either with his own family and friends, or with the fellow hirelings who joined him in fleshing out the Pink Floyd experience—guitarist Snowy White, bassist Andy Bown, keyboard player Peter Wood, and drummer Willie Weeks.

They too murmured of the discontent they felt, their status as hired guns often demeaned further by Waters's reluctance to even speak to them. When Snowy White found himself unable to make the 1981 shows on account of having joined Thin Lizzy in the interim, one can only imagine him uttering a sigh of relief. Now it was his replacement Andy Roberts's turn to endure a few nights with what Peter Wood once described as "the most miserable band in the world."

The cowriter of Al Stewart's "The Year of the Cat" and cofounder of Quiver with Waters's school friend Tim Renwick, Wood admitted he "endured" the tour more than he enjoyed it. But he was also quick to add that what other observers decried as Roger Waters's perpetual moodiness was rarely directed at anybody personally. "It was stress. He felt as though he was the only person in the band who actually cared about getting the job done properly. Everybody else just wanted to get it over with."

On more than one occasion during rehearsals, Waters found himself having to argue against the suggestion that *The Wall* be curtailed to just one half of the show, with the remainder of the evening turned over to more familiar favorites. On more than one occasion, too, he was threatened with one or other of his bandmates walking out on the whole affair. Those tensions did not lessen once the show hit the road, and rumors were circulating far beyond Pink Floyd's inner circle just weeks after the shows were announced that the first set of London gigs, at least, had come close to being canceled after one disagreement too many.

Out front, of course, witnessing the concerts in the jam-packed arenas, or hearing about them afterward from the folks who snatched up the tickets so quickly that even missing a bus could mean missing out altogether, there were few regrets.

True, the show paid no homage whatsoever to the band's past; but even if you didn't especially care for *The Wall*, there was no failing to be impressed by the performance itself. Pink Floyd had not even declared that the tour was over than demands were flooding in for them to play more gigs, with further bad blood being pumped into the pipeline when American concert promoter Larry Maggid offered Pink Floyd an unprecedented two million dollars to play just two further concerts at Philadelphia's RFK Stadium.

Gilmour, Mason, and manager O'Rourke said yes; Waters said no. *The Wall*, he explained wearily, was a reaction against stadium shows, not an excuse to play even more of them. It was a furious finger jabbed at the dawning age of corporate sponsorship, where you can have as much fun as you like at a show, so long as you use the correct credit card. Not even the threat of Pink Floyd performing without him, with Andy Bown stepping forward to handle his vocal duties, was sufficient to change his mind, and hardly surprisingly. Rather, Waters simply dared them to try, and he no doubt took immense satisfaction from the fact that ultimately, they either didn't have "the balls" (his words) or the enthusiasm to do it.

Richard Wright, after all, was not the only player on the stage for whom the relentless choreography of the production and the need to adhere unerringly to the musical script every night had traveled beyond tiresome into the realms of dread and boredom. Gilmour and Mason, too, were asking themselves what had happened to the idea of simply playing the music and were more likely to spend their offstage time reminiscing about the old days than looking forward to the next two hours of headphones, click tracks, and cues.

Neither were they especially good at disguising their discomfort. The *New Musical Express's* review of one of the Earls Court nights spoke of "guitar solos that smacked of clenched teeth and furrowed brows"; other reports admired the scale and perfection of the event but ultimately concluded that that was all it was. An event. Soulless, emotionless, and ultimately heartless. On the other side of the superstardom divide, a new wave of bands was growing up in the UK whose reliance on synthesizers and electronics was being described as inhuman, dispossessed, machine-like, and cold—acts like Gary Numan and Tubeway Army, the Human League, and Depeche Mode—but *The Wall* out-glaciered them all.

To those who were (and who remain) so disposed to spectacle, the sheer scale of *The Wall* remained astonishing. But so did its pomposity, as audiences forked out previously unheard of ticket prices, fifteen dollars in LA, eight pounds fifty in London, to listen to a near-identical rendition of the entire album, while the performers disappeared behind a pile of bricks. Animations and effects did lighten the vista somewhat, and there were some terrific moments, including, ironically, the inflatable pig. Even with all of the pomp and circumstance, it was hard to beat.

But they were effortlessly outweighed by the embarrassments, and when the ensemble launched into the hit "Another Brick," you suddenly understood that it was not that they didn't "need no education," it was the fact that they were incapable of learning from their mistakes. Following the commercial heights of *The Wall*, Pink Floyd would spend the brief remainder of their career in free fall.

But you cannot argue with the album's success. "Another Brick in the Wall (Part 2)" had effortlessly been established as Pink Floyd's biggest selling single of all time, and now *The Wall* was poised to overtake *Wish You Were Here* as their fastest moving (and, again, biggest selling) album this side of *Dark Side*, which itself had just (March 1980) overtaken Carole King's immortal *Tapestry* as the longest-running resident of the trade bible *Billboard*'s American chart, a 303-week span that dated back to its release six years previous.

The concerts had each sold out in record time, for record sums, and now the movie of *The Wall* was moving closer to release, heaving itself into shape around a vision hatched by director Alan Parker that was, if such a thing is possible, even more chaotic than Waters's.

No matter that Waters himself was essentially barred from the film studio by Parker—whose movie career was launched a decade earlier as screenwriter of the so charming schoolkids-in-love movie *Melody* before launching into a succession of peaks around *Bugsy Malone, Midnight Express*, and *Fame*—after a final and unwelcome bout of second-guessing the director. (The bassist decided to take a six-week vacation instead.) Parker and singer Bob Geldof, excellently cast in the role of the self-destructing Pink, both recalled the tension that seemed to walk hand in hand with Waters every time he did venture onto the set; Waters's seemingly frozen sour expression became almost a standing joke around the movie set, with one witness recalling, perhaps apocryphally, perhaps not, that when Waters walked in, all other work stopped "because he was going to find fault with whatever anyone was doing."

As much as the parent album was very much a collaborative effort between Waters and producer Bob Ezrin, so the movie was the result of a high-speed collision between Waters's view and Parker's realization of that view.

It was that conflict which hauled the movie away from the occasional navel-gazing of the audio experience. Swaths of *The Wall*, as presented on vinyl, were little more than eclectic filler, passages shoehorned in between the actual songs in order to allow the plot to move forward. On film, the visuals and the dialogue shifted such moments back to where Waters (who had always seen *The Wall* in cinematic terms) originally positioned them, as background or incidental music.

That was not a wholly intentional factor. The decision to abandon Waters's original notion of including live concert material in the film was made only after none of the five nights at Earls Court in June 1981 produced any workable footage. Pink Floyd's primary contribution to the movie would now be the soundtrack alone, as some half a dozen of the original album recordings were reworked for the soundtrack, together with one new song ("When the Tigers Broke Free") and one album outtake ("What Shall We Do Now").

Lost, too, were proposed appearances by Scarfe's monstrous puppets, while attempts to construct a robotic version of the schoolmaster were abandoned likewise—but only after several thousand pounds had been sunk into bringing the creature to life.

Arguably, the movie benefited from each of these calamities.

Just as Ken Russell's visionary reimagining of the Who's *Tommy* had somehow made sense of the deepest corners of the original vinyl albatross, so Parker, too, opened whole new windows into all that *The Wall* represented—at the same time as he was snatching it out of Waters's personal control.

—

The casting of Bob Geldof as Pink bordered upon the iconoclastic. Still a couple of years removed from his post–Band/Live Aid deification as Saint Bob, righter of all the world's wrongs, Geldof was lead singer with the Irish band the Boomtown Rats, a group that burrowed into the London scene in 1977 with the frenetic punk war cry "Looking After Number One," then made an abrupt body swerve to reveal themselves instead as one of the most witty, arty, and above all thoughtful bands on the entire scene. Hits "Like Clockwork" and "She's So Modern" established them as regular British chart contenders; the Springsteenesque street epic "Rat Trap" brought them their first number one; and "I Don't Like Mondays," based on what was then a truly shocking and all but unprecedented school shooting in the United States, left them looking, for a moment, untouchable.

Geldof himself was a spectacular performer, a hint of the young Mick Jagger bound up in a wiry, voluble, outspoken frame that contorted its limbs like the mouth twisted lyrics, and some of the most memorable musical moments of the day were the work of the Boomtown Rats: "Someone's Looking at You" was a masterpiece of paranoid suspicion and fear that truly rivaled any of Roger Waters's many ruminations on a similar theme;

"Diamond Smiles" remains the finest socialite-suicide song ever written (and the fact it has very little competition in that department should not be held against it); "House on Fire" absorbed post-punk convulsions and revived ska schematics in equal doses and emerged as one of the signature hits of 1982, one that was, in fact, still sniffing round the chart as *The Wall* began marching towards its premiere.

Yet Geldof's casting was itself fraught. The singer initially resisted Parker's invitation to try out for the movie, all the more so after he discovered that Roger Waters's first choice for the lead role had been . . . Roger Waters. The bassist failed his screen tests beyond even his own capacity for forgiveness, however, and so Parker cast further afield. Geldof was his first choice. All he needed to do was convince the singer of the fact.

In keeping with his punky peers, Geldof regarded Pink Floyd as a creature that had no place in the modern world, a bloated dinosaur whose musical crimes against humanity were only exacerbated by Waters's bleeding-heart-liberal-millionaire sensibilities. Geldof later admitted that he had not even heard *The Wall* when he was offered the role, that he had suffered so sorely at the hands of the hit single (which truly was inescapable for an inordinately long time) that he already knew he would hate the whole thing.

But two other factors were stronger than his dislike of Pink Floyd. On the one hand, the Boomtown Rats' career was definitely flagging after the peak of "I Don't Like Mondays," as their allotted time in the pink of their profession was gnawed away by even brighter, newer bands. And on the other, his ego was not alone in suggesting that he make the move into movies. As both a performer and a personality, Geldof had what the common vernacular described as "what it takes" to make a mark on celluloid, and as a purveyor of some of the most revolutionary music videos of the period, he had already proven himself capable of delivering as brilliantly on screen as he did on vinyl.

Plus, he was an Alan Parker fan.

Ultimately, everything worked out fine. Geldof's performance as Pink was peerless, and the movie itself would deserve all the plaudits that rained down upon it, as even seasoned Floyd haters converged to acknowledge a new admission into that select coterie of rock music movies that actually work. There is *Performance*, there is *Stardust*, there are *Tommy* and *Quadrophenia*, and there is *The Wall*. Five movies shot across a fifteen-year span that between them tell you the story of pop.

But Pink Floyd themselves were already placing *The Wall* behind them, were already back in the studio, working on an album whose topicality and immediacy has rendered it both the most dated-sounding record in their entire canon and, simultaneously, the most misunderstood.

It was called *The Final Cut*, and even people who didn't listen to the gossip about how the band had again ceased to exist knew that the title was not an idle threat.

5

The Great Gig in the Sky

Of all the songs that made up *The Wall*, perhaps the most significant, at least in personal terms, was the one that had not even been composed at the time. "When the Tigers Broke Free" was written for, and about, Waters's father, Eric Fletcher Waters.

Dispassionately, Waters understood that his father's death, as the war memorials put it, "was not in vain" — that without that assault on Anzio, World War II might have taken a very different turn at a time when, after almost five years of conflict, it finally felt as though the tide was turning. He knew that the horror he felt on a personal level was just one more manifestation of the increasingly prevalent modern predilection to look back at the major events that allowed the Allies to win World War II and denounce their perpetrators as criminals and madmen, without even considering that there had been no viable alternative. Not if they wanted to win the war.

But that was no consolation whatsoever for a withdrawn youth who was forced to grow to manhood without a father, and whose sense of loss only grew stronger with every passing year. Waters turned thirty in 1973, the year in which *Dark Side of the Moon* transformed him into a millionaire, a milestone that put into sharp relief his father's thirtieth year, dying on a foreign shore, cut down by a stranger whose only reason for the killing was that he wore a different uniform and spoke a different language.

Now the son whom the father never knew was nearing forty, and more and more his mind wandered to contemplate the years that had been stolen from his parent—stolen by the war that followed what the history books once called "the war to end all wars," stolen by vainglorious politicians and bungling generals, by orders that had haunted him his entire life and had helped shape his music, too. "Corporal Clegg" on Pink Floyd's second album, *A Saucerful of Secrets*, mocked the blinders through which we "see" war; and then there was that line in "Us and Them," eleven words that said more for the sheer randomness of battle than any royal scroll or military historian could ever tell. "Forward, he cried from the rear, and the front rank died."

The Wall, too, was shaped by the loss of Eric Fletcher Waters, and Pink Floyd entered the studio in early 1982, preparing to record a new clutch of songs that had either been omitted from, or weren't yet ready for inclusion on, *The Wall*. "When the Tigers Broke Free" was already a cornerstone of the project. The album would be called *Spare Bricks*, and as if to justify the "soundtrack now available" credit that ran at the end of the movie, it represented the closest the film would come to an official score.

And then Britain went to war again.

The 1982 conflict with Argentina was not the country's first military engagement since World War II had concluded—British troops battled alongside the United Nations in Korea at the dawn of the 1950s; they were engaged in Suez in the middle of that decade. Undeclared wars had been fought in Malaysia and Aden, and Northern Ireland had been a battleground in all but terminology since the beginning of the 1970s.

But the Falklands War was different. Those other wars were fought for principles and politics. The Falklands War was fought for something that everyone could understand: to protect an outlying corner of the old British Empire, the south Atlantic Falkland Islands, from an invader who cared naught for the wishes and lives of the inhabitants but simply wanted to subsume one territory into another.

The Argentinean claims were not wholly spurious. The Malvinas, as they knew the islands, had been disputed by the two nations for over a century and were a lot closer to the Argentinean mainland than they were to any other British territory. It was the kind of argument that takes place all around the world to this very day—North Korea, Japan, and China continue to make strident noises about so-called disputed territories whose destinies they each believe they alone should control. The question of Gibraltar, another British holding that is so close to mainland Spain that you can smell the food cooking, has rattled on for decades, and so on.

The difference was, Argentina had tired of rattling. Or, rather, General Leopold Galtieri and the military junta with which he ran the country had tired of the populace complaining about their oppressive reign and decided to give Argentina something to cheer about instead. Which, quite coincidentally, was the situation that British prime minister Margaret Thatcher found herself in at the same time, one term into her Conservative government's lifespan and already facing defeat in the next election.

There was no grand conspiracy between the two embattled leaders, the half-Italian military vet and the grocer's daughter from Grantham, no behind-the-scenes agreement that war would be great for their political futures. But a "winner takes all" scenario had presented itself, and neither side was going to back down.

On April 2, 1982, the two thousand Falkland Islanders, a million-plus sheep, and an indeterminate number of penguins awoke to discover their homeland was under Argentinean occupation. By June 14, they were free again, liberated by the vast British military force that spent almost as long chugging across eight thousand miles of ocean to the South Atlantic as it did actually fighting a foe whom the British tabloids had dubbed the Argies.

A thousand men died, the Argentinean junta collapsed, the British Conservatives were all but guaranteed reelection, and in a quiet corner of north London, Roger Waters was marshaling his forces through a new album's worth of songs that abandoned the *Spare Bricks* concept before the first bullet was even fired in anger, but which would provide a soundtrack for the war as exquisitely as it might once have for *The Wall*.

He had his own war to fight, as well. Sidelined rather than sacked, Nick Mason had joined Richard Wright in the ranks of the band's sidemen, to the point of being physically absent from one of the album's tracks (the concluding "Two Suns in the Sunset"). David Gilmour's expected role as coproducer, too, was snatched away as Waters announced that unless he was granted absolute autonomy, the entire project would be scrapped. Even more than *The Wall*, this was his album, and he had already designed its credits. *Requiem for a Post-War Dream*, or *The Final Cut* as it would ultimately be titled, was "by Roger Waters, performed by Pink Floyd."

Gilmour considered calling his bluff. He had little interest in the project and even less faith in the material, and his offer to take a few weeks away to work up some of his own musical notions could also have been taken as an offer to step aside altogether. Waters, however, dismissed the suggestion out of hand.

He ignored too Gilmour's insistence that four of the songs Waters now intended to record ("The Hero's Return," "One of the Few," "The Final Cut," and "Your Possible Pasts") had been dropped from *The Wall* so early on in the sessions that even their composer had acknowledged their lack of quality. Now, however, Waters behaved as though they were the greatest things he had ever written.

There was more. Waters declared that he would sing lead vocals on every song, utterly disregarding the protests—Gilmour's among them—that his voice was best experienced in small doses scattered across the course of an entire record. Ultimately Gilmour, whose voice to many people was as much a part of the Pink Floyd experience as any other individual instrument, the lungs behind "Time" and "Money," "Dogs" and "Echoes," would be heard on just one song, the raucous rocker "Not Now John," which, like "Comfortably Numb" the last time around, promptly became many people's favorite song on the album.

The greatest conflict, however, surrounded Waters's lyrics. All filters were off; all ambiguity was out. Listeners who possibly squirmed at the reference to English anti-smut protestor Mary Whitehouse on *Animals* five years earlier were now to be beaten over the heads with a collection of songs that were as contemporary as the newspapers that Waters read every morning over breakfast. And would be out-of-date almost as swiftly.

Both Margaret Thatcher and her political partner in crime, American president Ronald Reagan, were to be namechecked in song; so were Soviet president Leonid Brezhnev and his Israeli counterpart, Menachem Begin, names which every listener would recognize in 1983, but which might demand an awful lot of Googling thirty years on. Past Pink Floyd albums had been almost self-consciously timeless. *The Final Cut* would emerge time-locked instead.

With that in mind, the original working title, *Requiem for a Post-War Dream*, might have given the album a framework that its eventual titling evaded. As Waters explained, "*The Final Cut* was about how, with the introduction of the Welfare State, we felt we were moving forward into something resembling a liberal country, where we would all look after one another and slowly that dream had become eroded—maybe people discovered that wasn't what we wanted after all. There's a selfishness in us, and a lack of community spirit that led us, by the '80s, into a doctrine of a pragmatic, radical, Reaganite-Thatcherite economic system. That's the system of values to which, by and large, we still cling." Utopia had been avoided, to be replaced by what he saw as a society that could have stepped out of a Charles Dickens novel.

He felt, he explained, that the Falklands conflict should have been resolved via the diplomatic means that history later revealed were always an option, as opposed to the more headline-friendly option of going to war. But that was already old news by the time the album was completed, and so the Falklands became simply the last chapter, the final cut indeed, in a story that mourned the betrayal of all the young men and women who, convinced that they were fighting and dying for freedom during World War II, now saw their uniformed successors fighting for values that many of them did not even agree with. Wasn't World War II also supposed to have spelled an end to colonialism? Did anybody really consider one thousand lives (750 of which were Argentine) to be worth the preservation of a few lines on the map?

On the British home front support for the war was ambiguous at best, with probably the majority of people agreeing with Waters that a fair resolution could as easily have been reached over the negotiating table.

But there are no victory parades to be held after a few days spent sitting around a well-appointed conference room, no photo opportunities for peacock politicians, and no ticker-tape hailstorms or commemorative postage stamps. Thatcher required nothing less than a total military victory, and she rode roughshod over every objection to ensure she obtained it.

A lot like Roger Waters, in fact. Which, many people have said, makes his own ferocious loathing of the woman, and all that she stood for, seem somehow ironic if not downright hypocritical. In their eyes, in terms of *The Final Cut*'s actual creation, he accepted so little assistance from the other musicians in the studio that even affixing Pink Floyd's name to it was as much a betrayal of trust and belief in its own way as that which the album itself was condemning.

Again, however, Waters's dispute with the rest of the band was less due to him insisting they "do what I say," which is the mark of a dictator, than asking them to "do what I do"—a polar reversal of the familiar old canard, but ultimately no less of a stumbling block. All of which, and more that would be revealed in years to come, has erected a massive smoke screen across even the few things about *The Final Cut* that are worth treasuring.

Long-winded it might have been, but as a protest it was at least as effective as any of those more succinct offerings being transmitted at the time by such left-field talents as TV Smith (the pulsating "War Fever"), Billy Bragg ("Between the Wars"), and Crass ("How Does It Feel to Be the Mother of a Thousand Dead"). Dated it may quickly have become, but as a snapshot of a moment in time, *The Final Cut* is as elegiac as any early offering by Bob Dylan—whom Waters has never ceased to rank among his own favorite songwriters. Perhaps there is more universality to "Blowing in the Wind" or "Masters of War" than one could ever ascribe to "Not Now John" or "The Hero's Return." But the nature of the industry had changed since Dylan wrote those songs, and a Pink Floyd album that was built around atonal folk strummings would have been an even greater shock than the shattered minimalism with which *The Final Cut* echoed.

Recorded at some eight different studios, *The Final Cut* took the lessons learned from Bob Ezrin and amplified them. Downtime spent with Waters and Gilmour battling it out on the arcade game Donkey Kong was balanced by hours spent trying to get the most minute passages sounding just right. Sound effects dominate great swaths of the album, while a new recording procedure called Holophonics also caught Waters's attention, the invention, so ironically, of Argentine scientist Hugo Zuccarelli. Holophonics purportedly offered a quadraphonic effect through a stereo system by positioning every individual sound according to the dimensions of the average human skull, but whether it actually worked or not is down to the individual listener and the efficacy of his or her headphones.

But there is no denying that effects that on past Pink Floyd albums had been geared toward creating atmosphere and building a mood were, across *The Final Cut*, wrestled into the very frontline of the sonic stew, there to grapple with lyrics that were truly carving windows into Waters's own psyche—another reason why *The Final Cut* is often described as a "difficult" record. Because few people outside of psychiatric circles are truly comfortable being allowed that much access into the fears and fantasies of strangers—especially ones whose political complexion set them so firmly at odds with the beliefs and convictions of a sizable chunk of their intended audience, as was the case in the UK, or had very little relevance to it whatsoever, as was the case elsewhere around the world.

In June 1983, three months after the release of *The Final Cut*, the general election saw Thatcher's government return to power with the highest winning margin of any party since 1945, an absolutely unimpeachable 61 percent of the electorate. This meant there were an awful lot of people who disagreed with the politics that *The Final Cut* painted, which in turn added up to an awful lot of people who simply didn't buy it. Further afield, in the US, Japan, Australia, France, and all those other countries where Pink Floyd had hitherto been described as untouchable, the album struck even less of a chord. What did the average Italian record buyer care for the finer points of Britain's decaying welfare system? What possible difference did the Falklands War make to a Norwegian who just wanted to bliss out to the Floyd?

The Final Cut barely mustered sales of three million copies worldwide. Which isn't so bad by many artists' standards, and was certainly sufficient to push it to the top of the UK chart, and the top six in the United States. Unfortunately, that was all it could do. There would be no lingering afterlife for *The Final Cut* in the manner of *Dark Side of the Moon*, *Wish You Were Here*, and *The Wall*.

Richard Wright, who did not even appear on the record, once jokingly referred to it as the second volume of *Relics*, the budget-priced collection of self-confessed "antiques and curios" that was released back in 1971 and rounded up stray singles, B-sides, and outtakes. And David Gilmour apparently agreed, describing its contents as the kind of weak filler material that hadn't disgraced a Pink Floyd album in over a decade.

Somewhere, a dog named Seamus raised his head and howled vindication.

Rolling Stone's Kurt Loder awarded *The Final Cut* a five-star review, albeit judged as a Roger Waters solo album as opposed to a new Floydian masterpiece, but most reviews were contemptuous. A wholly unscientific snapshot of the used record stores of London in the months following *The Final Cut*'s release recalls racks overflowing with "played it once and hated it" copies, a blizzard of rejected vinyl that would not be repeated until David Bowie released a turkey called *Tonight* the following year. An artist's audience, both albums had discovered, can be trusted to accept a lot of things. But the complete abrogation of everything that made them that artist (and consequently, worthy of fandom) in the first place is not one of them.

The Final Cut's future reputation was scarcely assisted by the band's decision not to tour in its aftermath. Talk of a handful of select dates in November 1983 did surface, but it was also apparent that Gilmour and Mason alone had any enthusiasm for the notion. Waters was wholly and inextricably opposed to the idea, arguing instead for Pink Floyd to pursue the direction of *The Wall* and allow video to do the job for them.

It was the golden age of MTV after all, the American cable channel that was predicated, in those days, around a nonstop diet of music videos, and whose impact could be gauged every time the chart was topped by another band who looked and posed a lot better than they sounded.

"Another Brick in the Wall (Part 2)" was an early beneficiary of MTV's hunger for music video. Released during that brief hiatus between the advent of video as a potentially commercial proposition and MTV's consummation of that promise, it was one of the select handful or two of music videos that were even available at the time and was slammed into regular rotation. The advent of *The Wall* movie had increased MTV's interest in the band, and Waters was only being partially naive with his assumption that any further Floydian offerings would be grasped with equal enthusiasm by the powers that be.

Naive, because the rules were already changing. Now every band made videos, or so it seemed, and every band was fighting to outdo every other. The long-form video boom pioneered by Michael Jackson's "Thriller" was already on the horizon; so were the exotic landscapes and glamorous backstories that sustained the likes of Duran Duran, the gripping in-concert performances that let you taste the sweat on Bruce Springsteen's brow, and the sheer cachet of star directors coming in to helm three-minute mini-movies by the artists who could afford them.

Into that sea of wild creativity and hyperactive gimmickry, of towering hairstyles and leather-draped thighs, Waters dropped a video EP comprising four sets of moving pictures directed by his brother-in-law Willie Christie and apparently shot on a budget that would barely have plaited one of Boy George's signature dreadlocks.

Waters alone appeared in the four. No other member of the band was invited to participate, and they would probably have refused if they had been. And the choice of songs was equally shortsighted. "Not Now John," released as a single with its eyebrow-raising refrain of "fuck all that" replaced by a somewhat tamer "stuff all that" was the lead piece, but the single itself was already doomed to chart failure.

"The Gunner's Dream" and the almost painfully confessional "The Final Cut" were scarcely the most listener-friendly numbers on the album, while "The Fletcher Memorial Home" was essentially a call to assassinate every world leader with whom Waters disagreed, beginning with President Reagan and his secretary of state, Alexander Haig.

Yes, that would certainly have them tapping their toes down at corporate headquarters.

The video EP was released, the idea of touring was abandoned, and Waters went on the offensive. Even before *The Final Cut* was complete, *Rolling Stone* had caught him in a revealing mood, arguing that Pink Floyd's entire history was a matter that required serious revision, that "I started to get very resentful because I was doing a lot more [for the albums than the others] and yet we were all pretending that we were doing it. Well, we don't pretend anymore."

He could, he predicted, "very easily . . . work with another drummer and keyboard player," and it was likely, he continued, that "at some point I will."

That "some point" had now arrived. While David Gilmour took out his own frustrations on what would become his second solo album, the sublime *About Face*, Waters too was hard at work, resuscitating the *Pros and Cons of Hitch Hiking* idea that had been rejected in favor of *The Wall* and setting out to prove that no matter how much Pink Floyd needed him, he needed Pink Floyd an awful lot less.

A new coterie of musicians gathered around him: percussionist Ray Cooper (best known for his time with Elton John), Raff Ravenscroft on horns, and the now-stalwart Andy Bown on bass. Michael Kamen, too, was recalled, stepping into the role of Waters's main collaborator and sounding board, but anybody who regretted the absence of a familiar guitar-playing god from the proceedings would hopefully be satisfied by the appearance of a second.

Waters's second wife, Carolyne, had long been friends with Patti Boyd, the former Mrs. George Harrison and now Mrs. Eric Clapton. The two families often socialized, and it was following one such gathering, according to a legend that nobody has cared to deny, that the two husbands sat up late into the night, drinking, chatting, and laying plans that even Clapton's management was unable to believe once they got wind of what had transpired. Waters was recording an album, and Clapton would be playing guitar on it. He would then be going on tour, and Clapton would be playing on that as well.

No big deal, no name in lights. Clapton may have been one of the biggest stars in rock at the time, but he had also spent large parts of his career trying to dodge the spotlight and just be someone's bandmate. He'd tried it with Delaney and Bonnie, back in the wake of the Blind Faith breakup, but then it didn't work because he was a bigger name than either of the group's nominal leaders. He tried it again with Derek and the Dominoes, but that didn't work because even people without a rhyming bone in their body had figured out who Derek was the first time they ever heard "Layla."

But now . . . Roger Waters alone may not have had the same recognition as Clapton. But everyone in the world knew Pink Floyd, and it would presumably be easy to remind people that he was the voice and the energy behind that band. And besides, Waters promised, it would be fun.

Well, that's one word for it.

Much of the album Clapton would be gracing was already complete before he was invited to record; the basic tracks, which may or may not have grown out of the work that Gilmour, Mason, and Wright had put into them back in 1978 and 1979, were more or less complete, as Michael Kamen explained:

> Roger's demos were all there; he knew exactly what he wanted everybody to play. In fact, I think if he'd been able, he would have played every instrument himself and not needed any of us. The concept, which means the lyrics, was already so established that there was no room to improvise, nowhere for a musician to go apart from exactly where Roger wanted them to. It's an interesting way of recording because it is so disciplined, and Roger was smart enough to have surrounded himself with very disciplined players. But then he told us Eric was coming onboard and I think we all took a step back and wondered how that was going to work.

Clapton, too, would find himself surprised by Waters's requirements. Called in to overdub guitar and Dobro across the finished tracks, he would have made much the same observation as everyone else who heard the songs—that there was scarcely any room for more than the most modest instrumentation amid the hailstorm of lyrics that was *Pros and Cons'* frontal assault.

It was as if, after so many years spent as one quarter of one of rock's most virtuoso instrumental quartets, Waters had decided to flow in the opposite direction altogether, and in the process create an album whose twelve tracks devoured just over forty-two minutes in length, and which were so regimented that they were actually titled for their optimum

playing time: the album opens with, and at, "4.30 AM" and closes with
"5.11 AM."

But still, Clapton excelled with tight, economical bursts of sound and
melody, a constant backwash that swirls beneath the lyrics, creating tensions and undercurrents that aren't simply as compulsive as the words,
they are often even more descriptive.

Over the years Clapton had very much settled into a role as the kind
of guitarist whose latest flash of brilliance could be predicted by the first
notes he picked out at the start of the solo. *Pros and Cons* rebuilt him in
its own image, a guitarist whose savagery and spontaneity could never be
foretold from the mood of each track, whose invention still surprises as
much on the umpteenth play as it did on the first.

It would be absurdly hyperbolic to describe Clapton's performance on
Pros and Cons as his finest recorded performance of the 1980s. But at the
same time, when you line it up alongside everything else he did record
that decade, a clutch of almost tragically mechanical easy-listening solo
albums included, *Pros and Cons* emerges as the least Clapton-like sounds
he had made in years, which in turn took him back to the shock innova-
tions of his early days with Cream, or that first jaw-dropping exposure to
461 Ocean Boulevard—the album that ultimately wrote its own cliché, but
which was genuinely eye-opening when it first swung into sight.

Waters was inspired, and the album is inspirational in its turn. The
apparent drabness of the time-locked song titles was remedied by their
subtitles, each one of which spoke for the material concerns of the song.
And the overture grabbed from the outset, fading into "Apparently They
Were Travelling Abroad" on a hiss and a shimmer of guitar that spoke
only gently of the pastures that ignited "Shine On You Crazy Diamond,"
before moving into a rough approximation of the kind of epic storytelling
that Bob Dylan was expelling around the time of *Desire* and *Street Legal*,
his last two truly great albums (at the time), and not such a bad example
to follow.

But there were other spirits at large, too, a gentle vault that strummed a hint of John Lennon's "Working Class Hero," and the abrupt slam into "4.33 AM (Running Shoes)," a piece of almost incoherent rage that might be compared to listening to every song on *The Wall* at once.

Yet impressions and reviews that labeled *Pros and Cons* an almost unlistenable mélange of noise and verbiage, deprived of anything approaching a lasting melody, were almost tragically misaligned. It is not an album to relax to, nor one to put on in the hope of it soundtracking the dark side of your latest cocktail party. More than *The Wall*, or even *The Final Cut*, *Pros and Cons* is the sound of Waters unleashed, a collection that looks back to the days of "Take Up Thy Stethoscope and Walk," "Corporal Clegg," and "Several Species" in its absolute disregard for anything his audience might be expecting.

There are passages of sublime power—a minute into "4.39 AM (For the First Time Today, Part 2)" where guitar and sax duel for sonic supremacy only to be shouted down by Waters's impassioned cries of "stay with me"—and moments, too, when his pastime of adding sound effects to the sonic stew arose with almost spiteful vehemence.

Yet Waters did not abandon traditional signatures. Time and time again, you can hear the saxes of *Dark Side* renown, the sweet humming harmonies of Clare Torry and company, the vast palettes of electricity that most people assumed were Gilmour's preserve, and the moments when a snatch of an idea seems set to expand into a passage of sheer expansive beauty. The difference is that in the past, they would have been allowed to expand into lengthy songs; here, they are jettisoned after just a few seconds. Who can hear "4.41 AM (Sexual Revolution)" without thrilling to the closing chorus that toys with "How Much Is That Doggy in the Window," and the "ooooh-ooooh" harmonics that flare like freshly lit fireworks on the edge of "The Great Gig in the Sky"—only to be cut off before they have even taken another breath, for the whole thing to skew away in another direction entirely. One can almost imagine Waters grinning as he dangled such treats before the listener before snatching them away and dancing into another cavern entirely.

But Clapton demonstrated exactly why Waters brought him onboard with the exquisite near-instrumental blues of "4.47 AM (The Remains of Our Love)" and its Chicago shuffle into the overture to "4.50 AM (Go Fishing)," spectral and eerie behind Waters's soft speaking, and a snatch of a melody that you just know you recognize heaved itself into earshot, then slipped away again before you could grasp at its title.

Popular on the UK chart at the time was a series of singles called Stars on 45, essentially carving into irritating medleys a host of memorable chart hits of the past, and creating a whole new soundscape for them. Waters, like every other self-respecting music fan, probably hated them. But he hijacked their instincts regardless, and as if to prove that he knew precisely what everyone was going to say about the album, he waited until midway through side two and then dropped in a song so perfect for radio that it made "Another Brick in the Wall (Part 2)" sound like a slab of unlistenable avant-garde rubbish. "5.01 AM (The Pros and Cons of Hitch Hiking, Part 10)" has everything a hit single should have, from a chorus that lives in your ears forever, to a lyric that amuses as much as it intrigues. Sadly, few people heard it.

A Top 10 hit in several smaller European markets (it climbed to number three in Sweden), Pros and Cons struggled to number thirteen in Britain, and perished at number thirty-one in the US—a better return than those that had greeted solo albums by Mason and Wright, but only one position higher than David Gilmour's About Face—scarcely figures that could even pretend to compete with the peaks that Pink Floyd once took for granted.

Controversy, too, lurked. A Gerald Scarfe sleeve design depicted porn star Linzi Drew, editor at the time of the British Penthouse magazine, in a rear-view naked image that so mortified American CBS that her bare buttocks were gently censored from view, and so outraged British feminist groups that they announced a concerted campaign to tear down posters for the album wherever they might be hung. Not since the bound and gagged vixens portrayed in the Rolling Stones' *Black and Blue* album adverts back in 1976 had such fury been aroused, but whereas the Stones' office was gleefully poised to make fresh capital from the outrage, the Waters camp's grasp of PR was less inventive. They barely even responded.

Where outrage led, the reviews followed. No matter how cacophonous *Pros and Cons* may have been, still it was drowned out by the bile spouted by the music press as they railed against every aspect of the record, and even seasoned Floyd haters found themselves waxing nostalgic for the days of old.

Even Kurt Loder, *Rolling Stone*'s longtime resident Pink Floyd apologist, found no space in his heart for this "musical bilge," and one got the distinct impression that if the magazine's rating system had only permitted it, *Pros and Cons* would have received less than one star.

All of which did nothing but fuel Waters's conviction that every arrow he had aimed from atop Pink Floyd's *Wall*—at the dehumanization of the stadium concert, at the perils of mass appeal, and at the sheep herds whose bleating and babbling never changed its tenor even as the stun gun hit home—every one of those arrows had not only been well targeted but had also hit home with such brutal vengeance that he might never be forgiven again. In true medieval "shoot the messenger" style, or modern "sack the whistleblower" mode, Waters had shown the world what was wrong with it. And now the world was striking back.

6

Charade You Are

A tour was announced. Clapton, Newmark, and Kamen would be joined by keyboard player Chris Stainton, onetime King Crimson saxophonist Mel Collins, and guitarist Tim Renwick, Waters's fellow alumnus of Cambridge County High School for Boys, who had carved out his own career as one of the most distinctive and exquisite guitarists of the past fifteen years.

First sighted in a band called Junior's Eyes, Renwick haunted the last days of the London psychedelic scene before being snatched up to play in David Bowie's band on his second album *Man of Words, Man of Music* (better known today as *Space Oddity*). From there, Renwick moved on to the highly rated Sutherland Brothers and Quiver, at the same time as igniting a career among London's most in-demand session players. Behind Al Stewart, he was instrumental in the success of a string of early to mid-1970s albums, often playing alongside Peter Wood, keyboardist during Pink Floyd's *The Wall* concerts. He also recorded and toured with Mike Oldfield, Elton John, Gary Brooker, and, most recently, TV Smith, former front man with punk heroes the Adverts, now stepping out on a solo career kicked off by the seminal *Channel Five* album.

Renwick was actually closer friends with Gilmour than he had ever been with his old schoolmate and admits to suffering a shade of uncertainty when the call first came through to join the Waters entourage. But he accepted, and armed with a copy of Floyd's *The First XI* box set, a handsome vinyl collection of all their albums to date, Renwick would travel down to Waters's home one afternoon a week to comb through the catalog with him. Their mission: to seek out the songs that would be framed around the *Pros and Cons* album for an audience that even Waters acknowledged was there to hear the songs they knew.

"I was initially asked by Roger to write out all the Floyd material and, once a week, to meet at Roger's home to go through all the songs. This was basically an exercise to help Roger to decide what songs to perform—and how they went! He was not very adept at chord changes or arrangements himself."

Waters made all decisions concerning the songs themselves; Renwick's job was to "write out chord charts etc., in order to remind Roger of keys/ tempos and arrangements. I'm sure there were certain tunes that he had in mind to perform from the start." The only stipulation Waters gave himself was to look toward the shorter songs. "The longer pieces (*Animals*, etc.) would not have fitted into the hour-long (or so) set," Renwick explained. "So it would have been the shorter songs that he was interested in rehearsing."

Although Floyd's "big three" albums would all take a bow, Waters wanted to delve into the less frequented corners of the repertoire too: "Pigs on the Wing." "If." "Set the Controls for the Heart of the Sun." Even so, the result was a set that the most casual fan would know. Or that they ought to know. Renwick continued, "We went through everything. I recall it being quite fun. [But] he became a little sterner when it came to the actual band rehearsals!"

The greatest sticking point once the full band was together would be Waters's insistence that the most recent album be played as close as possible to the sound of the vinyl, with no space for any kind of extemporaneous expression. "He did adopt a rather 'schoolmasterly' approach when it came to the live performances," says Renwick, noting just how ironic that was "in view of his lampooning of 'the schoolmaster' in *The Wall*.

It was a case of 'keeping one's head down' really, which took away most of the fun at the time. He expected the tunes to be performed exactly as they were on record."

Which, of course, was a flapping red rag so far as Eric Clapton was concerned, and Waters sensitively (and, perhaps, sensibly) acknowledged that he was never truly going to rein his lead guitarist in. Just so long as Clapton stuck to the timing of each song . . . and *that* he generally did. But still, every night of the tour that has since snuck out on bootleg finds Clapton discovering new things to do and say with his guitar, and every one thrills in its own way as much as the album.

Renwick: "[Eric] took the guitar solos that David would have performed on the older material. I think Eric was intrigued by the prospect of the elaborate production and staging ideas that Roger had in mind. Playing along to synched visual images, etc., is something that would never have occurred to Eric, for whom a performance has always been about simply the playing."

Which is not to say that every night was as successful as it could have been. Even with the promise of a full set of Floyd numbers, and the expected array of special effects, even with onstage movies handled by both Gerald Scarfe and Nicholas Roeg, one of the most visionary moviemakers of the 1970s (with *Walkabout, Performance, Don't Look Now*, and *The Man Who Fell to Earth*, Roeg was the rock 'n' roll director of the decade, without ever making more than one rock 'n' roll film), ticket sales were slow and halls less than seething by the time the band came on stage. Afterward, when everything was tallied up, Waters acknowledged losing close to half a million pounds on the venture.

He also lost patience. Particularly in America, Waters had serious problems with the attention that Clapton was getting from the audiences, adulation that ranged from standing ovations for every solo to the ubiquitous cigarette lighters in the air whenever he stepped forward. Finally, in Hartford, Connecticut, Waters's frayed temper snapped.

Going into the intermission, the halftime break in the show, Waters threw his bass guitar to the floor in anger, then grabbed the mike to growl to the crowd, "Thanks to the fantastic Eric Clapton." He then stormed off stage.

Waters would later apologize to the band for what even he admitted was his unprofessionalism, an awkward moment that left everybody cringing in horror, but Clapton had had enough. He fulfilled his promise to complete the tour, but there was a distinct lack of camaraderie after that night. Even less than there had hitherto been.

Offstage, Waters kept his distance. He was traveling with his family in tow for much of the time, wife Carolyne and their children, son Harry and daughter India, and they generally booked into the most kiddy-friendly hotel he could find while his bandmates made do with more traditional rock 'n' roll fare. Occasionally, though, he would join his musicians hitting the sights of their latest halt; Renwick recalls "going on an outing to Buddy Guy's Checkerboard Club on the south side of Chicago . . . that was really good fun! Eric got up and played with Buddy, which was great, and there was also blues legend harp player Junior Wells who played a brilliant set (sober) and then came back on (hammered) and played like a wally!"

Still Waters continued to act the role of the ultragrumpy curmudgeon, apparently doing his thing because it was what he did, and not caring a toss for what other people might be saying or thinking. The media was all but frozen out as the tour did its rounds, and even when he did thaw a little, inviting an MTV film crew backstage at the London shows (ambitiously staged in Floyd's old Earls Court stomping ground), he then soured the waters by pointedly refusing to answer a gentle question about his old band.

The interviewer persisted; Waters resisted.

The segment was never aired, and MTV would never look kindly on Roger Waters again.

Waters toured through the latter part of 1984, took a six-month break, and then returned to the road in March 1985 for a second North American tour, albeit one with several major differences.

Clapton was no longer available, and he had also snagged Tim Renwick, adding him to his regular touring band. They were replaced in Waters's lineup by Jay Stapley and Andy Fairweather Low, who, as the implausibly cheerful-looking front man for Amen Corner, had toured with Pink Floyd back in 1967. Since that time, an occasionally successful and always enjoyable solo career had kept him in the public eye, but he was no Eric Clapton, and that was for the best. The spotlight returned to where Waters thought it ought to be.

The second leg of the tour was far more relaxed than the first, but the change in mood was not attributable solely to the lack of Clapton's fan club. Even more rewarding was the decision to abandon the barns and arenas of the first outing; smaller venues were the order of the day, a downgrading necessitated not only by the unsold seats the last time around but also by CBS's refusal to back the tour financially on the grounds that there was no new album to promote, and they'd already all but washed their hands of *Pros and Cons*.

So Waters essentially toured for the fun of it, a concept that his now eternally dour visage rendered somewhat oxymoronic, but which he was not going to abandon simply because the money men suggested it.

Still, one can only imagine the look on his face when he learned that the hierarchy at the label had no more interest in his solo albums than they did in Nick Mason's *Profiles*, recorded at Britannia Row and featuring a wonderful reunion with Gilmour, and just released to a smattering of applause and minimal sales.

Neither could he have been especially overjoyed when the office grapevine began murmuring that the same pair, Mason and Gilmour, were considering reconvening under a somewhat better-known brand name, with or without their recalcitrant Cranky Diamond. Pink Floyd had weathered the loss of one self-styled leader and songwriter, the remaining trio (Richard Wright was also onboard) was allegedly saying. It could survive the departure of a second.

Waters, however, wasn't so sure. In much the same breath as he and Fairweather Low shot their contribution to an upcoming BBC documentary marking the fifth anniversary of John Lennon's murder, a lovely version of "Across the Universe," Waters was also writing a letter to his British and American record companies, informing them that he was no longer a member of Pink Floyd. And, because he'd been more or less the sole source of the band's music for the past decade at least, that meant there was effectively no Pink Floyd whatsoever. If that didn't throw a wrench into this latest foolhardy idea, nothing would.

Yet it was not the musical differences that had soured the band's last two albums (at least) that prompted his announcement. It was his appointment of a new manager.

Earlier in the year, confirming the gulf that he believed existed between his solo career and whatever (if any) future Pink Floyd may have had, Waters declared that henceforth his affairs were to be handled by Peter Rudge, the notoriously hard-bitten businessman who tour managed the Rolling Stones through much of the 1970s. His personal management contract with Floyd's longtime handler Steve O'Rourke was at an end.

"Steve is an effective hustler," Waters reflected.

> A man in a man's world. And we should be jolly pleased with each other. And to give him his due, Steve O'Rourke never gave up his job of trying to get me to fill stadiums. But his attitude was rather summed up when I saw him giving an interview on TV, when he was still managing me. He'd taken on the task of managing a British Le Mans racing team. Steve said, "Management is management. It doesn't matter whether it's a pop group,

a motor-racing team or biscuits." I thought, "Oh, you arsehole."
He'd obviously got a little carried away with his role.

O'Rourke disagreed. His management contract was with Pink Floyd, and Waters was still a member of the band. Until such a time as that scenario shifted — and neither Gilmour nor Mason were at all inclined to terminate their contracts with him — O'Rourke would retain his interest in Waters's affairs.

There was no room for negotiation either, as Waters found himself up against a business brain that was just as rugged as his own musical mind. Neither were his erstwhile bandmates willing to budge their stances, not even when Waters offered them full legal rights to the Pink Floyd name, to do with what they would.

And that was the final straw. Vowing to combat their obstinacy with his own hardball politicking, Waters offered his so-called bandmates a taste of what life would be like if he was forced to remain a member of their band.

Among the myriad offers that came across O'Rourke's desk asking that Pink Floyd reconvene, there was one that not one of the band felt truly inclined to turn down — or even considered themselves in a position to. Live Aid was coming, the Bob Geldof–led gathering of rock's great and greatest that aimed to step in where the world's governments refused to tread and do something positive about the dreadful famine that was sweeping across Ethiopia.

Everybody was playing it. Led Zeppelin reunited for the first time in five years, the original Black Sabbath for the first time in seven. The Rolling Stones would not be present in total, but Mick Jagger, Keith Richards, and Ronnie Wood would all perform. Dylan was there, as well as Neil Young and Phil Collins. Prince sent a song. Pink Floyd, whose own relationship with Geldof was so firm in the eyes of *The Wall*'s viewing public, was a guaranteed headliner.

Or not. According to O'Rourke, interviewed three years later, Waters did not decline the invitation. He simply ignored it.

No matter that it was a decision that bruised him deeply. He would not budge. A matter of principle, more important than any other, was at stake. Ultimately, Gilmour's appearance alongside Bryan Ferry relieved Floyd of becoming the only truly major act not to be represented at the event by even a single member. But meanwhile, another conflict weighed in.

The band's contract with CBS appeared to contain a product commitment—that is, a clause that demanded a certain amount of new material be presented over a specified period of time. Failure to deliver would allow the label not only to sue but also to withhold royalties on existing releases until the shortfall in future products had been made up.

It is a fairly common clause, and one which the American band Boston, themselves no speed warriors when it came to releasing new records, fell foul of after just two LPs. But still, Waters was astonished to learn of it. There was no way, he insisted, that the group would ever have agreed to such a stipulation, and when he read the actual clause, his impression was that that was just one of several interpretations of the legalese. But his bandmates were resolute, in terms of both the label's likely reaction and the options that would be left open to them if that clause were ever sprung—namely, suing Waters not only for all their legal expenses but for any loss of earnings they suffered because of his refusal to make any more records.

"They forced me to resign from the band," Waters told *Uncut* magazine in 2004, "because, if I hadn't, the financial repercussions would have wiped me out completely."

So he sat down to write a letter, requesting that he be released from his contract with the band, while his lawyers made it apparent, in fluent legalese, that he had no intention of ever recording or performing with the group again. It was the final cut.

7

Reset the Controls for
the Heart of the Sun

Over a decade since he last set to work on a movie soundtrack, Waters's next project returned him to the arena in which Pink Floyd had once spent so much time, as he stepped in to replace David Bowie to score a full-length animated version of Raymond Briggs's *When the Wind Blows*.

Best known in early 1980s circles as the author of *The Snowman*, a book translated into a super-cuddly cartoon about a little boy and, indeed, his snowman, Briggs's latest work was as far from those Christmassy ideals as one could travel, a story set in the heart of the incumbent British government's own recent awakening to the perils of nuclear war.

The Cold War was at a saber-rattling peak; American missiles were being parked on British soil; the arms race appeared suddenly to have turned into a 100-meter sprint. Now, a government pamphlet, *Protect and Survive*, was being delivered to every home in the land, chockablock with helpful instructions about how to protect yourself from Armageddon. True, it contained nothing as asinine as the "duck and cover" instructions that were rammed down America's throat in the 1950s, wherein survival could allegedly be guaranteed by throwing yourself to the floor and putting a tablecloth over your head. But maybe it did. Painting yourself white and hiding under the table would probably be no more effective than a sheet of grandma's finest linen, although it would give you something else to think about during those final few seconds before you were incinerated.

Published in 1982, three years before work began on the movie, *When the Wind Blows* placed itself in the home of an elderly couple that has received such a pamphlet on the eve of the hard rain starting to fall. And, miracle of miracles, they survive the initial blast. But even tablecloths and white paint are no protection against the radiation poisoning that the pamphlet oddly forgot to dwell upon. And so, for the next hour and twenty minutes, we watch as this charming, grandparently pair slowly succumb to an even more horrifying death than the one the explosion itself would have meted out. And it has to be said, if you were looking for an artist who could adequately provide the soundtrack for such a harrowing document, who would you choose?

David Bowie, whose early 1980s were disappearing into a morass of grisly dance albums and moribund movies, making it merciful that he was ultimately unavailable for the task? Genesis, Paul Hardcastle, and Squeeze, who would also be appearing on the soundtrack album, without being especially noticeable?

Boy George?

Or Roger Waters, a man whose politics, intellect, and vision placed him so perfectly in the frame that the twenty-four or so minutes of music that he gifted to the soundtrack ranks as high as *Pros and Cons* in the annals of his career, and that despite comprising just two songs, "Folded Flags" and the epic "Towers of Faith" (which incredibly went unheard in the movie), plus eight shorter pieces that rank more as vignettes and sound clips than music, but which served their purpose regardless.

Lyrically, Waters was cruising, slashing out at the familiar old targets but with a concision and accuracy that confirmed *The Final Cut*'s status as little more than raw rhetoric. Who else would have commented upon the then-incumbent pope's recent visit to England by pointing out that you couldn't understand what he was saying because he delivered his words in Polish?

Who else could have lifted a lyric from the old Hendrix staple "Hey Joe," and made it his own?

And who else would have twisted Woody Guthrie's hymn of freedom, "This Land Is My Land" to a Middle Eastern point of view by draping "sand" across the land, and then thrown in a barb for any listening Pink Floyd fans with a brief acoustic interlude that is positively haunted by the old nugget "Brain Damage"?

He marked his new territory too, returning to the "this is my land" refrain and establishing "this is my band." But that was a dig not at his former Floydian friends, whom he still believed had nothing new up their sleeves, but at the fans who continued to consider him a member of one group, when he was now firmly the leader of another.

Wryly named with both a poke at Sergeant Pepper and at Waters's own reputation for sometimes over-sentimentalizing the underdog, the Bleeding Heart Band comprised guitarist Jay Stapley and sax player Mel Collins, with guest appearances from Clare Torry and Paul Carrack. Matt Irving, a keyboard player first sighted in the Lords of the New Church, as that band commenced delivering its own barrage of apocalyptic warnings upon the world, fellow keys wizard Nick Glenny Smith, Texas drumming dynamo Freddie "Steady" Krc, and bassist John Gordon completed the team. And the single side of music that they spread across the *When the Wind Blows* soundtrack album painted one thing very plainly. This was his band, and the old one was forgotten.

Andy Fairweather Low and drummer Graham Broad would soon be added to the lineup as Waters set to work on a new album—one that would retain the movie's fascination with nuclear war, but expand it sideways with a fresh story line that remains among his most expansive yet. And despite the commercial drubbing he had received at the hands of *Pros and Cons*, he was not about to let either finance or failure get in his way.

Radio K.A.O.S. was conceived, once again, as a three-pronged attack—an album, a stage show, and a movie were envisioned—while he also returned to *The Wall*'s unspoken debt to the Who by following *Tommy*'s lead in making a disabled youth its hero — Billy, a savant who was growing up in a mining town in Wales until the mine was closed down.

We join the story just as Billy's already beleaguered life falls completely apart. His older brother Benny, with whom he was living, was jailed for taking part in the industrial action that protested the mine closures, a deliberately nuanced shadow of the miners' strike that came close to paralyzing Britain in the mid-1980s, and the almost paramilitary response with which Margaret Thatcher set out to repress it.

For just a few days short of a year, beginning in March 1984, South Yorkshire was the epicenter of a conflict that placed workers, police, and even their families directly in the firing line. More than eleven thousand people were arrested, close to nine thousand charged with various offenses, most of them buried within that fine line of hypocritical legal posturing that has always divided civil liberties from civil disorder.

At its bluntest, it was class warfare; at its ugliest, the upper-crust government strove to crush the workers at their source, and once Thatcher authorized the police to use whatever means were necessary to bring the strikers to book, it became a page torn from the writings of Frederick Engels and brought chillingly to life on the streets of Britain. She had indeed "establish[ed] . . . a public power which no longer directly coincides with the population[,] organizing itself as an armed force." It was an impunity that arguably bred the corresponding contempt for law that permitted the same force to so ruthlessly rewrite the events of the Hillsborough disaster, in that same benighted part of the country, less than five years later, although Waters had no interest now in writing of current affairs.

For him, the state-sponsored misuse of the police was just one more straw on the allegorical camel's back, just one more brick in the wall. Across the world, and across every stage, government no longer even pretended to have the well-being of its subjects in mind. It cared only for power for power's sake, gaily attired in patriotic costuming, and not only answerable to nobody at all but ensuring that those elements who may once have questioned policy were securely on its side as well. Just one British newspaper sided with the miners while the strike went on, the left-wing *Morning Star*. The rest just sat back and let the authorities do their worst.

Billy got out. An uncle had gone to live in Los Angeles and agreed to take the boy under his wing. And there, Billy discovered that his mental and physical disabilities were not the only things that marked him as special. Unable to communicate in any conventional manner, his talent for electronics and computers allowed him to create a synthetic voice that fed off the radio waves that clogged the LA skies, and fed back through them as well. He began communicating with a local disc jockey (played by a real-life LA radio personality, Jim Ladd), one who shared Billy's growing disillusion with, and rage toward, the military-industrial complex that was turning the planet inside out.

And together, they fashioned a plan.

Expanding what was emerging as his psychic control over computers, the only force on earth that the world's governments seemed to unquestioningly obey, Billy seized command of the world's most powerful machines and staged a mock nuclear assault. Which may have conjured up shades of the movie *War Games*, in which a teenage computer nerd hacks into the American missile defense program and winds up playing a real war game with the central computer. But this, in the world of *Radio K.A.O.S.*, was no false alarm. A four-minute warning (heralded, of course, by a song of that title, and that precise duration) was the only cushion mankind seemed to have.

It is a fabulously prescient story. In 1985, remember, computers had barely even set a toe inside businesses, homes, and government offices, and those who had installed the ungainly monsters were still eyeing their toys with distrust. There were no Internet or networks to speak of beyond a few internal mail systems, and the idea that one rogue operator could take down, or take out, an entire nation's resources was still sci-fi at its most far-fetched, just one more in that long line of promises that the genre had made regarding our future (personal jet packs remain top of the list), but which technology never got around to delivering.

That might even have been the most common criticism of *Radio K.A.O.S.* when it was released: the fact it was so far-fetched and, after so much building tension, so idealistic. The bad men repented, the world was saved, and the final song, "The Tide Is Turning (After Live Aid)," compared Billy's actions to those that Bob Geldof strove for with Live Aid—a single day on which "technology's sword [was] . . . wrested . . . from the hands of the War Lords."

So far, so simple. Where *Radio K.A.O.S.* truly leaped ahead, not only of the standard conceptual framework but also beyond so much of the rest of the 1980s rock veteran pack, was in Waters's comprehension of the world in which it was set. Just as *When the Wind Blows* gained so much of its musical impact from the precision with which lines of seemingly harmless movie dialogue were inserted into the soundscapes (and none so powerful as Hilda Bloggs's repeated concern for the cake she had just popped in the oven), so *Radio K.A.O.S.* earned its spurs by the insertion of music that matched the action word for word.

No awkward shoehorning of space-filling story lines here. *Radio K.A.O.S.*, like *Pros and Cons* before it, is concise and crunching, with the crackling radio waves of the station itself modeled unapologetically upon exactly the kind of music that a genuine Los Angeles cutting-edge station would have been pumping out in the late 1980s.

It was the age of Guns N' Roses and the rising Jane's Addiction, the march of Metallica, and the consummation of the Cult as the best British hard-rock band of the decade, and whether Waters immersed himself in their music or not, one thing is certain: had any of those bands produced an album this powerful, and this dramatic, we would care a lot more about them today than we do.

The creation of *Radio K.A.O.S.* consumed a year of Waters's and the Bleeding Hearts' lives, sequestered in the studio Waters had built in his home in Barnes, west London, and christened—with a rare shot of becoming modest irony—the Billiard Room. As well equipped as any name studio, and with its equipment expertly manipulated by Nick Griffiths, engineer on *The Wall* at Britannia Row, the Billiard Room was everything that Waters had dreamed the Floyd's own studio could have been, with one major exception. Everything that took place in there did so by his volition and command. It was the outside world that he was having difficulty controlling.

In October 1986, a board meeting of Pink Floyd Music Ltd. brought all four musicians together with Steve O'Rourke, there to inform Waters that a new bank account had been opened into which all monies relating to the new Floyd project would be channeled. In other words, his own earnings from the group were being kept very separate from his bandmates' proposed new endeavors, a transparency that they hoped would keep him happy. Instead, he opened legal proceedings, with his first question being: Under what legal powers was Pink Floyd Music Ltd. even established?

He had certainly signed nothing that confirmed the partnership's existence, and he doubted that anyone else had either. The company had simply come into being of its own volition back in the aftermath of *The Dark Side of the Moon*, but it had no legal standing or status. Which in turn, his lawyers were quick to remind him, meant that any decisions regarding the band's future must be made by all the board members unanimously, a democracy that Waters had no intention of relinquishing.

Pink Floyd pressed on. On November 11, 1986, the corpse spoke publicly through a press statement signed by Gilmour, Mason, and the returning Wright that expressly stated, "although Roger Waters quit in December 1985, the group have no intention of disbanding." On the contrary, the three surviving members had regrouped with producer Bob Ezrin "[and] are currently recording a new album." Which, a furious Waters now discovered, was why Ezrin had been unavailable when he was asked to work on *Radio K.A.O.S.*

Naturally, Gilmour continued, they would "miss Roger's artistic input." But "the strength of Pink Floyd always lay in the talents of all four members. . . . We will continue to work together as in the past."

Waters had recently described the band as a spent force. Gilmour responded with incredulity. "We are surprised that [he] believes [that], as he'd had no involvement with the current project." No involvement meant no awareness. He was talking out of his ass. "The three of us are very excited by the new material and would prefer to be judged by the public. . . ."

So would Waters. He told the *Guardian* that fall, "My [lawyer] told me over a year ago that the kind of justice I was after I could only get from the public — the law is not interested in the moral issue bit in the name as a piece of property." Waters explains from behind his studio desk, "In the best of all possible worlds my public, the Pink Floyd public, will turn round and say, 'No, this is not the Pink Floyd; it meant more than this. No, it shouldn't just be a kind of franchise.' When does a band stop being a band? They presumably have the same sort of definition as the people going round calling themselves The Drifters. . . . I'm out on the road in competition with myself — and I'm losing. I'm sure I would be happier if I could murder them, professionally as Pink Floyd."

⌣

It was April 1987, with *Radio K.A.O.S.* on the brink of release, before Waters released an official response to Gilmour's goading, through the hyperbole-free auspices of his lawyers. It outlined, of course, his achievements and contributions to the band's past, how he was "the major songwriter and producer" of *Dark Side of the Moon* and *The Wall*, "as well as the lead singer and creative force."

It also reminded the world that "a dispute with the other members of Pink Floyd is proceeding in the courts to resolve the question of rights to the name and assets of Pink Floyd which include the many stage effects used in the past."

The ideal solution was that which had already been mooted by Gilmour, that the public should make the final decision. Would they accept Pink Floyd without the man who wrote so many of their best-loved songs, secure in the knowledge that his bandmates would write many more, which was Gilmour, Mason, and Wright's contention? Or, as Waters angrily argued, would the world agree with him that a band is not a franchise, is not a name to be worn by whoever felt they could, whether it be three former members reliving past glories or a friend of the roadie's, having a laugh?

Enough groups from the early to mid-1960s, and beyond as well, were already in that kind of situation, grinding around the circuit with a lineup that might not even have been born when their group was top of the pops, or with just one original member to establish some kind of lineage. As Peter Noone, the singer who helped shape the sixties at the helm of Herman's Hermits, once snapped: "There were people touring [as the Hermits], using the name, playing the songs, who I'd never even heard of! I went to some of the shows, and I'd see these fucking clowns on stage — 'Ah, here's one we recorded in 1965' — and my friends would have to hold me back. I just wanted to run up there and have a tantrum. 'You didn't record it . . . the only one of you who was even in the band back then was the drummer, and he never played on any of the records!'"

Was that how Gilmour, Mason, Wright, and O'Rourke wanted Pink Floyd to end up? Was that how anybody wanted them to end up? The beast was dead. Let it rest in peace.

But Waters was playing a dangerous game.

It would have pummeled Waters's ego to admit it, but there were a lot more Pink Floyd fans who didn't know the name of a single band member than there were who actually paid attention to such details.

A lot, too, could have made the same arguments for (or against) the band continuing on without Syd Barrett back in 1968. In 1968, after all,

Barrett was at least as dominant in Floyd's creative department as Waters was now arguing he'd been—more so, in fact, because at least Gilmour, Wright, and Mason now had two decades of experience of being in the band, and had played their own parts (however small Waters claimed them to be) in establishing the group's sound and vision. When Barrett departed in early 1968, Waters's sole solo credit on a Pink Floyd record was "Take Up Thy Stethoscope and Walk," universally regarded, even by its composer, as the least important song on their first album.

Even more damaging, however, was the fact that the argument had arisen now, as Waters was preparing for the release of his own new solo album. Ordinarily, he could have shunted the questions about Pink Floyd's future into the corner and talked his way through the new record's promotion. Now, *Radio K.A.O.S.* was guaranteed a backseat in any interviews he gave, as the media struggled instead to make sense of the death/non-death of Pink Floyd, and it was likely to be shoved even further back as Pink Floyd announced the release of their own next album, the pointedly titled *A Momentary Lapse of Reason*, for September 1987, just three months after *Radio K.A.O.S.*

On August 14, Roger Waters's *Radio K.A.O.S.* tour launched in Rhode Island, a six-week outing that would scour the United States before breaking for a month of recording in Nassau, the capital of the Bahamas, then pick up for another two weeks across the US, and finally across the Atlantic for two nights in London, where, to everybody's horror, he attracted just five hundred people to the cavernous Wembley Arena, a venue that the new Pink Floyd would effortlessly sell out the following year. Indeed, Waters's tour was just sixteen dates old when his old bandmates ignited their own tour in Montreal, Canada.

Mercifully, sensibly, the two tours never came within touching distance of one another; the closest was probably the night in late September when Waters played Seattle while his bandmates entertained Chicago. But often mere days separated the pair, and hostilities were never far from the surface as Waters had his lawyers contact promoters across the country, threatening dire repercussions should Pink Floyd be allowed to blight his outing. He never followed through on such threats, but still Pink Floyd had a legal team on standby in every city they played, briefed to defend them in the event of any action.

The war of words escalated. In the UK, *the Sun* tabloid announced that Waters had just commissioned an artist to make him 150 rolls of toilet paper, each perforated sheet decorated with David Gilmour's face. In the US, *Penthouse* came down solidly on Waters's side by comparing his "sadly conflicted sense of propriety" and sensitivity with Gilmour's "wire-pulling flair . . . an efficient and spiteful field marshal."

Which, in all honesty, was very much a reversal of most people's understanding of the two musicians' personalities, especially once they started talking to the media. Waters came across as bitter, spoiled, and ruthless, a pinchy-faced humbug who wanted to confiscate one of rock 'n' roll's most favored playthings, while Gilmour seemed a cheerful, affable fellow who just wanted to get on with what he did best, making people happy by playing their favorite songs.

And more than one observer remarked that Waters had created the rod for his own back in the first place. If he'd just sat tight as a band member, he could have killed the group by refusing to work with it, forcing the others to throw him out, while remaining fairly confident that they never would. Instead, he flung the door open and walked out. What did he expect the others to do?

As before, Pink Floyd would expand for the live shows, and one familiar face was called up. Tim Renwick recalls, "I got a call to do what was originally a short US tour—[and] the moment that the tickets went on sale, the tour became a sixteen-month-long twice-around-the-world event!"

There was, he says, no problem whatsoever that he had so recently worked in the enemy camp, and no lingering hangover from Waters's way of working. "It was, to my immense relief, a very relaxed affair and most enjoyable. The band got on really well, which proved that a rock tour can be tremendous fun as well as being highly successful!"

Pink Floyd did keep an eye on their nemesis, of course. Renwick reveals, "There were several secret visits to Roger's shows during this time; he sort of shot himself in the foot more than a little by booking his dates in various cities just before we were about to appear there. I have to report that we really blew him off, as our production was just (for those days) the biggest thing anyone had ever seen. Roger's production was more like an art school dance by comparison!"

Ticket sales, too, proved that the Pink Floyd name would always be much larger than any of its component parts. And ultimately, a lot of the squabbling was put to one side. Waters did extract one concession, that *The Wall* would remain off-limits to the band. But everything else . . . essentially the whole thing came down to money, a subject in which he was not especially interested, at least in this case. He did not want financial compensation. What he wanted was control over his own intellectual property, and that, he was finally induced to see, was a nebulous concept, the definition of which would have kept the lawyers in new yachts and country club memberships for years and years to come, years which would be better spent doing something else entirely.

Such as concentrating on his own tour.

As before, the show was divided into two halves, one devoted to the new album, the other allowing the Floyd fans to get their rocks off via what amounted to a potted history of the band from "If" to "Not Now John," and then on into *Pros and Cons*. Waters rescued "Pigs" from a decade's worth of concert oblivion and delivered all but "Shine On You Crazy Diamond" from *Wish You Were Here*. But it was the *Radio K.A.O.S.* portion of the performance that truly startled all comers, as Jim Ladd reprised his role on the album and introduced each of the songs via a stream of radio patter, while Waters sat down for a call-in show, taking questions from members of the audience.

Roger Waters in the Netherlands, June 1968. (Laurens Van Houten/Frank White
Photo Agency)

In the studio, 1967. Left to right: Richard Wright, Nick Mason, Syd Barrett, and Roger Waters. (Chris Walter/WireImage/Getty Images)

What is this ummagumma of which you speak? Left to right: David Gilmour, Roger Waters, Nick Mason, and Richard Wright. (Photofest)

Set the controls for the heart of Vesuvius: Pink Floyd, live in Pompeii, 1971. (Photofest)

Floyd of London. (Photofest)

Onstage at the Holland Pop Festival, June 28, 1970. (Laurens Van Houten/Frank White
Photo Agency)

Gilmour and Waters backstage at the Ahoy, Rotterdam, April 3, 1971. (Laurens Van Houten/Frank White Photo Agency)

Richard Wright. (Photofest)

Waters, '70s sideburns included. (Photofest)

Onstage, wishing you were there. (Michael Ochs Archives/Getty Images)

Ticking away the moments. (Michael Ochs Archives/Getty Images)

Piggies over Uniondale: live at Nassau Coliseum, February 28, 1980. (Frank White)

Waters at the Wall, Nassau Coliseum, February 1980. (Ron Akiyama/Frank White Photo Agency)

In terms of visual presentation, just as Renwick says, it was a lot less dramatic than some ticket holders might have hoped; in terms of ticket sales, too, the outing could not help but be sabotaged by the imminence of the Floyd tour. Waters even admitted that he was essentially out there competing with himself. But somehow it didn't bother him anymore. In terms of audience size and media exposure, Pink Floyd had the quantity. But, he assured himself, he had the quality—audiences who came to the show because they wanted to see him, not because their beer buddies told them there would be a flying pig and a shit-hot light show.

Gone, too, was the old impression of sourness, weariness, and rage with which Waters had once chosen to cloak his onstage persona. He laughed; he smiled; he became involved with the audience. Instead of studiously avoiding the hands that stretched out across the stage toward him, he would crouch down and shake them. When he sang "In the Flesh," he would engage even further, and while one does wonder how individual onlookers felt being singled out by a pointing finger as he condemned the "queers" and "coons" in the lyric, Waters's grin was so disarming that no offense could have possibly been taken.

"I'm completely different, and feel completely different about being onstage now," Waters later said of the change in demeanor. "I've come round to embracing the possibilities of that connection with the audience. Now I milk it mercilessly, just because it's fun and it feels good. Whereas back then I was so fearful that when I was onstage, I was the same as I was at a party—standing in a corner, not looking at anybody, smoking cigarettes, and more or less saying 'don't come anywhere near me.'"

The phone-in segment of the show, too, was astonishing, as Waters gleefully answered whatever was thrown at him, and made some wry observations, too, including the fact that he now thought about David Gilmour every time he sang "Pigs."

Enlivened, invigorated, Waters took the band to Nassau and, with just a month in which to work, essentially wrapped up a whole new album.

Amused to Death, he said at the time, was a return to the more personal struggles that he experienced, as opposed to the universal concerns of *Radio K.A.O.S.* But his hopes for a swift release (some reports claimed early spring 1989) were dashed as he clashed with his record companies, EMI and CBS, apparently over the quite disproportionate support they gave to the new Pink Floyd project, as compared with what they had done for him.

This was not about bitterness. This was about fair play. And, more than a few of Waters's sympathizers murmured, a matter of simple arithmetic. Who was most likely to deliver to the label a new *Dark Side of the Moon* or *The Wall*? Three of the guys who played on the records? Or the one who wrote them in the first place?

—

It was in the midst of all this that Waters was presented with what even he admitted was one of the most fascinating challenges of his professional career and given an opportunity to place all the other crap behind him for a while.

French songwriter Étienne Roda-Gil was working with top pop singer Julien Clerc when Waters first met him during one of Pink Floyd's Gallic sojourns in 1968. They had remained in contact ever since, and when Floyd's subsequent continental trips took Waters within a reasonable distance, he and his family frequently stayed at the home Roda-Gil shared with his wife, painter Nadine Delahaye.

Conversation was never less than stirring. Roda-Gil was the son of a Catalonian, a Spanish Republican who fled to France in the aftermath of the Spanish Civil War as it transformed from a purely local ideological struggle into a dress rehearsal for the military excesses of World War II. Roda-Gil was two years Waters's senior, and his instincts for and understanding of left-wing youth politics as they swept Europe that summer of 1968 played their own role in broadening the Englishman's feel for the subject, sweeping him out of the parochialism of his own upbringing and enabling him to see the struggle as a truly universal fight.

Roda-Gil's influence even prompted a new song, "Incarceration of a Flower Child," which would not be heard by the outside world until Waters gifted it to Marianne Faithfull in 1998 (she included it on her album *Vagabond Ways*), at which point many listeners painted it as an early lament for Syd Barrett. But Barrett's mental problems were scarcely a concern at that time and certainly had not committed him to any kind of psychiatric care. Rather, the song personalized the so-called hippy dream, and then internalized it, looking back over the idyll of the previous year's utopian fantasies and how cruelly they had been crushed in just a few short months. It would indeed "get cold in the 1970s."

Two decades had passed since those long, late-night discussions, but Waters and Roda-Gil remained close, and in 1987, the Frenchman approached him about a collaboration. Roda-Gil and Nadine had recently completed the libretto for a three-act French language opera, *Ça Ira* ("there is hope"), set during the French Revolution, an event whose two hundredth anniversary was already being prepared across the country.

Waters was asked to put the libretto to music, a monstrous task given all else that was percolating around him at the time, but one into which he threw himself with gusto. If nothing else, it took his mind off all the other business.

Spanning twenty-five years of turbulent drama, *Ça Ira* journeyed from "A Garden in Vienna, 1765," where the ten-year-old Marie Antoinette looked forward to her future, to the Revolutionary Tribunal of October 1793 which found her guilty of crimes against the people, crimes against the Revolution, and (apparently because it compounded her evil; there was no evidence whatsoever of it having taken place) the sexual abuse of her son. Waters's task was to set to music some of the most momentous, and best known, events in French history: the fall of the Bastille, the flight of the royal family, the establishing of the Commune, and the execution of both king and queen. And to do so without any recourse to his rock 'n' roll instincts.

He composed not on his usual guitar and piano, but by finding his way around a string synthesizer. And the music that he wrote was to follow the moods of history, not of himself, a discipline that was both unfamiliarly constricting, but also refreshing, invigorating, bold. It enabled him to take chances that he might never have dreamed of in his personal writing and to visualize structures that made *The Wall* look like a potting shed.

He conjured up gardens, palaces, and prisons. He gave momentum to the mob and fervor to the fighters. A lifetime of political discontent was channeled not into lyrics but into musical notes. And the three acts of the opera fell into place. It took him less than a year to complete his demo, and in late 1988, the tape was played to French president François Mitterrand. Impressed, Mitterrand asked for it to be performed during the bicentennial celebrations in July 1989 and approached the Paris Opera to stage the production.

Which is when it all fell apart. The Opera turned it down flat—doubtless they had their own musical and perhaps even logistical reasons for doing so. But Waters equally had no doubt whatsoever as to the true cause of their refusal. A celebration of the French Revolution should not be the work of an Englishman. And opera in general should not be the work of a rock musician.

Ça Ira was shelved, at least for now, the urgency of its completion defused not only by the Paris Opera's stance (which nobody doubted would be communicated throughout the remainder of the French musical establishment), but also by the death of Roda-Gil's wife, Nadine, the following year.

Besides, events elsewhere on the European mainland were now taking center stage in Waters's imagination.

—

Nineteen eighty-nine is the year that the Wall came down. The real wall, that is, the Berlin Wall, that literal construction of concrete and wire that had divided the former German capital since 1961, splitting it physically and ideologically between the Communist east and democratic west. And which now lay in rubble to be cleared away by the bulldozers that would make physical reality from what had once seemed an idyllic dream — the reunification of the city, the re-creation of Germany.

It was World War II that first halved the nation, the German defeat in 1945 being followed by the division of the country between the victorious Allied powers. To the west, the Allies restored democracy; to the east, the Soviets installed Communism, and, for more than forty years, those divides had become a fact of life.

But, from the moment President Gorbachev was elected general secretary of the Communist Party of the Soviet Union in 1985 to usher in policies and reforms that even his most immediate predecessors would have deemed impossible, a new sense of hope began to sweep across those lands that the "free" West deemed the Eastern bloc. A belief that they too could be free.

Free to consume, free to speak openly, free to wallow in the free-market economy that has worked so well across the West. Free to buy Pink Floyd records.

In truth, the Soviet Union and its satellites had never been the wasteland of rock-free squalor that the Western media liked to paint it. As far back as the late 1960s, British bands had been venturing into the East to play, and while certain acts would forever remain on the banned list (Pink Floyd was among those singled out for that honor in Bulgaria), the reach of Western radio ensured they all had a following, no matter how far underground that following was forced to exist. Western tourists played their own part as well, and while it would be 1987 before any Western rock band (Uriah Heep) received an official invitation to play the USSR itself, the East loved its rock 'n' roll just as much as the West. Now it wanted to be able to buy it.

The collapse of the Berlin Wall did not necessarily denote the end of Communism. Poland and Hungary had both held free elections before the Wall was demolished in November 1989, and Czechoslovakia and

Bulgaria would follow the East German lead within days. But Romania's Communist leadership held on for close to another month, Albania would not be free of Communism until 1992, and the Soviet system itself fought furiously against the reforms.

Still, the political tide had turned, and if Roger Waters had ever been asked, at some point in the preceding decade, whether there was one historical event that could possibly inspire him to restage his own wall, this was the one he would have chosen. In fact, he had already said as much, using the collapse of the Berlin Wall as a euphemism for "a cold day in hell" when he was asked if he would ever play a *Wall* concert again.

Well, the devil had just bought some leg warmers.

Or not. In fact, Waters had already abandoned his personal injunction on such a performance, and it was coincidence alone that decreed he should do so just a matter of weeks before the people of Berlin took sledgehammers and drills to the concrete barrier.

In September 1989, Waters was introduced to one of the Western world's greatest humanitarians, a British wartime group captain and pilot named Leonard Cheshire. The veteran of over one hundred bombing raids on Nazi Germany, and Britain's official observer at the atom bomb attack on the Japanese city of Nagasaki, Cheshire was so affected by the carnage that he both wrought and witnessed that in 1948 he founded the Cheshire Foundation Homes for the Sick, a charity dedicated to the long-term care of disabled former servicemen.

One hospital had become half a dozen by 1955, and four years later, Cheshire established a second charity with his wife, Sue Ryder, the Ryder-Cheshire Foundation. Now he had formed another. The Memorial Fund for Disaster Relief was established to provide funds for the victims of future disasters and wars, an ambitious aim for which Cheshire set an equally ambitious target. He aimed to raise no less than £500 million for the fund—a figure which boiled down to just five pounds for every life lost to war throughout the twentieth century.

It was Mike Worwood, one of the promoters involved in Live Aid, who suggested Waters's name to Cheshire, and when the two men met, the seventy-two-year-old war hero and the fifty-year-old war semi-orphan, it was as though they had known each other for years. Who suggested what to the other remains unclear. But Waters had already agreed to stage a fund-raising performance of *The Wall* weeks before the Wall itself came tumbling down. And the search for a suitable venue for the concert, which had already got underway, ended on the spot.

They would stage it in Berlin.

Waters explained:

> We're both passionate about the idea of the Family of Man and the idea of eradicating the idea of dying of hunger or being put up against a wall and shot or living a lonely drab existence. I have to say though that our response to that is completely different. I, by comparison to Leonard, am someone who lives an extraordinarily luxurious and indolent life. The way he works himself is beyond belief. I couldn't do that. I'm not . . . saintly and I never will be.
>
> I guess if I was as devout a Christian as Leonard is I might find it necessary to pursue the Christian ideal with the vigor that he has. Unlike most professed Christians he seems to take it quite literally. He is the Good Samaritan. My only connection to that is that in the broad sense at least I may be sensitive to the human situation. Some people close to me may say that's all very well, but it doesn't percolate down necessarily to the wife and the children. All I know is I'm working bloody hard on this.

Potsdamer Platz, essentially a no-man's-land between the two halves of the divided city, was to be the site of the event. Now all Waters needed was to formulate the concert itself—an all-star event as broad in its sweep as Live Aid had been, with a staggering array of guest performers that not only gathered force from across the spectrum of rock but stretched further afield, as well. An East German symphony orchestra. A Combined Soviet marching band. The US Seventh Airborne.

Impresario Tony Hollingsworth was brought in as producer; the previous year he had conceived and overseen Nelson Mandela's seventieth-birthday tribute concert at Wembley Stadium, London, a massive event that roped in some eighty performers and reached an audience of 600 million people via television broadcasts in sixty-five countries. The year before that, Hollingsworth had staged the four-day The Secret Policeman's Third Ball for Amnesty; in April 1990, Mandela personally commissioned Hollingsworth to handle his official international reception, a four-and-a-half-hour event celebrating the South African's release from prison.

Past Pink Floyd set designers Mark Fisher and Jonathan Park were recruited. They had handled *The Wall* in its earlier incarnation; now they could do it again, on a scale that even Waters had never imagined possible.

There would be a live audience of 350,000 people, swollen to almost half a million after the gates were flung open the night before the show and all comers were invited to take their own place. A live global television audience was expected to soar into the tens of millions. A new wall was constructed, eighty-two feet high and 550 feet long. Gerald Scarfe set to work on an array of fresh monstrosities, roundly and soundly acclaimed the largest puppets ever made. Eight million dollars worth of everything money could buy, all to ensure that this performance of *The Wall* would become the most lavish musical production of the century.

Which, whether you liked *The Wall* or not, it would be.

"When I came to listen to the album again after ten years, I thought, Christ, I hope I like it still," said Waters.

> Then I put it on in the car and it was, "This isn't half bad." I'm extremely proud of it. I'm proud of the fact that I get letters from school-teachers who use "Another Brick" as the basis of class discussions.

And there's a book about psychotherapy in which the author mentions *The Wall* and says how extraordinary it is that an English-man should write in this way. When I read that in an academic tome about child psychology, I did feel a warm thrill that some-body had taken it so seriously. So the payoff from having expressed myself before my peers and torn down my wall, if only to a limited extent, the payoff is . . . good.

Yet very little went to plan. Invitations were sent out to a clutch of name performers whom Waters especially wanted to involve in the production, to voice the songs that he selected for them. But Bruce Springsteen, Peter Gabriel, Rod Stewart, Eric Clapton, and Joe Cocker all turned down the opportunity to take part in the circus. Stewart actu-ally backed out after his name had been confirmed. So did Cocker and Huey Lewis.

Van Morrison did accept; alongside the Band, Bryan Adams, Sinéad O'Connor, Joni Mitchell, the Scorpions, Marianne Faithfull, Thomas Dolby, and Paul Carrack, all contributing to a lineup which certainly was not destined to glisten as brightly as was originally planned. At the same time, however, even Waters knew that the only absentees that anybody would really remark upon were the three men who had assisted with *The Wall*'s construction in the first place. They had pointedly not been invited, although wryly, their ex-wives were.

There were problems on the night of the show—typical in-concert gremlins who cavorted through O'Connor's rendition of "Mother," and galumphed around the other instruments too. The crowd was enthralled, but it was also frustrated—sight lines were poor and the amplification inadequate. Squeaky-squalling American pop singer Cyndi Lauper was (naturally) a contentious inclusion to begin with, and her assault on "An-other Brick in the Wall (Part 2)" only confirmed Floyd fans' fears for the song's safety. And so on.

Nonetheless, the inevitable video release, *The Wall Live in Berlin*, is routinely described as a sublime spectacle, and rightfully so. Onstage flubs were edited subtly away; sonic imperfections were redressed in the studio. And, of course, the cameras had the best seats in the house to catch every last moment of the admittedly powerful choreography and special effects.

But Waters was unhappy. Yes it was an astonishing event, one that burned its highlights into the memory of all who witnessed it, and one that only further confirmed the legend of *The Wall*. Demands for a repeat performance were deafening. But Waters would put it aside; once again, he announced that he would prefer to concentrate on new material, rather than continue rehashing the old.

Who did people think he was—Pink Floyd?

8

Wot's . . . uh the Deal?

Perfectly understandably, Operation Dinghy, the Memorial Fund's trading arm, went into *The Wall* expecting to make its money from the audio and video sales that all concerned were convinced would establish new records. Instead, increasingly aghast, they watched as neither even threatened to approach the estimated figures and wound up, in fact, incurring such heavy losses that the Fund itself would soon fold. It was a disappointing end to Cheshire's life—the grand old man passed away in 1992 after a battle with motor neuron disease.

Roger Waters has never been the kind of person to lose himself in regrets and lamentation. But his insistence that the production was a one-off event surprised many people. Eight million bucks is a lot to spend on a single concert performance, a huge bite to take from a budget that could have easily been restored with a few other choice locations. The Great Wall of China was one prospective venue that other folks' wishful thinking floated. Hadrian's Wall, in the north of England. The Vietnam Memorial Wall in Washington, DC.

Or even the vast barrier that was about to be constructed in occupied Palestine, the separation fence that would divide Israeli from Arab with great slabs of concrete, stretching for miles across the land. A construction, in other words, that would make the Berlin Wall look puny by comparison.

The Arab world and its struggle to find both political and cultural equilibrium in the Middle East and beyond was a cause Waters had never felt truly comfortable espousing, no matter how deeply he sympathized. Even without delving into the so-called rights and wrongs of the situation, there are lines that the very nature of the Western world, and in particular its media and political structure, will seldom permit to be crossed. Too many vested interests, too many financial power plays, too many knee-jerk responses. It was not even as though he was scared to raise his voice. He just knew it would be drowned out too quickly. But sometimes, it is impossible to remain silent.

Waters's personal life was undergoing another of its occasional upheavals as his second marriage, to Carolyne Christie, broke down after sixteen years and two children, Harry and India. Neither party would air their dirty linen in public, although keen-eyed paparazzi delighted in filing pictures of Waters with the new lady in his life, American actress Priscilla Phillips. A striking blonde whom certain camera angles gifted with a hint of Jerry Hall around her facial structure, Phillips's career was still in its infancy at the time—a minor role as a supremely bitchy customer in *Frankie and Johnny,* and an appearance in an episode of the British TV series *The Big One.*

The pair, Roger and Priscilla, would announce their engagement on April 30, 1992, and would wed on July 28 the following year. And in the meantime . . . Waters had a new album to work on.

Amused to Death was the collection he had cut in the immediate aftermath of *Radio K.A.O.S.* Titled for a favorite book, Neil Postman's damning critique of the influence of Western television *Amusing Ourselves to Death,* the album was all but complete. But he continued tinkering with it, carting the tapes from studio to studio, and wondering sometimes whether events unfolding in the world outside would ever relent sufficiently for him to deem it a finished work. Whenever he turned on the television news, which the nature of the album insisted he did, he found himself increasingly spellbound as great elements of the Postman book were transformed into a living theater of current affairs, masquerading as prime-time entertainment.

In 1989, TV coverage of the Tiananmen Square massacre in Beijing had mortified Waters, and not only for the carnage that was wrought that day. The image of the lone man advancing on a Chinese tank, armed only with a plastic grocery bag, was seared into the minds of everybody who witnessed it. But how soon after that did it become the only image from the fateful day that anyone would recall? Everything else that happened in the Chinese capital, and that includes the massacre itself, was forgotten behind that one image, that one feel-good moment on a day that left the world with nothing to feel good about whatsoever.

Worse was coming. History recalls the Vietnam War as the first conflict ever to be broadcast on television, as the American military granted the media more or less open access to every aspect of the conflict, and then sat back in mounting horror as the expected images of courage and heroism were instead supplanted by gut-wrenching footage of suffering and carnage. More than any other event on the home front, the generals grimly agreed, it was television that had turned the tide of public opinion against them. They would not make that mistake again.

The Gulf War, pitting an American-led coalition of nations against what was being painted as the rapacious Iraq, was also to be fought on television. But this time, the media was locked down tight. There would be no enterprising camera crews straying off piste in search of napalmed babies and slaughtered villages. There would be no lingering shots of American servicemen breathing their last as their guts flowed around them. The Gulf War was a clean war; the Gulf War was a choreographed war. Set to music — which you sometimes felt it might as well have been — so anodyne was the coverage, so bland was the footage, you could almost have called it a fun war.

Particularly once the handful of reporters that were permitted to visit the frontline seized their own little moments of stardom, grasped their own media-friendly nicknames (the Scud Stud was an especially memorable one), and viewers found themselves exhorted to admire a whole new wave of superstars, the bold and brave reporters who showed such commendable courage while under faraway fire.

Even the bombing of Iraq's cities took on an almost balletic quality, with a lightshow that rivaled Pink Floyd's most ambitious assaults, and a soundtrack that all but overlaid patriotic orchestration over the muffled thump of the bombs raining down.

Amused to death indeed.

Tiananmen Square and the Gulf War would both enter into Waters's lyric writing. But whereas his past attempts to seem contemporary had merely dated themselves within months of composition, this time his verbiage was built for the long haul. True, *Amused to Death* does sound quaint today, naive and even a little old-fashioned. But that is not because its sentiments have been at all displaced. It's because even Waters, like Postman before him, could never have foreseen how much worse things could get.

There were no television reality shows in 1992. Simon Cowell–shaped searches for stars with the X factor were still popularly known as "talent shows" and were the makeweights of the broadcaster's schedule. Strangers were not routinely bundled into houses together and told to act out their sickest childhood tantrums. Documentaries still attempted to tell stories that were true. Paranormal investigators did not routinely misuse the word "debunk" and devour countless hours of broadcast space every week on hapless searches for realities that would, were they to find them, necessitate the immediate cancellation of their own show.

Newsreaders still read the news, as opposed to impersonating fourteen-year-old boys on their first visit to Hooters . . . or their older sisters applying for a job there.

MTV still showed music videos.

And so on.

Viewed from twenty-plus years down the road, 1992 actually feels like a halcyon era. And *Amused to Death* is the lone stagecoach rider, disgruntled by the advent of the very first railroad.

But what a beautiful stagecoach he rides.

The Bleeding Heart Band was still in evidence. But so was a crop of guest stars that was, if anything, even more impressive than those who had helped build the wall in Berlin. Jeff Beck followed his Yardbirds predecessor Eric Clapton into the lead guitar slot, and perhaps gave us a glimpse into what might have happened had one of Waters's oldest dreams come true and Beck had joined Pink Floyd instead of Gilmour. The pair became friends, Beck later laughed, after a visit to the bassist's house ended with the vintage-car-crazy guitarist being allowed to take Waters's Maserati for a spin.

Pat Leonard, perhaps best known as a songwriter for Madonna, was brought in to play keyboards and coproduce, following Tim Renwick as the latest in what would soon become a small tide of changing allegiances (five years before, Leonard had played keyboards on the last Pink Floyd album). Don Henley of the Eagles and country singer Rita Coolidge were onboard as well, while Waters typically allowed himself space to namecheck a few absent friends . . . who just happened not to be friends any longer:

Bob Ezrin, producer of *The Wall*, had fallen out with Waters over his decision to work on *A Momentary Lapse of Reason*, having already apparently agreed to produce Waters's *Radio K.A.O.S.* He was rewarded with the lyric "every man has his price, Bob, and yours was pretty low."

Director Stanley Kubrick refused Waters permission to use a few snips of dialogue from *2001: A Space Odyssey* and was likewise repaid with a mumbled chunk of backward speech. Although one could also say that Kubrick was himself just exacting a form of revenge; years before, he had approached Floyd's office for permission to use a piece of *Atom Heart Mother* in his then-gestating *A Clockwork Orange*. They turned him down.

Waters had learned one lesson, however. Aware that two (three if you counted *When the Wind Blows*) previous albums had been largely lambasted as musically difficult and conceptually convoluted, *Amused to Death* was a considerably less sonic experience than its predecessors. Rather, it emerged as an album that was comprised of songs as opposed to soundscapes, radio friendly in a manner that only occasional moments of *Pros and Cons* and *Radio K.A.O.S.* had been, and imbibed, in fact, with the same moments of yearning and emotion that had been lacking since the days of primal Pink Floyd—and which, correspondingly, many people assumed were the province of Gilmour.

"Perfect Sense," both parts one and two, certainly stands as one of Waters's most emotive compositions, as he and coproducer Leonard discovered the secret that had, perhaps, eluded Waters across all his past solo efforts—that of seamlessly weaving the sound effects (in this case, the near-constant babble of television commentary) into the music. The impression, though he probably would not have thanked anybody for pointing it out, was not that dissimilar to the use of a baseball commentary during the make-out scene of Meatloaf's "Paradise by the Dashboard Lights," an exquisite superimposition that pulled along the song like a super-souped-up tow truck.

Reviews responded accordingly, and so did sales. Reaching number eight in the UK, *Amused to Death* was Waters's highest-charting solo album yet. But sales of a million were nowhere close to the three-to-four-million target that he had deemed necessary before he would consider touring the album, and he was not being bitter when he casually noted that, had *Amused to Death* been a Pink Floyd album, it would have sold ten million without even blinking. He was being truthful.

He might have had another reason, however, for not planning any kind of live outing. Across town, the noisy neighbors were preparing their own next move, a new album called *The Division Bell*, and a tour—which would be preserved on the *Pulse* CD and DVD—that not only promised to be their most grandiose yet, it would also climax every night with a full performance of *The Dark Side of the Moon*.

And so the 1990s and, correspondingly, the twentieth century ran out of the hourglass, and one of the most vocal and vociferous of the entire era's lyricists maintained a stoic silence that apparently nothing could penetrate. Not the invitation, in the summer of 1994, for him to rejoin Pink Floyd for an evening at Earls Court for the night's rendition of *Dark Side*, nor even the band's long-overdue induction into the Rock and Roll Hall of Fame in January 1996—a night, incidentally, that spoke aloud of another rift forming within the band, as Nick Mason also absented himself after falling out with Gilmour over the band history the drummer was then writing. (*Inside Out: A Personal History of Pink Floyd* would eventually be published in 2004).

"The line they give you is, 'If you don't get another record out they'll all forget you,'" Waters shrugged.

> [Genesis guitarist] Mike Rutherford was telling me this, not about me but about himself, a couple of years ago when he was furiously working on a solo album that meant he couldn't go on holiday or something like that. What's the problem? Who cares if they forget you? How much money do you need? If you're locked in the studio and you can't go on holiday with your family because you have a desperate need to get the feelings out, that I can completely understand. But to go into the studio because you're worried that people are gonna forget you seems to be nonsense.

There was a brief flurry of media interest around 1995, with reports that a full recording of the French Revolution opera was finally nearing completion and might be out by 1996 (it wasn't), and another when Waters was said to be contemplating a stage production of *The Wall*. That, too, vanished into the ether.

But finally, in 1999, Waters stirred once more, convening a new band lineup around Andy Fairweather Low and Snowy White, keyboard player Andy Wallace, and another graduate from the recent Pink Floyd camp, keyboard player and vocalist Jon Carin, and heading out on a tour that triumphantly proclaimed him "the Creative Genius of Pink Floyd," appearing In the Flesh.

The set list confirmed the title. Waters's solo career was more or less sidelined behind a repertoire that went all out for Floydian grandeur. He reinstated "Shine On You Crazy Diamond", with Snowy White snatching back all the mantles that Gilmour's Pink Floyd had draped over the song, and he handed unfamiliar vocal lines to Carin to perform.

Which meant yes, it did seem somehow strange watching a live band performing "Dogs" every night, and knowing that only the bassist had ever played it before, but there was a sense, too, that a lot of water had now flowed beneath Waters's bridge. The tour was a new beginning, and he was finally willing to embrace once again his entire past, and not just those elements of it that spoke for his own most obvious contributions.

There were moments when it even felt like a Pink Floyd show.

His reasoning was simple. It was seven years since Waters had last played live, when he added his weight to a charity concert being staged by Don Henley's campaign to save Walden Woods in Massachusetts, back in 1992. A handful of Floyd numbers was all he needed to play, but the audience response to the concise little set reminded him that he did still have an audience, even if the low turnout for *Radio K.A.O.S.* had done much to convince him otherwise.

In the Flesh was no scaled-back performance. The size of the screen behind the stage, onto which Waters's customary array of short films and images would be projected, was large enough to discount many of the venues he had played last time around, while ticket demand forced other halts to be rearranged so that a new, larger venue could be found. For the first time since the *Pros and Cons* tour, Waters found himself performing in American stadia, and for the first time since *The Wall*, he was selling them out.

He rewarded audiences with a set that was heavy on nostalgia and heavy, too, on the kind of extended soloing and extemporizing that once characterized Pink Floyd, a hits-heavy set that played out like the greatest Floyd collection you could possibly imagine and that reached a stunning, and utterly unexpected, climax with the one new song on display, the starkly moving, and utterly Floydesque "Each Small Candle." A song that would never find an album to live on, but whose encapsulation of the world to which it was played was itself a vast, sweeping canvas that wrapped up so many ideological concerns.

Elements of the lyric were drawn, in a manner Waters had not really approached since the days of "Set the Controls for the Heart of the Sun," from a poem by Danish poet Halfden Rasmussen. "Ikke Bødlen" ("Not the Torturer") was first published in 1979 in a book of poetry commissioned by Amnesty International. Waters opened the new song with a verse from the poem, but then shifted the focus to his own observations and a story he heard of a young Serbian soldier fighting in the Kosovo War who broke ranks to aid a wounded Albanian woman. In a conflict that, to Western media eyes, was dominated by the torture and massacre of civilians, that single act of sacrifice stood out, indeed, as one small candle in the darkness. The song implored mankind to light many more.

If "Each Small Candle" represented a shift in Waters's songwriting style, away from polemic and into the realms of more studied observation, it also coincided, like the tour which it dignified, with him taking a more hands-on approach to the fruits of past labors.

In 1992, Pink Floyd stepped into the world of extravagant CD box sets with *Shine On*, an outsized package that served up a not-exactly-conventional selection of past albums, neatly remastered, with an assortment of bonus bits (a hardback book, a couple of postcards, a fold-out display case) and an extra disc retelling the group's early history through the five singles they released between 1967 and 1969.

For a group that had kept such a tight lid on its archive, with only *Relics* (and possibly, if you agree with Richard Wright, *The Final Cut*) truly breaking their embargo on revisiting the archive, *The Early Singles* was a fairly grand gesture. Of course it was not enough for the fans who had spent their entire Floyd-loving lives seeking out alternative versions, live cuts, and outtakes, and all of whom could compile their own wish list of releases that the band could/should have unleashed alongside it.

Now, with a new century upon us, the twentieth anniversary of *The Wall* would see at least one of those dreams come to fruition. All four past band members agreed to roll out to discuss the old album with the media, and although they did it separately, with the old disagreements regarding its quality still bubbling close to the surface, nevertheless there was a genuine understanding of what *The Wall* meant to its audience.

Waters was especially enthused, throwing himself not only into some of his most revealing interviews yet but also into the remastering of the movie for DVD, complete with a new commentary track that paired him with Gerald Scarfe. And then he delivered the live album that topped so many fans' personal Christmas lists.

Is There Anybody Out There? The Wall Live: Pink Floyd 1980–81 was recorded over the seven nights the band played at Earls Court, London, and represented only the second official live recording that the "classic" band lineup had ever sanctioned (following *Ummagumma* three decades earlier). More such ventures were in the pipeline, however, while Waters's In the Flesh tour would also be preserved on both CD and DVD, adding its weight to a growing mountain of "post-Floyd" offerings from individual and collective alike.

A thirtieth anniversary edition of *Dark Side of the Moon* was in the works, exquisitely remixed for 5.1 sound by James Guthrie, the studio whiz who had now worked alongside the band for over two decades. And before that, a twenty-six-track compilation, *Echoes: The Best of Pink Floyd*, swaggered out of the vault, a two-CD collection that reached back to the Barrett era and then moved forward (to Waters's undisguised disgruntlement) to *A Momentary Lapse of Reason* and *The Division Bell*.

All four band members were involved in the track selection, and maybe Waters was correct in his assumption that the rest of the group ganged up against him when it came to some of the more contentious selections. Gilmour, one assumes jokingly, accused Waters of wanting to include no less than half a dozen cuts from *The Final Cut,* but nobody got things their own way—the guitarist's own insistence that "Fat Old Sun" be featured was soundly voted down by the others, and Richard Wright recalled pushing, equally unsuccessfully, for "Summer '68."

No matter. The finished package did indeed serve up a Floydian feast that it was very hard to argue with, with the expected jewels being beautifully balanced by some genuine surprises. And Waters maybe had the last laugh when he added a brand new song, "Flickering Flame," to another retrospective, this time examining his three solo albums. No matter what else was taking place around him, the song pledged, he would be "the last one to lay down my gun."

Like "Each Small Candle," "Flickering Flame" is first and foremost a song of hope. Yet sadness also permeated it: After eight years and one son, Jack Fletcher, Waters's marriage to Priscilla had now ended (a new relationship was already in place, with actress and filmmaker Laurie Durning). His first wife, Judy Trim, had passed away on January 9, 2001. Tony Howard, the band's former booking agent and tour manager, too, had died.

Waters had said good-bye to Philippe Constantin, the French journalist whom he counted among his closest friends. Longtime Pink Floyd manager Steve O'Rourke and Waters's recent collaborator Michael Kamen would pass before year's end, as would author Douglas Adams, a close friend of Gilmour's too. In an age when Pink Floyd's sole reason for existing appeared to be so that they might reflect on their musical past, the individual members were being given cause, too, to reflect on their personal pasts, each death adding its imponderable weight to the band members' own awareness that they had probably enjoyed far more yesterdays than they could ever have tomorrows.

Flickering Flame, as Waters's solo compilation was titled, is a fascinating introduction to the world of his solo output, albeit one that frustrates, too. "Knockin' On Heaven's Door," the old Dylan song, is rescued from the obscurity of the 1999 Israeli thriller *Ha Dybbuk B'sde Hatapuchim Hakdoshim*, for which it was originally recorded (and where it was otherwise ignored). The demo "Lost Boys Calling" teases the potential of Waters's short, sweet songwriting collaboration with Italian soundtrack giant Ennio Morricone (the finished track appeared on the movie score *The Legend of 1900*, and adds guitar by Eddie Van Halen), while "Each Small Candle" and the title track both make the listener yearn for the fourth solo album that Waters kept insisting was underway. But which he was keeping very close to his chest.

Either that, or he'd decided to release it in installments.

Two more new songs emerged, a single of sorts that was made available for download in 2004. Of the two, "To Kill the Child" sounded a little too much like Dire Straits to bear repeated listening, with the backing chorus that keened the title drowning the lyrics' naked thoughtfulness beneath way more bombast than they required. Plus, it really was all rather mawkish, a charity sing-along that left most listeners silent.

"Leaving Beirut," on the other hand, blazed. Onstage in Sydney, Australia, he introduced the song to the audience. "When I was . . . seventeen years old, I travelled in the Middle East with a friend of mine and our car broke down in Beirut, in the Lebanon, and we had to hitch-hike back to England. For the first night of that journey I was taken in by an Arab family who treated me with such enormous kindness that I've never forgotten them. They changed my life, to some extent. This song is about that night . . . among other things."

The separation barrier was a reality now, the division that cut a physical line through Israel that could only strengthen the psychological walls that already split the inhabitants of Israel and Palestine. "Leaving Beirut," whose early verse could as easily have been the tale of any young man in the Mid East of the early 1960s, trying to hitchhike home from any of the cities, asked just one question: Would an Arab family be as willing to care for a young Westerner today, knowing all that his mind would have been filled with by the media? And then answered it with a list of all the reasons why they probably wouldn't.

Rapprochement was in the air. Vacationing on the Caribbean island of Mustique, Waters found himself face-to-face with Nick Mason — or, rather, face to back. Mason was not even aware Waters was in the hemisphere until he felt two hands on his shoulders, and then his neck. He turned to identify the silent strangler, and the pair were inseparable for the rest of the afternoon. A month later, in February 2002, Mason was backstage at London's Wembley Arena, preparing for possibly the most unexpected gig of his entire recent career, playing behind Roger Waters for the first time in twenty-one years.

The reunion was brief, just a performance of "Set the Controls for the Heart of the Sun" (which went so well they repeated it the following night), but it opened a door that had felt closed for so long. One through which Bob Geldof was about to march.

By mid-decade, 2005, twenty years had passed since Live Aid, twenty years throughout which the memory of the event itself had at least been bruised by the infighting and politics that surrounded the dispersal of all the money raised, but in which the very concept of the show had become the blueprint for rock 'n' roll's capacity to "do good."

Long memories will recall how, in the immediate aftermath of the original event, a host of other "aids" were launched — Sport Aid, Farm Aid, Ferry Aid — each with its own worthy agenda, each drawing in a clutch of sympathetic superstars to sing a verse, or play a show, or in some other way make their participation public. There was even an all-star record made to try to convince Britain's BBC not to cancel the long-running television show *Doctor Who*.

Some, of course, were less successful than others; some even prompted industry observers to suggest that the public was running dangerously close to charitable burnout. But the long-term wheat was separated from the "yester-day's headline" chaff, and by the early 2000s, the causes that most demanded longevity were established as a vital and vibrant part of the rock calendar.

David Gilmour, a longtime philanthropist (in 2003, he was awarded one of Britain's highest civilian honors, a CBE—Commander of the British Empire—for his services to both charity and music), was heavily involved in the homeless charity Crisis; Roger Waters was vocal in his support of War on Want. Now Bob Geldof was back on the charitable scene (not that he had ever left it), declaring no less than ten benefit concerts to be staged around the world on July 2, 2005, under the banner of Live 8, to mark both the anniversary of Live Aid, and also to raise awareness of the Make Poverty History campaign.

Awareness, not money. There would be no grinning MTV telethon hosts demanding that viewers of the internationally televised event dig deep and call in to pledge cash to the cause. No slickly edited video pathos to be screened between the songs. No all-star singing-circus singles to push forgotten former somebodies down the watching public's throat. There would simply be music, music, and more music.

Geldof already had a sizable coterie of artists onboard. Sir Paul Mc-Cartney, U2, and Madonna all agreed to perform. So did Elton John, Stevie Wonder, Neil Young, and German superstars Die Toten Hosen. Now, as Geldof cast around for other headline acts to draw into his web, he remembered something he'd read in the British *Q* magazine the previous year, an interview with Nick Mason in which the drummer mused aloud on the kind of event that could possibly bring the fab four back together again. Another Live Aid, maybe. Something significant, something life changing. Something that felt bigger than the band.

Geldof made the call, to Gilmour first of all.

Gilmour turned him down.

But Geldof persisted, even taking a train down to the guitarist's home, then calling again to ask for a lift. Gilmour picked him up, heard Geldof out, and then asked for a few days to think about things. Not, he assured Geldof, that it was his decision alone. There were other people involved, after all, and maybe the way he said it was intended to push the idea out of Geldof's head forever.

Nick Mason was already onboard, after all, and nobody doubted that Richard Wright would join him. That just left Roger Waters.

It was Mason who e-mailed Waters to let him know of Geldof's offer, and really not knowing how the news would be received. He was astonished to learn that Waters called Geldof immediately after, catching him just as he was about to go out for dinner with his wife. The ensuing conversation was disjointed then, but it ended with Waters giving his assurances that, if it could be brought together, he would be happy to play a part.

Now it was Gilmour who was holding out, for what his bandmates could only guess. So finally Waters called him to ask, the first time the pair had spoken together since they argued at an acrimonious meeting a few years before, while discussing a documentary on the making of *The Dark Side of the Moon*. Prior to that, they'd not said a word to each other since 1987.

This time, tempers were calmer, and the only real impediment was Gilmour's surprise at even receiving the call. But it did the trick. Twenty-four hours later, the guitarist called Waters back to say he would play the concert. It really was going to happen.

Now they had to marshal the troops—Tim Renwick, Dick Parry, Jon Carin, and Carol Kenyon, one of the backing vocalists from *The Division Bell*. A band meeting at London's Connaught Hotel sorted out the set list, four songs that would eschew Waters's suggested selections from *The Wall* alone in favor of what could be called essential Floyd—"Breathe," "Money," "Wish You Were Here," and "Comfortably Numb."

Tim Renwick: "Initially I heard from David that Floyd had been invited to appear, but he told me that there was no way that he wanted to do it. Several weeks later, I had a call from him saying that he had changed his mind and that it would be 'fun' to have Roger back on bass. He appeared to find the whole thing very amusing (at the time). . . . He may have regretted it later. . . .”

Rehearsals were tense. Waters's immediate instinct was to alter the tempos and arrangements of some of the songs, a trick that had worked well for him on his recent solo tours. Gilmour was equally adamant that they play everything as it ought to be. This was not about art or artistic expression. It was about reuniting the band for a single good cause. And finally, Waters relented.

For the accompanying musicians, Wright and Mason included, “it was a matter of keeping out of the way really!” Renwick continues. “There had been legal wrangles/ threats of legal actions/overturned injunctions, etc. ever since Floyd had announced their decision to carry on without Roger.” Even with Live 8 a reality, “I heard that there were still legal proceedings afoot.”

Somehow, they put all the extraneous stuff behind them. And then it was showtime—some seventy thousand people crushed into London's Hyde Park, the same expanse in which Floyd's former management, Blackhill Enterprises, had once staged free concerts back in the late 1960s and early 1970s. Something else remained the same, as well. The acts were still faced with the same interminable wait while the other performers went through their paces.

Elton John and Pete Doherty. Snow Patrol. U2. Madonna. All ran through their scheduled sets, until finally, only two acts remained to be heard: the headlining McCartney, from whom nobody expected a single surprise, and Pink Floyd, whose very presence on the bill was a shock that no one had ever anticipated.

Darkness had fallen, and a heartbeat thumped through the crowd—a heartbeat and the opening voices and sound effects from one of the biggest selling albums the world has ever seen. Figures were on the stage. The crowd was in ecstasy. And then the music began, and the sound was as crystalline as the greatest hi-fi in the world. It was really happening, and two vast screens on either side of the stage made sure that nobody could deny it. Gilmour, balding and bulking but unmistakable, leading the vocal line. Waters, graying and equine, looking more like actor Frank Finlay than one-quarter of a rock band, but looking like he was having fun, too, almost bouncing behind his bass. Wright, as stately as the sounds he created, and Mason, half-invisible behind his drum kit, but you could see his smile for miles.

"Money," tight and funky, coiling around a bass line that is as familiar as your own pulse beat. Geldof apparently requested they perform it, but it's unlikely that they would have omitted it regardless. Dick Parry's sax was flawless; Tim Renwick and Jon Carin were perfect. Carol Kenyon sang like an angel. And twenty-three minutes went past so fast that, even rewatching the footage again and again, it's hard to believe that it actually took place, and harder still to resist throwing yourself around the house like the overjoyed idiot dancers at the front of the crowd, captured forever on global TV with their faces creased like *South Park* Canadians, and their own disbelief written large in their eyes, only to be slowly nudged aside by the realization that they were there.

Nobody has ever estimated how many different people Pink Floyd had appeared before over the course of their original fourteen-year in-concert lifespan. But it is unlikely any were as happy to see them as the audience at Live 8.

Later, rumors would insist that the event was somewhat less celebratory than it could, or should, have been. Tim Renwick recalls, "There was a fair amount of 'jockeying' for the final slot of the evening—Paul McCartney wanted to perform twice. We were hanging around for what seemed like an age, finally going onstage at the end of the evening. It was all a terrible shambles I'm afraid. I personally had to walk back to the hotel after the show as there was no transport organized—and there was no 'thank you' or anything for the work done! I think all concerned were just happy that the show was over frankly!"

For the duration of the show, however, all seemed blissful. Pink Floyd closed with "Comfortably Numb," solid and soaring, blissful and hopeful. But it was the performance of "Wish You Were Here" that saw grown men break down and hardened rockers in tears, that song of inter-band bitterness that the years had translated into the ultimate lament for sadness and loss, for the years that had raced past since the first time you heard it, and everything that had vanished as they did so.

Not only for the audience, those people who had now grown old to the sound of Pink Floyd, but for Pink Floyd, the musicians themselves. Which is why Roger Waters took it upon himself to speak the only words that any of the musicians would utter from the stage until it was time to say good night, a brief introduction to the song that probably ranks among the most heartfelt he has ever told an audience.

"It's actually quite emotional standing up here with these three guys after all these years.

"Standing to be counted with the rest of you.

"Anyway, we're doing this for everyone who's not here. But particularly, of course, for Syd."

PART 2

During times of universal deceit, telling the truth
becomes a revolutionary act.

—misattributed to George Orwell; original source unknown

9

Emily, Playing

On June 5, 1975, a very fat, very bald man clad in gray polyester pants and a nylon shirt with a glaringly visible string vest beneath it passed the elderly security man in the main reception of Abbey Road Studios. He made all the correct turns down the ensuing maze of corridors, past the gold discs and awards that hung on every wall, past the other doors that might have opened into offices, closets, or someone else's album, and walked into the studio where Pink Floyd was recording.

Nobody looked up. Roger Waters, David Gilmour, and Nick Mason, the three band members present at the time, were clustered around the console, talking about the track they were currently working on and cuing up the tapes for another playback. Maybe they noticed the newcomer, but they were too engrossed in their own work to pay him any mind. Besides, it was the mid-1970s, and the British chart was positively overflowing with weird comedians and novelty acts. This was probably just another one. A Wurzel looking for his next shot of cider. A Womble in search of a garbage bin. Telly Savalas's brother. Well, they had the same hairline.

But Andrew King, one of Pink Floyd's oldest friends, paying his own visit to the studio that day, was just going to ask the visitor what he wanted, when suddenly the stranger didn't seem quite so strange. And as King's brain struggled to strip almost five years of fat from the smiling cue-ball face of the new arrival, his lips mouthed a name he'd not spoken in ages.

Perhaps he said "Roger," which was the apparition's given name. Or maybe he said "Syd," the nickname with which he had been saddled since school, ever since (according to one of so many legends) he turned up to his scout troop's field day clad in a flat cap. The sort of hat that old working class men named Sid would wear. The name stuck, but the boy changed the spelling because he thought it looked a shade more exotic.

Whichever name King spoke, the sound of the word, and the tone in which he said it, had a galvanizing effect on the musicians around him. For they, too, suddenly realized that they were once again in the presence of an old friend, an old bandmate, and the nearest any of them would ever come to true genius. And they were stunned to silence. For it is not true simply to say that without Syd Barrett there would never have been a Pink Floyd. Without Syd Barrett, half of what we take for granted in the history of rock might never have come to pass.

He's been immortalized as the Crazy Diamond, and in concert, David Gilmour and Roger Waters still bid him to "shine on." He's been touted as a principle influence from as far afield as Julian Cope and Michael Stipe, his songs have been covered by everyone from David Bowie to the Jesus and Mary Chain, and according to the legend to which he ascended some forty years ago, and which persisted even after his death in July 2006, he was as nutty as a Snickers bar, and raised mushrooms in his basement.

Brief though it was, Syd Barrett's legacy was impressive. In the course of three years—1967 to 1970—he recorded one full album with Pink Floyd and contributed sufficient material for a second. The uneasy solo career that he undertook following his departure from the band spawned two further official albums, and another pair's worth of outtakes and run-throughs. And after that? Silence. He had said all he was going to, and maybe all that he wanted to. By the time of his death, he had not thought of himself as a musician (or a former musician) for years. He was an artist, a painter. The same thing he'd wanted to be in the years before he joined a band. Before he formed Pink Floyd.

The first time Pink Floyd played London's Marquee Club, in February 1966, they were essentially still making exactly the same kind of noise they'd been unleashing since the various members first started playing together a year or so before, after meeting through what English rock history insists was the traditional route during the early to mid-1960s, university.

A native Londoner, keyboard player Richard Wright was the oldest, born on July 28, 1943; drummer Nick Mason (born in Birmingham on January 27, 1944) was the next to youngest. But the heart of the band were two Cambridge boys, Roger Keith Barrett (born in Cambridge on January 6, 1946) and Roger Waters, an almost impossibly serious-seeming youth who was just a couple of months Wright's junior, but had a demeanor that made him seem by far the most senior.

It was Waters who planted the seeds of the band. Having Letrasetted the phrase "I believe in my soul" across his guitar, he first formed a folk duo with fellow student Keith Noble in 1963. The Tailboard Two played a handful of gigs in the Polytechnic's assembly hall, sharing the bill with sundry like-minded enterprises, but more of Waters's time was spent with fellow students Richard Wright and Nick Mason.

They bonded over typical teenage pursuits of the age: regular trips down to Charing Cross Road, the hub of London's community of music stores, to drool through the glass at the instruments arrayed out of reach and certainly out of budget on the walls. They went to the movies—the cut-price matinee performances, of course—and any money they did deem spare was saved away for clothes. Nick Mason recalled regular visits to Anello & Davide, a world-renowned ballet-shoe maker in nearby Covent Garden, who had recently branched into custom-made Cuban-heeled cowboy boots. The height of hipness!

By late 1963, the Tailboard Two had expanded to half a dozen, as Mason, Wright, guitarist Clive Metcalfe, and Noble's singing sister Sheila came onboard in a band sensibly titled the Sigma 6. Occasionally Wright's girlfriend (and future wife), Juliette, would join them for a few of her favorite blues numbers, while other players came and went.

They were called the Ad-Dabs for a while back then, occasionally the T-Set, and sometimes the Meggadeaths, and the lineup began to stabilize: a residual core of Waters (now playing bass guitar), Wright, and Mason, plus another of Waters's Cambridge connections, guitarist Bob Klose, and, briefly, a vocalist named Chris Dennis, who worked as a dental assistant for the Royal Air Force.

But then Waters's old friend Roger Barrett arrived in London to study painting at Camberwell Art School in Peckham. Naturally, he contacted Waters, and soon the pair, plus Nick Mason and another friend, Dave Gilbert, were sharing a flat at 39 Stanhope Gardens in Highgate, north London, and writing songs as well. Nothing they would have dared play in public, of course (the best recalled of Waters's efforts was a novelty duet designed to be sung by Barrett and Juliet, "Walk With Me, Sydney"—Barrett was Sydney), but it was an education all the same.

Klose and Dennis were short-lived band members; they departed in late 1965, around the same time as Barrett's burgeoning interest in American bluesmen prompted him to rename the band after two of them, Floyd Council and Pink Anderson, and around the same time, too, as the group began distorting and distressing their R & B repertoire into something else entirely, stretching "Louie Louie" out as long as it would go, riding "Road Runner" round to the peyote plantation, chasing "Cops and Robbers" till their legs begged for mercy. That was the set they took to the Marquee, and any other venue that would book them, and almost immediately upon their emergence, Pink Floyd caught the capital's attention.

A Canadian radio interview from late 1966, shortly after the band appeared at an Oxfam benefit at the Royal Albert Hall, captured the intensity of their performance, as the female interviewer warned her audience, "Some call it free sound; others prefer to include it in the psychedelic wave of isms already circulating around the western hemisphere. But this music, here and now, is that of the Pink Floyd, a group of four young musicians, a light man, and an array of equipment sadistically designed to shatter the strongest nerves. The Pink Floyd are new on the London scene, they've stupefied audiences at all-night raves, in church halls, at the Albert Hall, and on various tours throughout Britain."

Nowhere can that stupefaction be better gauged than by listening to the music which Syd Barrett was suddenly, feverishly composing.

According to (admittedly inaccurate) legend, Barrett had written just two songs before the Floyd's newly recruited management team, Andrew King and Peter Jenner, suggested the band try developing some original material. One was "Effervescing Elephant," a poem he wrote at age sixteen and had vaguely set to music sometime since then; the other was a melody intended to accompany a favored fragment of James Joyce's *Ulysses*, "Golden Hair." In fact, these were written later, but there were plenty of others already in place. "Butterfly" and "Remember Me" are among the early prolusions that his old friends recall, while he also had a jokey song about the students' favorite drug, marijuana, which he called "Let's Roll Another One."

But all of a sudden, the floodgates opened, and as if the songs themselves were not spectacular enough, the brilliant blaze of inspiration which consumed Barrett as he created them dazzled everybody. It was, in hindsight, as though he knew his time in rock 'n' roll would be limited, and he was getting everything in while he could. At the time, it was simply a staggering achievement. "Syd was an incredibly prolific writer," future producer Norman Smith later reflected. "Everything we recorded together, the albums, the singles, and many of the songs on his solo records too, was written in one six-month burst. I'd never met anybody that young, who was that prolific."

Christening themselves Blackhill Enterprises, managers King and Jenner set up shop at 32 Alexander Street in Bayswater, an unremarkable storefront in a row of old brick dwellings that had seen better days. Most of the band at one point or another moved into one of the flats upstairs (King and his girlfriend, Wendy, too, lived there), while downstairs, secretary June Child (the future Mrs. Marc Bolan) attempted to wring order from the chaos of ringing phones, unpaid bills, unanswered mail, and all the other detritus of a slowly building management agency.

By contemporary music business standards, they were an unconventional pair, utterly uninterested in traditional industry habits and methods. While other agencies scrabbled to book their bands into the clubs and pubs that had always comprised the English gig circuit, King and Jenner constantly sought out new venues to play: All Saints Church in nearby Notting Hill, the Commonwealth Institute down the road in Kensington, Hornsey Art College.

In December 1966, Pink Floyd headlined the opening of a new club in London's Tottenham Court Road, the basement beneath the Blarney Club, which would, seven days later, be renamed UFO, and become a legend within its own lifetime, immortal after its death.

Like the Cavern in Liverpool five years before, or the Covent Garden Roxy ten years later, UFO was not simply the focal point of the latest musical movement; it was the heart and soul of it too. A churning, burning potpourri of mayhem, mysticism, art, and electricity, incense and dope, into which the songs flooding out of Barrett's imagination found (or were founded upon) instant fertility. "Astronomy Domine," perhaps the premier piece of period space rock; "Chapter 24," based upon a favorite segment of the I Ching; "The Gnome," oozing the imagery of Tolkien's Lord of the Rings. "Percy the Ratcatcher" touched upon T. S. Eliot's Practical Cats saga (the song would later be retitled "Lucifer Sam").

"Arnold Layne," which would become Pink Floyd's debut single (backed by a rerecorded "Let's Roll Another One," judiciously retitled "Candy and the Currant Bun"), daringly immortalized a pervert who stole underwear from people's washing lines, and which took its initial inspiration from the Waters household. Barrett explained, "I pinched the line about 'moonshine washing line' from Rog, because he has an enormous washing line in the back garden of his house."

There was the childlike wonder of "Matilda Mother"; there were "Sunshine" and "She Was a Millionaire," "Flaming" and "The Scarecrow," "[The] Bike [Song]"; and there was "Interstellar Overdrive," composed by Barrett around a guitar riff borrowed from Love's "Little Red Book," built up by his bandmates into a full-blown sonic extravaganza, and emerging as a veritable talisman for the early Pink Floyd.

"The Pink Floyd is the underground's house orchestra," proclaimed *Town* magazine. "Their music sounds more like Thelonious Monk than the Rolling Stones. Projected slides bathed the musicians and audience in hypnotic and frenzied patterns of liquid-colored lights. Honeycombs, galaxies and throbbing cells whirl around the group with accelerating abandon as the music develops."

Other people were impressed by their diction; Waters and Barrett, already established as the group's lead spokesmen, were almost breathtakingly well-spoken, holding their own against BBC TV interviewer Hans Keller in spring 1967; the heavily accented Austrian musicologist sounded almost churlish interrogating these two charming, polite, well-dressed young men. If the pop music business ever went belly-up, either could have found a new career as a BBC TV announcer in his own right.

It was very early in this process that Pink Floyd made their first attempts to land a record deal; but the two Barrett compositions which made it onto the band's first demo tape — "I Get Stoned" and "Let's Roll Another One" — although typical of the drug-induced whimsy that was slowly sweeping England's capital, were quickly forgotten. The most encouraging response it received was from Joe Boyd, one of the leading lights at UFO, and all he suggested was that they make another tape, and that this time, they try spending some cash on it.

An American-born producer who had relocated to London in late 1965 as a roving producer for Elektra Records, Boyd was now striking out alone at the helm of his own Witchseason production company (named for Donovan's all-pervading "Season of the Witch.") Hurling himself into the hubbub of the London underground scene, he swiftly located its epicenter, photographer John "Hoppy" Hopkins, and two aspiring young entrepreneurs named Andrew King and Peter Jenner. It was they who first sensed Pink Floyd's potential and snatched the group up as their first (and, for a time, sole) managerial client, and they who introduced the band to Boyd.

The producer's first instinct was to sign the band to Elektra. But label head Jac Holzman was not interested, so Boyd turned his attention to Polydor, a long-established player on the German scene that was just beginning to make inroads into the UK by contracting the country's established musical giants to link their own stables to the company. Impresario Robert Stigwood had already contracted his newly formed Reaction label to Polydor, bringing with it a catalog that included the Who and Cream, plus sundry Bee Gees–related projects (Stigwood also managed the brothers Gibb).

Giorgio Gomelski, another giant on the UK scene, was launching his own Marmalade label, again through Polydor; Who managers Kit Lambert and Chris Stamp would soon establish Track Records via the same lofty portal. The parent label itself was signing up all and sundry, and Witchseason was destined to follow. Boyd passed the good news on to the band, and they set to work rehearsing what would become Pink Floyd's debut single, "Arnold Layne."

In the event, Polydor's overtures came to naught. The contract was still awaiting signature when King and Jenner introduced a new player to scene, promoter Bryan Morrison, an experienced veteran whose first move was to scrap both the Polydor contract and Boyd's proffered Witchseason deal. Morrison's own agency would finance the recording of the Pink Floyd single, and Boyd would remain onboard as producer. But he would be the band's employee, as opposed to the other way around, and across two nights in February 1967, the re-signed, but still unhappy Boyd led the band into Sound Techniques studios to record both the A- and B-sides of the band's debut.

Tony Baws, the Morrison Agency's accountant, recalls the day he first heard of this new band—courtesy of Morrison's father Joe. Bryan was handling the Pretty Things at the time, but a couple of years had passed since that band's last hit, and, while they remained a vibrant musical concern, commercially Joe felt they "have probably had their day. It's all underground music now."

Baws admits that he was none the wiser, and he doubted whether Joe was either. Underground music was a new phenomenon, one that even the music press was still struggling to get its head around. But Joe had done his homework. "The Pink Floyd—they're kings of that scene. And Bryan's their agent."

"'So, they're doing well then?' I hoped that I sounded confident saying 'they' because in truth I had never heard of Pink Floyd.

"'Oh yes' enthused Joe. 'They go out for two-fifty, three hundred pounds now. Just need a hit record, that's all.'"

Joe Boyd was the man who would give it to them.

The Morrison Agency offices had recently moved to that grubby little corner of London's west end that has forever been enshrined as Tin Pan Alley, a short block called Denmark Street, into which the entire British music industry seemed to have been shoehorned. Promoters, publicists, studios, producers—they all had their offices on Denmark Street, all re-splendent in a kind of bohemian shabbiness that itself epitomized the nature of the local industry at the time.

Morrison's agency, a partnership with a diminutive Glaswegian named Jimmy Duncan, planted itself at 142 Denmark Street—through a doorway that had probably not seen a new coat of paint since before the war, up a flight of rickety stairs, and the first door you saw led to the bathroom. Continue up the stairs and there was a members-only drinking club, but take a sharp left turn through the glazed door, and there was the two-room Morrison-Duncan agency.

One room was the domain of the agency's founding namesakes, a single shared desk with a pair of telephones, a typewriter that was probably as old as the paintwork, and a Dansette portable record player that had seen a lot better days. Later, a Grundig reel-to-reel player would find its own way onto the premises, but for now, as Baws laughs, "considering the nature of the business, the music reproduction system at the time was pretty basic." With Baws and Morrison senior squeezed in there as well, the same could be said for the working conditions.

The other room belonged to the agency staff, bookers Tony Howard and Steve O'Rourke, likewise seated around a single table. Occasionally Duncan's sister, singer Lesley Duncan, dropped by to help out with the secretarial work, but the Morrisons had no intention of expanding until they had no choice. As Joe used to put it, "I've always worked on the boot-strap principle. Suffer in discomfort for as long as you can — it saves money. Only move when you can't expand one single inch more inside the space you already have."

This was the world into which Pink Floyd was shuffled once the Morrison Agency took over their diary, although right now they were too busy to really register the surroundings. A deal with Columbia Re-cords, a subsidiary of EMI best known for the long-term residency of singer Cliff Richard, brought "Arnold Layne" onto the streets in early 1967, a minor UK hit sustained almost wholly by the band's London audience — the BBC, supreme arbiters of the country's pop radio, played it occasionally.

But the so-called free spirits at Radio London, one of the pirate radio stations that hovered just outside Britain's territorial waters and blasted a nonstop diet of music into the country, banned the track outright, so strongly did they feel about its subject matter, and there was a general sigh of relief among broadcasters and management alike when "Arnold

Layne" had finally run its sordid course, and the group announced its next single, "See Emily Play."

According to Barrett, the song was inspired by a night he spent sleeping in the woods after a gig somewhere, when a girl appeared before him. That girl was Emily, and according to Floydian apocrypha, the sixteen-year-old Honorable Emily Kennet was a familiar sight around the UFO circuit, where regulars had nicknamed her "the Psychedelic Schoolgirl."

Unfortunately, it is equally likely that this charming tale is as fanciful as so many of the others surrounding Syd Barrett's time with the Floyd. Mick Farren, vocalist with another of UFO's most regular performers, the Deviants, recalls, "When not playing, I used to oversee the door and run the security at UFO, and I never heard of the Hon. Emily, who I would absolutely have noticed since she would have been a bust waiting to happen. The cops would have liked nothing better than to nail the organizers for contributing to the delinquency, etc., etc. She could have been a Syd schoolgirl groupie, but she never hung out at the club."

The Bryan Morrison Agency had moved at last, to Bruton Place in Mayfair, directly above one of the clubs which they handled bookings for, Revolution—they also took care of the entertainment at the Speakeasy, Blaises, the Black Sheep, and the Pheasantry, a convenience that would be reflected in Pink Floyd's social life. Free admission to each of those venues was a welcome perk of their contract with Morrison, while his own proximity to one of the beating hearts of socialite swinging London saw the agency itself become a fulcrum for creativity.

Gold and purple, the predominant colors of Revolution, continued up the stairs. The walls were adorned with pop art; a new, hiply lettered logo and masthead were splashed across the agency's stationery. Two dolly-bird receptionists greeted visitors, blonde Annabel and brunette Melissa, and Tony Baws continues, "A reception/lounge area was established to accommodate the increasing foot traffic: musicians, agents, band managers, publicists, journalists, groupies and so on.

"Some individuals stood out by virtue of the frequency of their visits or the amount of mayhem or excitement their appearance caused or their notoriety warranted." The duo Tyrannosaurus Rex—Marc Bolan and Steve Peregrin Took (plus Bolan's wife, the charming June Child). Sundry Pretty Things. Blues legend Alexis Korner, and most of Eire Apparent, a Northern Irish band whom Jimi Hendrix had taken under his wing. Disc jockeys Jeff Dexter, Simon Stable, Pete Drummond.

"Mick Farren was a regular but I can't say whether that was in his role of a member of the Deviants or as a nascent journalist and author." Agents and managers: Joe Boyd of Witchseason; Tony Secunda of New Movement; Laurie O'Leary of the Charles Kray Agency; Derek Block, Andrew King, and Pete Jenner of Blackhill Enterprises. Members of the graphic design team Hipgnosis, who designed the album covers for many of Bryan's signings.

Baws:

> Bryan supported some of the acts financially in their start-up period but little cash passed hands in the office. A certain sheepish look came over musicians on the scrounge, and they were usually sidetracked by the ever-so-innocent secretaries. Nor was there much sign of flirting—I think that in the main, Annabel and Melissa saw musicians as slightly grubby and not at all glamorous. There were, of course, exceptions. Marc Bolan and Syd Barrett in particular seemed to set their hearts and other parts aflutter. At odd moments the girls would warble delightedly, "I've got a bike you can ride it if you like."

Barrett's attraction, Baws continues, like his talent, was

> real and obvious. He often appeared in the office, usually on his own, and unannounced. He had great self-confidence and

wandered around at will, usually with a big smile on his face. He was courteous, charming and softly spoken. There often seemed to be no specific reason for his visits, other than to say "hello" and be involved.

But he had an aura of disquiet about him, a fragility that was hard to ignore. Bryan was always pleased to see him and the two of them chatted in an easy fashion, with many chuckles and smiles. While Bryan could be cold blooded and mercenary when the mood took him, Syd seemed to be almost in the nature of a "special project," someone who appealed to Bryan on more than a purely commercial level.

If his own management regarded Barrett as the standout attraction in the band, it is scarcely surprising that media and audiences should have felt the same way. Baws recalls,

Unlike the other band members, Syd seemed at ease in satin shirts and velvet trousers as casual day-wear, his long, unkempt hair sported as a natural feature rather than an imposition of fashion.

For a band that turned out in both creative and commercial terms to be far and away the most successful to be handled by Bryan Morrison, I have to say in all honesty that as individuals, in those early days, Pink Floyd were the most ordinary, bordering on boring. They still looked ill at ease in the gaudy clothes worn on the *Piper* cover. Syd Barrett was an exception and had an aura of excitement about him. Nick Mason and Richard Wright came across as solid, middle class citizens, with Nick being the more outspoken of the two.

Unusually, however, the band members not only realized this criticism, they went out of their way to encourage it. Waters explained, "We give the public what they can see for themselves. We don't want to manufacture an image. We dress as we feel at the time."

Too many bands, past and present, have been hamstrung by their adherence to an early image that ultimately proved impossible to shake. By remaining in the stylistic shadows, Waters proclaimed, Pink Floyd was not going to make that same mistake, and it was this thoughtfulness, this consideration for moments beyond the present, that caught Tony Baws's attention as Floyd continued their upward motion. "Roger was not yet the troubled soul or deep thinker that he appeared to be in his later career." But in terms of being the sole member who appeared to care deeply about the ins and outs of the band's career, whose "yea" or "nay" was the one that management knew could sink or sail any new business idea, and who actually cared about the future ramifications of decisions being made on the spur of the moment, "Roger was definitely the leader of the band."

By spring 1967, with "See Emily Play" on the brink of release, Pink Floyd's name was now oozing out of the underground and into the cold light of the media mainstream. A suitably alarmist story in the tabloid *News of the World* numbered Pink Floyd among the sinister ringleaders of the drug-demented "Psychedelic Experience"—and that experience was only going to get louder.

On April 29, 1967, Pink Floyd headlined the Fourteen Hour Technicolour Dream festival, hosted by the stately Alexandra Palace.

Some days before, the police had busted the London basement offices of the *International Times*, the alternative newspaper that both dominated and influenced what the mainstream media was now dubbing "countercultural" thought processes. *IT* swore to fight back, however, and the underground rallied to its side. Alexandra Palace, a gorgeous slab of Victoriana dominating a hill over north London's Wood Green, was procured at very short notice, and with it, the services of every freak in town.

Artists and poets offered their support. Frank Zappa associate Suzy Creemcheese was there, as were Yoko Ono, Ron Geesin, and more.

Fairground amusements sprang up in every corner of the building; slide shows flickered on every surface; fireworks lit up the night sky. And then there were the bands, forty-one of them, all playing for free on two separate stages.

Some were known quantities with nothing to prove—John's Children, the Soft Machine, the Move, the Syn. Others were total unknowns, still searching for a lucky break—a full year before "Fire" gave them a worldwide number one hit, the Crazy World of Arthur Brown fell into that category. And others still were one-off, ad hoc conglomerates drawn together for the thrill of the evening and nothing more.

Floyd was set to take the stage as dawn broke over London, hot off the ferry from some shows in the Netherlands. And of course they joined in with the spirit of the event, but, according to the Move's manager, Tony Secunda, as showtime drew closer, it was impossible not to notice that something was going seriously awry for Syd Barrett.

Barrett was no stranger to LSD. He had long since passed beyond the "experimental" stage and now resorted to the drug as both a recreation and an escape. Until Gilmour purchased the rights in 1994 and promptly withdrew it from circulation, you could even buy a grainy home movie purporting (probably wrongly) to show Syd's first acid trip. But even at his wildest—and his friends talk freely of the violent moods which the drug was capable of inducing in the normally mild-mannered singer—Barrett always maintained some sort of control. He knew how much he was taking, and generally, he knew what it would do.

The dose which was slipped into his drink at Alexandra Palace, unbeknownst to Syd (but witnessed by several other people), then, represented unknown territory, and the guitarist reacted badly, so badly that those same witnesses distinctly recall one of Floyd's own entourage forcibly pushing a very reluctant Barrett onto the stage.

The sun was creeping in through the huge windows as Pink Floyd started to play, pitting its own increasing might against the man-made lights which still swirled around the cavernous hall, reflecting off Syd's mirrored guitar. "Syd's eyes blazed as his notes soared up into the strengthening light," wrote journalist Barry Miles, one of the era's most visionary chroniclers; packed tightly around the stage, ten thousand people bathed in the music, holding hands with whoever was alongside them. It was a magical moment.

And then the strobe lights started up.

Syd didn't falter, but something had changed. If he'd looked uncertain before, when he first took the stage, now his expression was one of pure panic. Something was happening in his mind, something which went far, far, beyond the natural effects of the acid-spike, and whose effects would linger long after the drug had worn off. After just four songs, his bandmates nudged him off the stage and continued their set without him.

Historically, the "Crazy Syd" stories started right there. But at the time, everybody was too busy to notice.

10

The Death of Amusement

On May 12, Pink Floyd marked the release of "See Emily Play" by staging the Games for May (titled for a line in the song) concert at London's Queen Elizabeth Hall.

Games for May was arguably the single most important show Pink Floyd had played, the moment which blew them out of the last lingering confines of their underground cult and into the mainstream at large. "See Emily Play" only narrowly missed out on a top five placing; the band had been "discovered" by the serious newspaper critics; they even received the blessing of the Beatles, as the two bands dropped in on each others' sessions to see how things were progressing.

Of course, not everybody was impressed, with many continuing to agree with Hans Keller's almost gleeful demolition of the band: "I don't want to prejudice you, but there are four quick points I want to make before you hear them . . . to my mind, there is continuous repetition, and proportionately, they are a bit boring. My second point is that they are terribly loud; my third point is that perhaps I'm a little bit too much of a musician to appreciate them; and the reason why I say that is, four, they have an audience, and people who have an audience deserve to be heard. So perhaps it's my fault that I don't appreciate them." But of course, you knew that he didn't really believe that.

Such controversy, of course, was grist for the rock 'n' roll mill. At a time when British pop and rock were deliberately widening the generation gap through the use of drugs, free love, and musical anarchy (or the general public's perception of such wild abandon), Pink Floyd's public alienation by a figurehead of BBC broadcasting could not have been better staged.

Reviews were harsh too about *Tonite, Let's All Make Love in London*, a documentary on the unfolding scene that is both an indisputable psychedelic landmark, but is also pretty boring. Segments dedicated to such themes as the decline of the British Empire, fashionably clad young ladies, making music, painting, and protest strive to bring some form of cohesive documentary overview to the hour-long film, but director Peter Whitehead's short-form genius deserts him here, as he simply tries too hard to nail the zeitgeist of Swinging London, 1967.

In short bursts, there are some fascinating sequences: footage that merges Floyd's "Interstellar Overdrive" with sundry psychedelic effects and some revealingly static shots of Waters, beavering away on his bass guitar; Andrew Loog Oldham working in the studio with the duo Twice as Much and singer Vashti Bunyan; some neat Stones performance, and Eric Burdon's performance of "When I Was Young," merging with news footage from Vietnam to create what would, in modern parlance, be regarded as a seriously thought-provoking video. The Marquis of Kensington's sadly whimsical "The Changing of the Guard" likewise fits perfectly with footage of that same ceremony.

Interspersed with this, however, interviews with Mick Jagger, Julie Christie, Edna O'Brien, Michael Caine, and sundry others entertain only as slices of quaint kitsch, while Vanessa Redgrave journeys from radical to shrill in less time than it takes to chant "Guantanamera." And they all go on for way too long. But so did a lot of what passed for art at that time, as artists of all persuasions seized upon the era's predominant notion of self-expression and somehow confused it with self-indulgence. Anything was passable so long as it was "trippy," and many of the ears turned toward the sessions that Pink Floyd had been undertaking at Abbey Road Studios labored beneath the misconception that they, too, would be pushing the frontiers of recorded sound by creating a vérité soundtrack to the underground's most protracted experiences.

Instead, they made an album of pop songs.

Almost. There was one major exception — "Interstellar Overdrive," of course, as it pushed beyond even its live boundaries to herald (although none could have known it at the time) the extremes that the future Floyd would make their own.

The song surfaced on several occasions during the recording of *The Piper at the Gates of Dawn*. The first couple of times, they laid down short, but sonically shattering takes, which remain in the vault to this day. As the sessions progressed, however, so did the performance, and by April 18, 1967, the band and producer Norman Smith knew what to do with it. In the end, two different takes were double-tracked together, one on top of the other. The result was quite unlike anything the Abbey Road Studios had ever heard before.

In later years, and despite the productivity that none could deny, producer Smith remembered the sessions as little less than a nightmare. He told author Karl Dallas, "When I look back, I wonder how we ever managed to get anything done. It was sheer hell. There are no pleasant memories. I always left with a headache."

Barrett, he said, was the problem. "Trying to talk to him was like talking to a brick wall, because the face was expressionless." Even worse, he was "undisciplined, and would simply never sing the same thing twice."

But Smith also acknowledged that at least part of Barrett's attitude might well have been spawned by mere artistic hubris. The band had wanted Joe Boyd to remain their producer, only to have staff producer Smith (chief engineer on the Beatles' *Rubber Soul*) foisted upon them by Columbia. "I knew they weren't happy and neither was I. I didn't think that highly of them as musicians, and the songs struck me as very infantile in a lot of ways. There were personality clashes. Syd was the worst, but all of them made it clear that they were working with me under sufferance. Later I think they understood better what I was trying to do, or some of them did at least. But at the time it was a nightmare."

In fact, Peter Jenner later confirmed that without Smith to guide the band into an arena of cleanly cut musical performances, they would indeed have tried simply to recapture their live sound, and the corresponding performance of protracted improvisation. And that would have been the end of them.

The Piper at the Gates of Dawn was scheduled for release on August 5, 1967, hitting the streets (as was the wont of the era) in both stereo and mono formats. The stereo is the one that everyone knows today. But the mono is the one that the band intended to be their statement.

There is something oxymoronic about that picture. If any band was tailor made for headphone parties, it was the Floyd, with their extravagant soundscapes flying from side to side, ear to ear . . . the closing moments of "Interstellar Overdrive," as the guitars ricochet wildly between two blaring speakers remains one of rock's most inviolate memories, and the very idea of the whole thing being stuck "in the middle," mono style, seems absurd.

And then you play the thing.

Bereft of stereophonic gimmickry, the first thing you notice is the sheer depth and clarity of the recording. In truth, the actual mix barely deviates from the familiar stereo: there are no secret guitar solos screeching out of the disc, as is the case (for example) with the Who's seminal *Sell Out*; no dramatic rerecording, as with Arthur Brown's eponymous debut. No, the benefits lie in more intangible joys, hearing the album as it was originally intended and, with its thirtieth anniversary reissue, remastered to standards which no previous reissue had even touched upon.

From the opening proto-space-rocking "Astronomy Domine" to the closing nursery mania of "Bike," *Piper at the Gates of Dawn* not only retains its historical reputation among the finest albums Pink Floyd ever made, it also stakes its claim for even loftier accolades.

Sadly, Barrett would not be around to reap them.

His disintegration was slow, but marked. It started with the weekend he failed to join the rest of the group at a scheduled session for the BBC. A deputation sent out to locate him returned empty-handed; he was not at any of his usual haunts, or any of his more unusual ones. He had simply vanished, and, when he did return on the Monday, something . . . nothing you could put your finger on, but something . . . was different.

Worse was to come. With the album complete, Pink Floyd's attentions necessarily turned toward stockpiling new material. There was the all-important follow-up to "See Emily Play" to be considered; sessions for a new album were already looming later in the year. The musicians themselves were hankering for new pastures to roam. But when they turned to Barrett for guidance, he simply stared blankly back at them.

They grasped what they could. Based around an instrumental piece which the band had hitherto used to open their live set, "Reaction in G" was an essentially free-form piece that the band themselves described as a protest against being expected to play their hits in concert. "Vegetable Man" was a nonsensical inventory of the clothes Barrett was wearing at the moment he wrote the song. "Apples and Oranges," inspired by a girl Barrett saw while shopping one day, was a nonstarter even before the band recorded it.

Waters eased himself into the breach. He did not consider himself a songwriter; he saw his role more as the glue that pulled Barrett's more fanciful notions down to ground and ensured that a song would emerge from around the lyrics. "Take Up Thy Stethoscope and Walk," his sole songwriting contribution to the debut album, had universally been declaimed as the dullest song on the entire disc, while his only other composition of note, "Set the Controls for the Heart of the Sun," had been similarly dismissed by Norman Smith the first time he heard it performed.

A slow, repetitive mantra springing from the same stellar fascinations as "Astronomy Domine," "Set the Controls for the Heart of the Sun" epitomized Waters's uncertainty regarding his lyrical prowess. Much as Barrett had lifted swaths of the *I Ching* for "Chapter 24," so Waters turned to a collection of poems by the ninth-century Chinese poets Li-Shang Yin and Li Ho, borrowing and reshaping lines of verse to fit a song whose title was taken from Michael Moorcock's novel *Fireclown*.

But an early attempt at recording it was abandoned, and while Waters later described "Set the Controls" as the first of his songs the band ever taped, it would be circumstance more than enthusiasm that allowed it to live on in the repertoire. Circumstance, too, that declared Waters's desperate scrabbling should emerge so prophetic. Pink Floyd would not deviate away from the basic mood of that song—swirling, atmospheric, almost symphonic in its simplicity—for the next five years.

Even in these dog days of his writing career, however, Barrett was still capable of pulling out all the stops when he needed to, and in the late summer of 1967, he came up with the two songs that, according to all those people who must chart such things, testify to his mental disintegration: "Scream Your Last Scream" and "Jugband Blues."

"Scream," subsequently described by journalist Nick Kent as "a masterful splurge of blood-curdling pre-Beefheartian lunacy," was totally unlike anything Pink Floyd had ever recorded before—or ever would again. It remains unreleased. "Jugband Blues," on the other hand, was the ideal choice of follow-up to the hit "See Emily Play"—or so the band reckoned. On October 24, they headed down to De Lane Lea Studio to record "Jugband Blues" and Richard Wright's "Remember a Day," specifically for their next single.

"Jugband Blues" is a remarkable song, a nonsensical sing-along that only gradually sags first into melancholy, and then into the freeform madness that John Lennon had in mind when he (allegedly) invited Barrett to join George Harrison, Mal Evans, and himself at Abbey Road the following

August to record "What's the New Mary Jane." Midway through "Jug-band Blues," a Salvation Army band appears out of one speaker, marches cacophonously across the studio floor, and then vanishes out the other side, leaving Barrett alone with his acoustic guitar to mourn the song's final verse.

Columbia was not impressed. They refused to have anything to do with "Jugband Blues" and turned down "Scream Thy Last Scream" as well. Then, when Barrett did come up with something the label deemed release worthy, the aforementioned "Apples and Oranges," the single bombed out completely. For the first time in what had hitherto been a mercurial career, Barrett experienced rejection, and though he tried to put on a brave face, his words—"all we can do is make records we like"—could not disguise his dismay.

Less than a year earlier, Barrett had been writing songs in his sleep, lyrics and melodies flooding out of a faucet he barely remembered turn-ing on. Now something had turned it off, and with it, the desire to carry on had vanished as well.

—

In October 1967, Pink Floyd visited the United States for the first time, an outing which has spawned more than its fair share of legends. Recording an appearance on crooner Pat Boone's show, Barrett simply stared down every question his genial host tried to ask him. On *American Bandstand*, he refused to even pretend to play (or pretend to pretend to play—the show was mimed). According to manager King, he apparently wasn't into moving his lips that day. Waters took over vocal duties for the occasion.

There were other pitfalls. Floyd was the epitome of the UK under-ground, but they achieved that at a time when it was still struggling to match the extravagance of its American counterpart. Three days at Win-terland, San Francisco's heartbeat center of the new psychedelia, could scarcely impress locals raised on the marathon aural and visual freak-outs of the Dead and the Airplane, while Barrett's increasing dislocation left management frantic, pulling out every stop to cancel the tour and bring the band home. Now, while they waited for their flights back to London, Pink Floyd made their way to Venice, California, where they were put up at the home of local promoter Sheryl Cotter, alongside a local band called the Nazz, but later better known as Alice Cooper.

It was in LA, incidentally, that one of the most legendary of all Barrett's onstage outrages took place. "The Cheetah Club was the occasion that Syd decided his permed hair was too curly and had to be straightened before he could go on," Nick Mason recalled in his autobiography, a tale that Glen Buxton confirmed with his memory of being sent out to a nearby drug store to pick up a tub of hair gel, which Barrett proceeded to empty over his head. He stepped out onto the stage, and the audience stared aghast as Barrett's head appeared to melt in the heat of the stage lighting.

Days later, having canceled shows in Chicago and New York, the party flew home, with Barrett's future in Pink Floyd very much up in the air. Clearly, things could not continue as they were; clearly, too, Barrett needed either to get help, or get out. But the luxury of doing anything at all would have to be postponed for at least another couple of months, as the Pink Floyd road show hit the tour circuit once again, taking part in the last great package tour of the sixties.

They warmed up with a clutch of European dates, preserved by enterprising microphones that shrugged off the illegality of recording a live concert by farsightedly pondering how grateful fandom would be in years to come. At the Star Club, Hamburg, in October, "One in a Million" and "Stoned Again" were granted their only known recorded outings. And in Rotterdam on November 13, we got a glimpse into what a second Barrett-led Floyd album might have comprised, its five songs rounding up three then-new numbers, plus first-album freak-outs "Pow R Toc H" (expanded to a marathon eleven minutes), and "Interstellar Overdrive." The opening "Reaction in G" and "Scream Thy Last Scream" were new to most ears, while "Set the Controls for the Heart of the Sun" would need to slow down considerably before it could be preserved on *A Saucerful of Secrets*. Even so, at nine minutes, it remains an astonishing performance — it's not often that we get to hear Barrett's bass playing.

Then it was back to Britain.

Top of the package tour bill was the Jimi Hendrix Experience, playing a forty-minute set that highlighted virtually everything the band had recorded to date. Next up were the Move, still riding high in the chart with the anthemic "Flowers in the Rain." They played half an hour. Pink Floyd came third, with a seventeen-minute show that seldom got beyond a savage "Interstellar Overdrive"; Andy Fairweather Low and Amen Corner got a quarter of an hour, the Nice had twelve minutes, and Outer Limits and Eire Apparent got eight minutes each.

From its opening at London's Royal Albert Hall on November 14, 1967, the tour stretched for a little over two weeks, two shows a day in towns and cities which are little more than afterthoughts on a modern British tour — Bournemouth, Blackpool, Chatham, Newcastle, Portsmouth, Coventry.

There was some surprise expressed that the Floyd should be so far down the bill; with two top thirty hits to their name, they could easily have supplanted the Move, and maybe even taken co-headline status. But Move manager Tony Secunda insisted that management knew exactly what they were doing. "Basically, they were worried about Syd. They needed to keep the band's name out there, but nobody knew whether Barrett was up to it. The general feeling was that he wasn't.

"Once Floyd started having hits," Secunda continued, "Syd changed dramatically. I remember different members of the Move, and the other bands as well, tried to get through to him but it was like he had this shell around him. Personally, I think the best thing that could have happened to him would have been a night out with the Move."

Noel Redding, bassist with Hendrix's Experience, agreed. "I wouldn't say Syd was in a bad way, but he wasn't at all with us. On the bus, he'd just sit quietly; if you spoke to him he'd smile and nod maybe, but he kept himself to himself." He rarely spoke to anybody, simply sat on the bus immersed in his own thoughts, while all around mayhem reigned. Occasionally, someone would ask one of the other Floyd members if anything was ailing their front man, but the responses were almost as noncommittal as Barrett's own. "I know they were worried," Redding continued, "because at that time he was their meal ticket. But you also knew they had more going on than just Syd, because they were already using sound checks to try out new material, and I guessed that Roger Waters was behind a lot of that."

As Redding remarked, the bands traveled together in a tour bus, but even after they arrived in a new town, the question always remained— would Barrett make it to the show? Most nights, the guitarist would turn up at the venue hours after his bandmates, and minutes before he was due on stage. Then, once there, he'd play out the next act in the drama, real or imagined, which has fueled his legend ever since.

There was the time he surrounded himself with so many echo boxes that the rest of the band couldn't even make out when he was playing, let alone what.

There was the show when he didn't touch his guitar all night, and another when he played a completely different set from the band.

And there was the night he didn't show up.

David O'List was seventeen, the youngest member of the Nice, the youngest musician on the tour bus. But he was a brilliant guitarist, a genuine prodigy, psychedelia's first true child star. He'd been about to join John Mayall's band, successor to the recently errant Peter Green, when the Nice came calling, and when this new band taped its debut album, O'List didn't just compete with virtuoso organist Keith Emerson, he all but wiped him out.

But he was willing to learn all the same, and every gig of the tour, he revealed, "I used to stand by the side of the stage to watch the Floyd. They only used to play that one number in their set, and because it was a fairly straightforward guitar thing, I was able to pick it up quite quickly. So when Syd didn't turn up one night, Floyd asked me to go on instead."

O'List agreed. He'd already changed out of the clothes he'd worn on-stage with the Nice, so he slipped on a new jacket and went out there. At first, the crowd was fooled. O'List kept his back to the crowd, and it seemed like the whole hall was shouting messages to Syd. "Then I turned around and they all shut up immediately."

On December 22, Pink Floyd returned to London to play the Christmas on Earth, Revisited festival at London's Olympia exhibition hall. Hendrix, Eric Burdon, the Move, Tomorrow, and the Soft Machine were also playing; Barrett, however, wasn't. He spent the entire gig standing with his arms limp at his sides, while Waters tried to keep the show alive by thumping out a repetitive bass line.

He needn't have worried. "There was a real feeling that the Christmas show was for the kids who wanted to hear the hits, rather than for the scenesters," Tony Secunda complained. Psychedelia was now a high-street commodity, with the Fleet Street tabloids publishing guides on "how to be a hippy," and peace symbols flashing in department-store windows. "Groups were [beginning to] worr[y] about the way things were going, losing their original audience and having to play to kids who didn't give a shit about their airy fairy space music."

A little over two months later, Syd Barrett played his last gig as a member of Pink Floyd.

David Gilmour, a Floyd friend from their Cambridge hometown, was drafted into the band, ostensibly as a fifth member, but more accurately as Syd's replacement. Davy O'List was also considered, and Jeff Beck was invited, but Barrett and Waters's old friend Gilmour was always in with the loudest shout. Not only did they know him, but it was he who taught

Barrett to play guitar in the first place. If anybody could offer a seamless sonic transition, it was Gilmour—plus, he could sing, which was something neither Waters nor Wright were yet comfortable with. On March 18, 1969, Gilmour signed to EMI as a member of the band.

Tim Renwick: "I did see Syd once or twice after the band had started up and thought to myself how unhealthy he looked! I remember Dave telling me that he had been asked to join the band (I was amazed as they had already had a massive hit single success) to cover for Syd, and I gather they only played a handful of shows before David took over completely!"

The band played just five shows as a quintet (or quartet with passenger) and then one day on the way to a gig at the University of Southampton, opening for Tyrannosaurus Rex, the band's Bentley paused. The rest of the group was already inside, and someone asked, "Shall we pick Syd up?" Someone else replied, "No, let's not bother." And according to Gilmour, "We never went to pick him up again. It's as simple as that."

Despite all the difficulties exploding around him (and them), Barrett's last months with Pink Floyd were not completely unproductive. On December 20, two days before the abortive Christmas on Earth, Revisited festival, the band recorded another *Top Gear* session for broadcast on New Year's Eve, taking the opportunity to introduce the best of three most recent compositions—"Scream Your Last Scream," "Jugband Blues," and "Vegetable Man"—and serving up just one track from *Piper*, the group composition "Pow R Toc H."

The band was also in and out of the recording studio with some regularity, although just one "new" Barrett song would be attempted, a quirky call-and-response song titled "Have You Got It Yet?" It looked simple on paper: Barrett would call out the title, and his bandmates would reply "No no no." It would be some time into the session before the others realized why the song just wasn't working—and why Barrett had given it that particular title in the first place. They hadn't "got it yet" because he was changing it slightly every time they tried, making certain there was no way that they ever would.

For a time, Pink Floyd had considered keeping Barrett on in an advisory capacity, the songwriter taking the same sort of role in the band as Brian Wilson had lately adopted in the Beach Boys. The original plan for Pink Floyd's second album, after all, had been to compile together an audio diary of the band's musical history so far, through outtakes, oddments, and old songs they just hadn't gotten around to recording.

With Barrett's writer's block showing no sign of lifting, that particular scheme continued apace, even as the other one, the notion of retaining his services in a behind-the-scenes capacity, fell apart. Suddenly, the band members themselves found it easier to come to terms with Barrett's incapacitation than they had ever expected. And with that realization, a whole new vista of creative possibilities raised its head. Norman Smith recalled, "We were in the studio and every day someone would ask Syd if he had anything for us to do and he would mumble something and then disappear. So other people started bringing their own ideas in and we'd work on them, and out of that, we found enough material for the second record."

Richard Wright brought in a pair of delightfully plaintive little ditties, "Paintbox" and "See Saw," which his bandmates promptly retitled "The Most Boring Song I've Ever Heard Bar Two" (its original title would be reinstated in time for inclusion on the new album); Waters introduced the pulsing "Let There Be More Light" and "Corporal Clegg," a daft, but nevertheless potent, presentiment of his future obsession with the hypocrisy of war and the men who wage it.

Two other pieces, "The Boppin' Sound" and the tantalizingly mysterious "Untitled," were completed between January 11 and mid-February; and on February 12, 1968, work began on another Waters song, "Doreen's Dream." Retitled "Julia Dream," the song would mark David Gilmour's first recorded appearance as a member of Pink Floyd. Syd Barrett did not attend the session.

But he may have been in the studio waiting room, a place that legend insists he spent much of the album session, holding his guitar and waiting to be invited in to lay down his parts. Occasionally, he'd get bored waiting and go home. Other times, he would be called in to the control room, just in time to say good-bye to his bandmates.

Whatever the truth of the matter, the recording of "Julia Dream" marked the dawn of the "new" Pink Floyd, a four-piece convened without any regard for Barrett, and *A Saucerful of Secrets*, the band's second album, reflected this new hierarchy. Only one Barrett composition was included on the LP, "Jugband Blues," serving up a soft, sad coda to the thirty-five minutes of spaced-out psychedelia that preceded it. The remainder of the record looked only into the future.

Norman Smith was utterly nonplussed by it all. His instructions from on high remained the same as ever, to record a string of three-minute singles, and half of the new album reflected at least one half of that re-quirement—the songs were three minutes (or thereabouts), but it would have been a courageous decision to release any of them as singles. But when the band began spreading out, reiterating what Smith argued they had already accomplished with "Interstellar Overdrive," he lost patience. The new music, he pronounced, was rubbish and wouldn't sell a single copy. "But if that's what you want to do . . ."

It was. The ball, as David Gilmour put it, had stopped rolling with Barrett's departure. They needed to set a new one in motion, one that would allow for growth, ambition, and most important of all, perpetual change. Traveling on the underground from his local station, Goldhawk Road, Waters had been struck by a piece of graffiti art sprayed onto the walls alongside the track: "Same thing day after day, get up, get on the tube, come home, watch TV, go to bed," repeating over and over again down the platform and into the darkness of the tunnel. The faster the train traveled, the faster the words shot by. It was, he mused years later, a great piece of art. But it was also a great piece of truth. Life moves too fast to stand still. Pink Floyd needed to move.

On April 6, 1968, Barrett's departure from the band was formally announced. Three years later, Barrett confronted his removal in the pages of *Melody Maker*: "I suppose it was really just a matter of being a little off-hand about things," he smiled. His exasperated erstwhile bandmates' response to that was not recorded, although neither Mason nor Waters have pulled any punches in revealing their side of the story.

"It seemed his whole bent was on frustrating us," Mason admitted to *ZigZag* in 1973. "We staggered on, thinking to ourselves that we couldn't manage without Syd, so we put up with what can only be described as a fucking maniac. We didn't choose to use those words, but I think he was." Waters, characteristically, was more circumspect, refusing to speculate on whether or not Barrett was sick, insane, or whatever. "All I know is, he was fucking murder to live and work with."

He was also, it seemed, a lot more cunning than anyone had expected. On May 6, precisely one month after he was ejected from Pink Floyd—and some six months after he last offered the band a new song—Barrett returned to the studio with Peter Jenner in tow to begin working on his first solo album.

Like the rest of Pink Floyd, the King/Jenner management team had long doubted whether the band could even continue to exist without Barrett; unlike the rest of Pink Floyd, they concluded that they couldn't. When Barrett left the band, King and Jenner followed him out, persuaded EMI to finance a return to Abbey Road, and got to work on what would become *The Madcap Laughs*.

The band he left behind, of course, never forgot him. As late as 1970 to 1971, "Interstellar Overdrive" and "Astronomy Domine" were still turning up in Pink Floyd's live set, with the latter proving one of the highlights of both the band's first (partial) live album, 1969's *Ummagumma*, and their most recent, 1995's *Pulse*. In 1996, a solo Gilmour performed Barrett's "Terrapin" (from *The Madcap Laughs*) at the Tibet Festival at Alexandra Palace, and a decade later in 2006, he induced David Bowie to step out of self-imposed exile to perform "Arnold Layne" with him onstage in London.

In vinyl terms, too, Floyd has kept Barrett's name alive. In 1971, the band released the *Relics* compilation, rounding up several of its early, Barrett-era 45s and associated rarities, while the interest aroused by David Bowie's 1973 cover of "See Emily Play" was certainly instrumental in two further archive releases in 1974: the *A Nice Pair* double album, which brought *Piper* and *A Saucerful of Secrets* together in one package; and *Syd Barrett*, a similar pairing for the solo sets *The Madcap Laughs* and *Barrett*. Barrett compositions are a guaranteed bet on Floyd's compilations, and Gilmour himself curated a Syd Barrett "best of" compilation.

It is creatively, however, that Barrett has maintained his greatest influence over Waters, Gilmour, Mason, and Wright. Every time a new Floyd album was released, at least one critic was guaranteed to mourn Barrett's departure, and Waters was being brutally honest when he confessed that, for a long time, he felt threatened by Barrett's continued hold over the band.

Threatened, but also inspired. We may never know for sure just how deeply Barrett's plight impacted upon *Dark Side of the Moon*, Pink Floyd's blockbuster 1973 creation, nor whether his memory really did assist in the building of *The Wall*, six years later. But "Shine On You Crazy Diamond," from 1975's *Wish You Were Here*, is clearly Pink Floyd's own tribute to their founding father, and with a synchronicity that the best fiction in the world could never hope to get away with, this was the song the band was working on that June afternoon in 1975 when their past popped round to see them again.

Having been the first to recognize the big, bald vision, Andrew King was also the first to speak. He wanted to know how Barrett got so fat. "Well," the visitor replied, "I've got a very large fridge at home, and I've been eating a lot of pork chops."

Apparently, Barrett spent much of his time in the studio clutching his toothbrush and brushing his teeth. Richard Wright recalled how he had been the last to arrive in the studio, some time after his bandmates had accustomed themselves to Barrett's presence, and he still recalls how nobody bothered to introduce him. So he acknowledged the presence of a stranger in the room and just got on with whatever he was doing. It took him forty-five minutes, he said, before he finally realized who he was ignoring.

Conversation was stilted, even as the afternoon wore on. Storm Thorgerson, the band's art director, recalls one or two people crying softly as Barrett sat before them; Roger Waters, too, later admitted, "To see this great, fat, mad, bald person . . . I was in fucking tears." But Barrett himself seemed remarkably nonplussed, both by his effect on his old bandmates and by their music. Listening to one playback, Waters asked Barrett his opinion of the song. Barrett shrugged. "I dunno. Sounds a bit old."

Later, somebody suggested they hear the track through again. "Why bother?" Barrett asked. "You've already heard it once." And then he seemed to remember where he was, and maybe even what he had come for. "Right," he said. "When do I put the guitar on?"

The band members looked at one another, then at him. "Sorry, Syd, the guitar's all done."

11

The Near Side of the Moon

Syd Barrett's years at the helm of Pink Floyd ended not with a bang, but a silence. His growing distance from both the band and his bandmates had been taking its toll for months, leaving the rest of Floyd dangling indecisively over his future: Should he stay? And, if he did, what further acts of unreliable rebellion would he conjure before the entire group finally shattered beneath the weight of its own contradictions? Or should he go—in which case, what chance of survival would they have anyway?

Neither did the first vinyl prolusions of the new regime suggest that the doomsayers, which amounted to most outside observers and fans, were wrong. That most floral of Richard Wright compositions, "It Would Be So Nice" was a pleasant enough song, but it also had a hint of desperation to it, a sense that the band had been sat down and told to write a hit single— and this was the best they could manage. Even the band admitted that it was probably doomed long before the record label agreed with them, and "It Would Be So Nice" is best remembered today for the spurt of minor controversy that erupted around the BBC's refusal to play it on the radio. A reference to the newspaper the *Evening Standard* was construed as free advertising, and while the band did return to the studio to overdub the offending lyric (it became "Daily Standard"), it was not enough to render the record instant turntable fodder.

The band itself was not especially disappointed by the single's failure. They had scarcely enjoyed the year or so as top thirty hit makers that both preceded and possibly precipitated Barrett's departure; their attention was focused far more on their hopes for their second album.

Recording sessions in May 1968, however, indicated that the band was already moving away from the sounds that had established their name during 1967. A lengthy guitar- and atmosphere-led piece, "The Murderotic Woman," made it onto the soundtrack to director Peter Sykes's *The Committee* movie, alongside what Nick Mason describes as "a collection of sound effects."

Around the same time, the band was also seriously considering their own movie project, to be financed by an Arts Council grant and revolving around a story line ("like the Iliad," Waters said), as opposed to the traditional cinematic pop fare of the day.

A narrator was discussed, and John Peel's name arose—the disc jockey had recently made his vinyl debut reciting a short story on the first Tyrannosaurus Rex album, and while he later claimed not to remember ever having been approached by Pink Floyd, "that's not to say it didn't happen. A lot of people had a lot of ideas in those days, and it's not like we were strangers or anything."

Indeed, the story itself was presumably developed enough that one of its characters, the Demon King, was already in place. Waters envisioned Arthur Brown playing that role.

It is uncertain whether the band ever wrote any music toward this presumably ambitious project, but though the film came to naught when the applied-for grant was turned down, the group itself continued to drive forward.

Peter Jenner and Andrew King were out of the picture now, concentrating their managerial efforts on Syd Barrett. The partnership was dissolved on March 2, 1968, with the agreement that Blackhill Enterprises would receive twenty percent in perpetuity for all recordings made during the term of their management. Pink Floyd picked up the credit on their equipment, and then asked Bryan Morrison to manage them. He agreed.

A session recorded for BBC radio disc jockey John Peel's show in late June offers up a very cogent portrait of Floyd in the immediate aftermath of Barrett's departure. Already an established live favorite, "Let There Be More Light" was the only recognizable number in sight; the aptly titled "Julia Dream" was the only "conventional" one, a moody, spooky ballad whose unsettling vista of fearful paranoia was certainly an indication of composer Waters's future preoccupations.

The bulk of the session, however, was consumed by "The Massed Gadgets of Hercules," a wordless—and almost formless—semi-improvisation that would (once its title had been changed to "A Saucerful of Secrets") become the new album's title track, and a revised rendition of "The Murderotic Woman," a spectral sketch of what would, later in the year, emerge as "Careful with That Axe, Eugene."

Vast, sprawling, and absolutely improvisational, "A Saucerful of Secrets" remains one of the most pivotal numbers in the Pink Floyd catalog, not for what it is, but for what it represented. Gilmour later pointed out that it set the stage for future epics "Atom Heart Mother" and "Echoes," while Waters described it as the first thing the band had recorded without Barrett that the musicians, at least, believed to be of value.

They were certainly in the minority with that opinion, however. Producer Norman Smith hated it, and once the sessions were complete, was very vocal in his opinions of them. "After this album," he said, "the boys will really have to knuckle down and get something together."

The media, too, was uncertain, with the New Musical Express complaining about "basically good tracks being ruined by the now mandatory extended psychedelic electronics," while the International Times, the underground magazine that had developed almost hand in hand with Pink Floyd, merely shrugged. "There is little new here."

In fact, A *Saucerful of Secrets* swiftly unspooled as one of the band's most influential discs, personally if not otherwise. Those two solo Waters compositions, "Let There Be More Light" and "Set the Controls for the Heart of the Sun," not only shook off the shuddering memories of "Take Up Thy Stethoscope." They would also be responsible for the band's role as figureheads of the space-rock movement (however that is defined; opinions still differ), while it was here, too, that the band arrived at one of its most distinguishing features, that of using the singer whose voice most suited the song, regardless of who wrote it.

So vocals on the opening "Let There Be More Light" fell to Gilmour and Wright (Gilmour alone handled the non-album B-side "Julia Dream"), and while Waters would take control of his rampaging "Corporal Clegg" and the sibilant "Set the Controls," the general perception of him as the least of the band's three vocalists was already falling into place.

Still, with so much attention paid to the longer, spacey numbers, it was a hard album for listeners. Tony Baws recalls, "The whimsical, fey songs of Syd faded away as Roger's influence became more marked. There were still attempts at a number one hit and for a while there was still something to sing in the office; 'Arnold Layne' and 'See Emily Play' moved on to 'Corporal Clegg'. 'Another drop of gin?' became a bit of a catchphrase." But it was one of very few in sight.

Sonically, too, A *Saucerful of Secrets* proved challenging. Moving a year or so behind the United States, UK record companies were still producing new releases in mono as well as stereo, and the majority of record buyers still preferred the old format, for reasons of cost if nothing else—stereo LPs retailed for as much as a dollar more than mono. But as bands grew ever more adventurous with sound effects and the like, mono was becoming increasingly redundant.

Floyd stuck with it, though, and great swaths of A *Saucerful of Secrets*—those moments that rush from speaker to speaker and fill your head with unimaginable effects—take on an entirely different texture in mono, with the vast, spacey title track certainly feeling the absence of the stereo effects.

But there's also a totally different mix at work here that should send every Floyd fan rushing out to invest in a copy. As a listening experience, the mono A *Saucerful of Secrets* might not be as well known as the mono *Piper at the Gates of Dawn*. But it's just as dramatic.

A week after the album's release, Floyd played their biggest show since Barrett's departure, when they headlined the first ever free concert in London's Hyde Park. Days later, the band departed for their second US tour, a six-week outing that itself preceded lengthy European and British outings. And by the end of the year, nobody denied that Floyd had survived Barrett's departure and was, if anything, looking even stronger than they had twelve months before. True, they were still unable to score a hit single—the raucous "Point Me at the Sky" flopped so abysmally in December that it became their final UK single for over ten years. But *A Saucerful of Secrets* peaked only three spots lower down the UK chart than its predecessor, while the live show was soaring higher every time out.

In the past, Floyd concerts had walked an unsteady tightrope between the band members' own improvisational instincts and their audience's demands for the hits. With those hits now receding ever further into the past, however, the more voluble onlookers had drifted away, to find other acts to scream at. Floyd's core constituency of hippies, students, and "serious" music fans rushed in to take their place and, over the last months of 1968, the group's live repertoire had completely shifted.

Only a couple of Barrett-era oldies remained in the set now, and both were numbers that allowed the band to rush out into space: "Astronomy Domine" and the lengthy "Interstellar Overdrive" freak-out. New numbers, on the other hand, were flooding into view. "Careful with That Axe, Eugene" was still developing, to be joined by "The Embryo" and "Baby Blue Shuffle in D" (both of which were previewed during a John Peel radio session in December).

Waters wrote "Incarceration of a Flower Child," that wonderful, if somewhat cynical, number that could, had Floyd not already embargoed 45s, have finally presented the band with that elusive post-Syd hit single. And the band was working on no less than three new albums: a soundtrack for French director Barbet Schroeder, *More* (to be followed, later in the year, by Michelangelo Antonioni's *Zabriskie Point*, a mélange of halfhearted mood pieces that the director largely rejected); Syd Barrett's solo album *The Madcap Laughs*; and their own next studio set, *The Massed Gadgets of Auximenes*.

More, although it is frequently overlooked on account of its soundtrack origins, remains a stunning album. It opens gently, Waters's "Cirrus Minor" floating in on birdsong and organ, Gilmour singing like a gentle angel, and the whole thing lulling the listener into such a sweet spot that there was only one place the band could go in its aftermath — to the opposite end of the musical spectrum altogether, and the battering bruising of "The Nile Song," a hard rocker that would find no true equal in the Floyd canon until *The Wall*'s "Young Lust."

Hard to believe that both tracks sprang from the same author's pen or that the next cut on the original vinyl, the lightly jazz-inflected "Crying Song," should also be the work of a writer who, if one judges only from his previous recorded efforts, had scarcely even glanced in such conventional directions in the past. Only "Julia Dream" could be compared to the simple song structures from which Waters hung *More*'s opening triptych, although he would revert to what could be called type, via "Green Is the Colour" and, best of all, "Cymbaline," two pieces that remained in the band's live repertoire until well into 1971. In fact, it took the birth of the epic "Echoes" to finally displace "Green Is the Colour."

Of all the ultimately abortive projects associated with Pink Floyd, from their attempts to follow *The Dark Side of the Moon* by recording an entire album using kitchen utensils, to a projected ballet movie starring Rudolf Nureyev and directed by Roman Polanski , *The Massed Gadgets of Auximenes* might well be the most legendary, because it is the one that came closest to fruition.

Elements of the project were debuted at the band's first live show of 1969, an all-nighter at the Roundhouse on January 18. Further snippets from the project continued appearing in the band's live set as they toured through the early part of the year and, on April 14, the new material—under the auspicious title of *The Massed Gadgets of Auximenes: More Furious Madness from Pink Floyd*—received its official premier, in quadraphonic sound, at the Royal Festival Hall in London.

Both new and older music had been incorporated into the set, albeit suitably retitled: "Careful with That Axe, Eugene" was now known as "Beset By Creatures of the Deep"; a passage from "A Saucerful of Secrets" was revised as "The End of the Beginning." And "Work" saw the band predict the age of industrial music by building a table on stage, and then relaxing for a cup of tea—an idea that would be revisited on "Alan's Psychedelic Breakfast."

Much of the *More* soundtrack (recording of which had by now been completed) was incorporated into the concept, again under alternate titles: "Sleeping" ("Quicksilver"), "Doing It" ("Up the Khyber"), "The Beginning" ("Green Is the Colour"), and "Nightmare" ("Cymbaline"). Other numbers that would ultimately be salvaged from the project included "Daybreak" (which subsequently developed into *Ummagumma's* "Grantchester Meadows") and "Afternoon" ("Biding My Time"), while shards of "The Labyrinths of Auximenes" were incorporated into "Money," from *The Dark Side of the Moon*. Clearly, here was a band that hated to waste good ideas!

Three of these numbers ("Daybreak," "Nightmare," and "The Beginning") would be recorded for the band's next John Peel session in May 1969; "Labyrinths of Auximenes" would be contributed to BBC TV's coverage of the Apollo 11 moon landing later in the year. But the bulk of this most fascinating and (if live recordings are anything to go by) groundbreaking album was simply divided piecemeal all across the discography—"Biding My Time" is one of the highlights of the 1971 *Relics* compilation of rarities and curios; "Oenone" was reworked for *Zabriskie Point*.

Such untidiness is regrettable, but understandable. Still uncertain precisely how their career was going to pan out, Pink Floyd was throwing themselves into every project that presented itself—by late 1969, they were discussing another soundtrack, this time to a cartoon series called *Rollo*, designed by artist Alan Aldridge, although it was nothing to which Pink Floyd would be returning for the time being. By September 1969, with a handful of revisions, the *Massed Gadgets* show was on the road in Europe, now operating beneath the title *The Man and the Journey*, and comprising two musical suites, sensibly titled "The Man" and "The Journey."

It was not a concert for the hit-happy casual viewer. Although many of the songs, or at least elements thereof, were now familiar, others were all more or less new back then. Other "oldies"—"Pow R Toc H" (restructured as "The Pink Jungle") and an improv based around "Interstellar Overdrive" ("Behold the Temple of Light")—were only marginally recognizable.

But the audience's silence (respectful or confused—you decide) that hallmarks the best bootlegs of the show works to the band's advantage. *The Man and the Journey* never made it into the studio in its own right, but the lack of interruption on the live recordings is so pronounced that it might as well have.

It's not all brilliant. The conceptual percussion of "Work" went on way too long, and, in and around some moments of sublime loveliness, the band was clearly still struggling to locate the thin line that divides masterful improvisation from pointless noodling. There was also, clearly, a lot more going on onstage than the microphones picked up ("Sleep" was very aptly titled). But an electrifying "Afternoon"/"Biding My Time" was a genuine treat, nailed down by a Gilmour guitar solo that transforms the now familiar *Relics* ballad into a full-fledged rocker, and "Green Is the Colour" (aka "The Beginning") is an absolute treat.

Indeed, so much was either in the works or in the air that, coupled with the group's now prodigious appetite for ever more adventurous live shows, they seem to have quite forgotten to deliver a new album. EMI released *More* in July 1969, but, although it was wholly a Pink Floyd creation, the label never viewed it as the conventional third LP that it was awaiting. When Pink Floyd was switched to the newly launched Harvest label later in the year, then, it was to discover that they owed the company not one but two new albums, at a point where they personally felt they had scarcely an EP's worth of release-worthy material on hand.

So they scrambled, but if the resultant double album now seems an undignified gesture from such a perfectionist act, it was not solely the result of their haste. It was also their contribution to the new label's raison d'être.

The birth of Harvest Records was EMI's belated, but so welcome, acknowledgement of the words old Joe Morrison spoke to accountant Tony Baws almost three years earlier: underground music was the next big thing, and Pink Floyd was the king of the scene. That it had taken EMI so long to arrive at the same conclusion is no condemnation of the label's own vision; every other label in the land had taken almost just as long, but now the release schedules were overflowing with specialty boutique labels.

Decca's Deram, Philips's Vertigo, Pye's Dawn, and B&C's Charisma also came into being around the same time as Harvest, and all shared a similar vision of releasing records that may or may not have been destined for the chart, but which demanded to be released regardless—the unknown and unsigned groups that dominated the festival and university concert circuit and provoked high-and-mighty discussions in student common rooms the nation over. An arena into which Pink Floyd effortlessly slipped.

For Pink Floyd, then, the shift was as natural as breathing. Columbia had been good to Pink Floyd, but that was all. There, the band had rattled around a massive stable, as the label's penchant for dabbling toes in every musical current that passed by left it with a hopelessly unwieldy roster of acts, far too many and far too varied for even the best-intentioned PR department to handle. In late 1968, therefore, EMI staff producer Malcolm Jones was given the go-ahead to launch a new label that would eschew such diversification once and for all, a role that Harvest would effortlessly fulfill.

With its catalog dictated exclusively by what Jones, and fellow Harvest heads Peter Jenner and Andrew King, considered worthwhile, as opposed to any corporate notions of commerciality, Harvest's early catalog roamed the underground far and wide. The freak-form Edgar Broughton Band, singer-songwriter Michael Chapman, folkies Shirley and Dolly Collins, and former Cream songwriter Pete Brown were among the label's initial signings, to be joined by the handful of renegade spirits that had hitherto toiled on EMI's more established labels—Deep Purple, the Pretty Things, and Pink Floyd.

Now all they had to do was make music that matched Harvest's founding ideals, a process that would hopefully begin as Waters joined Gilmour in the studio to coax a solo album out of Syd Barrett. Sessions for what would eventually be released as *The Madcap Laughs* began in early 1968, before Barrett's departure from Pink Floyd was even public knowledge. Over a year later, they were still winding on, with Gilmour only the latest producer to try to bring the process to fruition. According to Malcolm Jones, who had been overseeing the majority of sessions so far, "Syd had maintained fairly constant contact with Dave . . . , whose amp we were using. When he delivered the tapes for the *More* album to me, David quizzed me as to how the sessions were progressing . . . by April he had completed most of his . . . contributions to [the new Floyd album] and had more time to spare."

It was Barrett, apparently, who asked that Waters also become involved, although Jones continued, "Much of what [they] were to produce was little more than guitar and voice tracks, which any of us could have supervised." Gilmour and Waters would ultimately share the production credit, but according to the sessions' own paperwork, the latter appeared in the studio only for the final session in late July, and only really became involved once the mixing process began.

Waters was, in any case, busy scheming the band's own Harvest debut, a new album titled *Ummagumma*—a set whose own completion was frustratingly to take precedence over the Barrett album. Neither was Jones especially thrilled with the final appearance of the album, as the duo chose to include false starts that, in Jones's opinion (and that of a lot of other listeners) showed Barrett "at best, as out of tune (which he rarely was) and, at worst, as out of control (which he never was). When I first heard [them], my reaction . . . was first, one of anger that they were left in, and secondly, boredom!"

Neither Waters nor Gilmour has ever spoken publicly of their decision to include such moments on the album, although several subsequent generations of rock psychologists are glad that they did. The saga—or, perhaps, the verisimilitude—of the Crazy Diamond would be a lot weaker without these unscripted moments of chaos.

Yet given what Pink Floyd themselves were preparing to unleash, in the form of their next album, perhaps chaos was what they sought. To the back-room staff who had journeyed alongside Pink Floyd since the early days, the band, and the sounds it was making, were certainly unrecognizable.

Tony Baws:

> The change I noticed most was one of self-confidence. Looking at *Ummagumma*, the back cover photo reveals a marked change of attitude from the shifting unease of the band members on the front cover of *Piper at the Gates of Dawn*. Pink Floyd are on the runway with some very expensive kit, for the time, carefully arranged. They were not about to turn back.
>
> The music also began to reach new heights, although it was still feeling its way to the great creative works. David's guitar had a distinctive voice and I suppose he acted as a pace-maker for Roger,

who in turn blossomed instrumentally, vocally, and creatively in
a way that he seemed unable or unwilling to do as long as Syd
was "the main attraction."

Ummagumma, the fourth Pink Floyd album, was divided into two
distinct halves, the first a live disc recorded at shows in Manchester and
Birmingham earlier in the year, the second a series of four "solo" recordings, one by each member of the band.

Waters reworked the aforementioned "Daybreak" as "Grantchester
Meadows," dedicated to one of the rolling green corners of Cambridge
where he had spent much of his teenage leisure time; Gilmour self-con-
fessedly "just bullshitted" through "The Narrow Way" (the fourth track
premiered during the summertime John Peel session), Wright threw in
an overbearing keyboard piece, "Sysyphus," and Mason offered up "The
Grand Vizier's Garden Party," a duet for his percussion and his wife Lindy's
flute playing. It was perhaps the least pretentious, and most unexpectedly
enjoyable, part of the entire disc.

But it was Waters, again, who offered up the album's most surprising
piece, a track that boasts the most attractive title in the entire Floyd catalog,
while ranking among the least listened to performances.

"Several Species of Small Furry Animals Gathered Together in a Cave
and Grooving with a Pict" was Waters unleashed with way too many tape
machines, and way too much time on his hands. The kind of experimental
collage that so many people (most of whom should have known better)
indulged in after the Beatles' "Revolution 9" made such indulgences at
least vaguely acceptable, it looped tape noises in and around themselves, at
different speeds and in different directions, threw in some atrocious poetry
and an even worse Scots accent, and perhaps the kindest thing that could
be said about it was that played backward (as was de rigueur in those days
of vinyl and turntables), it actually made as much sense as it did forward.
You at least got a sense of Waters's own opinion of the track, as he is heard,

at different points, demanding "bring back my guitar" and "that was pretty avant-garde, wasn't it," before concluding with a whispered "thank you."

For listening? Or for stopping? That is the question.

The live disc, on the other hand, was a revelation from start to finish. A far cry from the future luxury, as Richard Wright put it, of "recording every night of the tour and then selecting the best notes from the ensuing stockpile," the band taped just two nights from their latest tour, and made their choice from there.

Versions of "Astronomy Domine," "Careful with That Axe, Eugene," "Set the Controls for the Heart of the Sun," "A Saucerful of Secrets," and "Interstellar Overdrive" were all prepared for the disc (the latter was ultimately dropped when they ran out of room on the record), and American radio flipped.

Recent US tours had introduced the country to an act that was many miles removed from the old Pink Floyd that was available on record. Only *More* hinted at the sonic extremes that the band was capable of touching in concert. The first two sides of *Ummagumma*, on the other hand, put the sound of the live show straight onto your stereo, and listeners from the day can still recall blissful evenings spent absorbing all four tracks as FM radio jocks let them play without any more interruption than was required to flip the disc over.

Piper at the Gates of Dawn had charted in 1967, at a very lowly number 131. *Ummagumma* would become Floyd's Top 100 debut in January 1970, and if its ultimate placing of number seventy-four seems unimpressive, remember *Meddle*, the following year, climbed no higher than number seventy. (*Ummagumma* is also the earliest Floyd album to have been awarded a platinum disc).

Of course, the chaos of 1969 would not haunt the band forever. *Ummagumma* was still rising up the charts (it went to number five in the UK), and Floyd was already working on their next set, *Atom Heart Mother*. They were learning, too, how to streamline their ideas, to build several themes into one piece of music rather than try to develop each of them into a living song of its own, and if that did eventually lead them into some genuinely stultifying pastures later in life, still it also permitted them to produce some of the most important music of the new decade.

12

A Slice of My Pie

In summer 1969, with his marriage to his high school sweetheart, Judy Trim, now imminent, Waters finally got out of the rented apartment at 13 Pennard Mansions, on the Goldhawk Road in Shepherds Bush, where he had lived for the past two years. The money was coming in now, and in sufficient quantities for him to put down a 30 percent deposit on a home of his own.

Tony Baws: "In the wake of financial success, some acts behave badly, throwing their new-found weight around and generally being difficult and demanding. I never found that the case with Pink Floyd. They remained approachable and polite, comfortable with themselves and apparently enjoying every minute. Financially the group were now secure. Proceeds from gigs might be eaten up in expenses and equipment but their track record of album sales was established. The peaks and troughs of cash flow could be bridged by advances."

Waters's own income, from all sources, was estimated at £7,500 per annum, at a time when the average wage in the UK was a considerably more modest £1,607.

Number 186 New North Road, in Islington, north London, was a three-story terraced house (row house in American terminology) built in 1865 and priced at a competitive £8,365 sterling. It needed work, but that was where Waters's architectural training came into play. He set about renovating the entire house, shifting the kitchen to the basement—indeed, the kitchen was the basement, a vast space that his Burmese cats promptly claimed for their own.

The old wooden floors were polished back to something approaching their original glory; furniture was imported from (or designed in the style of) Scandinavia, at a time when such lines and simplicity were considered the height of chic. Out back, in the garden, he rebuilt the original ramshackle shed, soundproofing one half as his own demo studio, then throwing the other open to Judy's career as a potter and sculptor. In the years that followed, Judy (who retained her maiden name for her artistic career, signing with a distinctive, circled *JT*) would become one of the country's most respected potters, exhibiting in numerous galleries and museums.

It was there, with his three Revox tape machines seated on a simple workbench, that he schemed the future. And from there that the blueprint was laid for Pink Floyd to bestride the 1970s like no other band of their generation. "Several Species of Small Furry Animal" was one of the shed's earliest offspring, but the most impressive was a collaboration between Waters and performance artist Ron Geesin, destined to become yet another soundtrack, to the movie *The Body*.

The same age as Waters, although he seemed to have been around for many years more, the Scots-born Geesin was already well established on the avant-garde scene when he met Pink Floyd, befriending Nick Mason first and, through him, being introduced to Waters and Judy; Geesin and his wife, Frankie, became regular visitors to New North Road, while Roger and Ron even teamed up for golf, with Pete Townshend often completing the party.

Waters was fascinated by Geesin's reputation for literally doing whatever he wanted to within his own vision of a musical framework—fascinated and inspired. Suddenly his personal creative impulses were bubbling into the kind of improvisational territory that Geesin had long since staked out. A collaboration was inevitable, even before Geesin was offered the soundtrack to *The Body*.

Oft overlooked in discussions of Floyd, and Waters's, canon, *Music from The Body* is very much one of those albums that actively enjoys its obscurity, if only because that will heighten the delight of any unsuspecting soul who finally gets round to listening. Saddled as the soundtrack to a movie that has few admirers outside of anatomy classes, and famously recorded with the two musicians working absolutely separately from each other (Waters recorded his contributions in his garden shed; Geesin utilized his home studio in Ladbroke Grove), *The Body* comprises twenty-two tracks, and the opening "Our Song" is a dislocating dance indeed, a gurgling baby and a rhythmic pattering that isn't a song at all.

But "Sea Shell and Stone" is the kind of persuasively pensive ballad that Waters was now beginning to trademark, while the interjection of Geesin's only slightly off-kilter strings ("Red Stuff Writhe") serves as a haunting interlude before the almost Iberian flurry of "A Gentle Breeze Blew Through Life." And so on, through vignette after vignette that may, to some ears, peak with the inclusion of three further Waters vocals, but serves too as a dry run for ideas that Waters would still be expanding upon three years later. And others that would persist even longer.

The childhood reflections that drift through "Chain of Life" would not have been out of place among Waters's earliest sketches for *The Wall*, at the same time coming closer than anything else he has written to the lyrical pastures through which Syd Barrett once led the band. It is the longest song on the album, and it remains one of Waters's most revealing, nostalgia ("memories . . . drifting down") perched just on the edge of sadness as the song's narrator is slowly revealed as an old, old man coming to uncertain terms with his own imminent mortality.

The sudden segue into the scratchy instrumental "The Womb Bit" feels like nothing so much as a wordless coda to those impressions, a suggestion of rebirth that drives toward a musical peak before being subsumed by a flickering "Embryo Thought" and then "March Past of the Embryos," a minute or so of sound that stands darkly redolent of the more frightening elements of John Cale and Terry Riley's *Church of Anthrax*.

The Body twitches on, through the staccato choir of the immortally titled "More Than Seven Dwarves in Penis Land," a tip of the hat toward Frank Zappa in both name and execution, and then we leap into "Dance of the Red Corpuscles," which occupies almost precisely the same place and space as some of Richard and Mimi Farina's most evocative material, the ghosts of familiar melodies jigging and jogging in and around one another, and disappointing only in its brevity.

"Breathe" is not a dry run for the opening cut on *Dark Side of the Moon*, but it could have been, as Waters acknowledged when he borrowed a lyric for the later song, while also composing a gorgeous lament for air pollution. "Old Folks Ascension" is a fine rocking instrumental, "Bed Time Dream Climax" a reminder of the earlier corpuscular dance, and "Piddle in Perspex" is the irony-rich sound of a tinkling piano; we're into the final stretch now, and *The Body* makes another of its occasional stabs toward contemporary sound with the distinctly Gong-like "Mrs. Throat Goes Walking," a recurring bass riff over which Geesin's harshly accented voice scats and gibbers its way toward a lovely reprise of Waters's first vocal number, mildly retitled ("Sea Shell and Soft Stone") and restyled to allow the cello to sing.

And then it's into the grand finale, the one song to feature the full Pink Floyd lineup, and the one with the least Floydian title of them all, "Give Birth to a Smile." Gilmour's guitar carves chunks behind a warming vocal and angelic female harmonies, and the closing refrain could be a gospel rocker, the entire studio raising their arms into the air, swaying and swinging and indeed smiling, and so infectious that it completely realigns your every preconception about Roger Waters's worldview.

An amazing album, a fabulous collaboration, and wholly a child of the era into which it was born. The psychedelic boom of the late 1960s certainly produced a landslide of talented eccentrics who between them are responsible for some of the most startling sounds of the age. But few were truly to survive into the next decade with both reputation and commerciality intact, and fewer still would stamp their imprimatur onto that decade with the same forcefulness as Pink Floyd.

And *Atom Heart Mother* was Pink Floyd's first almighty triumph, the sound of the band emerging from the varying states of metamorphosis exemplified by past recordings, confirming their ambitions through the band members' own developing capabilities. With its first side devoured by a single musical piece, and its second spread across four more-conventional songs, *Atom Heart Mother* was the first album on which those capabilities rose above the musicians' uncertainty and inexperience to present a vista that any future Floyd fan would recognize. Technically, all four members of the group have since acknowledged that it left a lot to be desired in terms of both conception and execution. But it was the best that they could do at the time, and it was arguably better than anybody else had achieved.

The first suggestion that Pink Floyd's fifth album would be an epic came on June 27, 1970, three months before the LP released, when the band headlined the Bath Festival in Shepton Mallet. Fully backed with choir and orchestra, "Atom Heart Mother" was the centerpiece of the performance, and few who witnessed it were anything less than blown away. Three weeks later, on July 18, Pink Floyd repeated the exercise at the Garden Party free concert in London's Hyde Park, on a bill that also featured Kevin Ayers, the Edgar Broughton Band, Roy Harper, and Formerly Fat Harry.

In 1969, the Rolling Stones officially opened up Hyde Park, London, to the notion of free concerts; now Blackhill was stepping into their shoes with a second, even greater event. Both the Broughton show and Ayers set have seen official releases over the years, while footage of the event also circulates. It was, all these sources agree, a magical day.

Pink Floyd's set largely adhered to material that the audience was already familiar with—"The Embryo," "Green Is the Colour," "Careful with That Axe, Eugene," and "Set the Controls for the Heart of the Sun." But then Roger Waters stepped to the microphone to introduce "The Atomic Heart Mother," as the piece was then known; a brass ensemble and choir appeared alongside the band on stage, and for the next twenty-five or so minutes, an outdoor audience larger than any the band had ever entertained before was held spellbound.

"The piece began with an arrangement for the brass, and then switched into a lengthy choir pattern," *Disc and Music Echo*'s review of the Hyde Park show documented the following week. "Followed by a dash of marvelous Floyd rock-jazz. In came the brass again, pursued by incantations from the choir and swirling special effects in twin-channel stereo. A reprise took up the original theme and group, choir and orchestra projected it together in fine combination."

The following day, another performance of the majestic leviathan was broadcast on the BBC from a recording made earlier in the week for DJ John Peel's *Sunday Concert* show, and across a string of European summertime festivals, the now-renamed "Atom Heart Mother" became a familiar and often dynamic presence in Pink Floyd's live show. Even if the presence of the choir in the touring party did provoke some bizarre reactions from band and audience alike.

On September 12, Pink Floyd appeared before an estimated half a million people at an open-air event in Paris, the *Fête de l'Humanité*. A regular event in the French artistic calendar since 1930, the *Fête de l'Humanité* was originally staged to raise funds for both the radical left-wing newspaper *l'Humanité* (whose publisher Marcel Cachin organized the event) and for the families of the nation's then-striking coal miners.

A low-key event at the beginning, and forgotten during the war years, the festival returned in the 1950s and by the 1960s had become a focal point for revolutionary French youth, an often contentious but seldom less than invigorating day of music headlined, through the 1960s, by some of the biggest names in French music. Pink Floyd, in fact, were the first international rock performers ever to appear at the event, headlining over local heroes Michel Polnareff and Boby Lapointe at the Bois de Vincennes.

European audiences adored the new music, applauded its ambition and execution. America seemed less certain, and Pink Floyd responded with an admirable, if perhaps self-defeating, bloody-mindedness. At the old Fillmore West in San Francisco, for example, the group decided to forgo their usual encore and send the choir out instead, to perform "Ave Maria." Their efforts were roundly greeted with boos and cries of "We want Floyd" from the crowd, and, while *Rolling Stone* did leap to the band's defense ("if [people] don't understand what Pink Floyd's music is all about, it's a bit puzzling why they spent $3 to come to see them"), one can also sympathize with the bemused masses. If you go to see a band, and reward their efforts with an encore, you really don't expect somebody else to appear on stage in their stead, to perform music that has nothing to do with the main attraction. Pink Floyd obviously saw their point as well—they never made the same move again.

From the US, the tour returned to Europe for dates that would carry the band through until the end of 1970. The album was out now, topping the charts in the UK and elsewhere across the continent, and another song from the set, "Fat Old Sun," moved into the show. It would be December, however, before the full *Atom Heart Mother* album presentation hit the road, with a UK tour that opened with what remains one of the most unconventional pieces of music in the band's entire repertoire (at least since the solo sides of *Ummagumma*), "Alan's Psychedelic Breakfast." Which was, essentially, the sound of one of the band's roadies, the eponymous Alan Stiles, preparing his breakfast. In concert, he would even fry egg and bacon on stage, to add scent to the sense of occasion.

For all its invention, "Alan's Psychedelic Breakfast" is the one track on *Atom Heart Mother* that really didn't take off. The album version was recorded too hurriedly, Waters later acknowledged, although he furiously denounced those reviews that dismissed the track as just another mass of sound effects. What, he demanded, is really the difference between a sound made with a conventional instrument, and one created from something else entirely? That was a conundrum that would continue to exercise his mind, later in the decade. For now, he simply growled, "The differentiation between a sound effect and music is all a load of shit."

Elsewhere, however, *Atom Heart Mother* was unimpeachable. The latest in Waters's grab bag of pretty folk songs, "If," would return to his live repertoire in the 1980s as a reminder of just how important the self-flagellatory lyric was to him, while the sweet nostalgia of Gilmour's "Fat Old Sun" and, even better, Wright's "Summer '68" both drifted on such beautiful moods and melodies that one still wonders why it was Waters, and not Wright, who took Barrett's place as the group's principle songwriter.

Sharing a similar sense of English whimsy to that which inspired Barrett, early classics "Paintbox," "Remember a Day," and "See Saw" were all Wright compositions, and even after the balance of songwriting power had shifted, Wright's contributions to the ongoing saga of Pink Floyd remained crucial.

Atmospheric, thoughtful, and wholly unimpressed by the flash and pizzazz with which other period organists plied their trade, Wright was often regarded as the very quietest of an already all but silent group of musicians.

But it was his musical abilities that brought reality to so many of Waters's musical notions, and he who supplied the glue that held together the band's first attempts at long-form compositions, "Atom Heart Mother" and (later) "Echoes." It is also worth remembering that, when the four Floyd members chose to contribute one solo work apiece to the *Ummagumma* album, Wright's "Sysyphus" was the only one that really bore repeated listening.

Yet even these gems were overwhelmed by the sheer majesty of *Atom Heart Mother*'s title piece.

For many people, their first understanding of what, or who, the Atom Heart Mother was came from the LP's so distinctive cover portrait of a cow—snapped by Storm Thorgerson, of the Hipgnosis art studios, after hearing artist John Blake rave about some cow motif wallpaper that Andy Warhol once produced. It was not an image that immediately appealed to everybody; back at the Morrison Agency office, all observers were distinctly underwhelmed by it, while Harvest's Malcolm Jones admitted that the cover art received approval more because of the terms of the band's contract with the label (which provided them with complete control over such things) than because anybody else thought it was a good idea.

Still, the artwork conjured impressions that were furthered by the subtitles appended to the various movements within "Atom Heart Mother" itself, "Breast Milky" and "Funky Dung" among them. One could even, at a stretch, see the piece as an early precursor to Floyd's later *Animals* album, where sheep, pigs, and dogs would be unleashed to cavort with the brown-eyed ladies of the meadow. It was also an immensely influential piece. Photographer Chalkie Davies, remembering his friend following Thorgerson's death in April 2013, recalled, "The original sleeve for *Atom Heart Mother* made me want to become a photographer. I was fifteen, and the idea you could photograph a cow instead of the group seemed the best job in the world."

In truth, however, there is little to connect the dots. "Atom Heart Mother" was, is, and always will be, a piece of music quite unlike any other in Floyd's catalog.

The piece originally developed from a chord sequence that Gilmour was tinkering with, which he called "Theme from an Imaginary Western" (a title that Jack Bruce had already employed on his *Songs for a Tailor* LP). Waters was intrigued by it, and over the coming months, both he and Wright set about adding further themes and variations to the initial concept, both working hard to retain the vast cinematic feel of Gilmour's original notion.

It was, Wright later remarked, something akin to doing a jigsaw, "without any idea what the picture is of, how big it is, or even what dimension it is in. We were just searching for a shape." A shape that they titled "The Amazing Pudding," and in which, as early as January 1970, they were sufficiently confident to try it out on stage in France. It was already the longest single piece of music they had yet attempted, but it was soon to become the most ambitious as well, as the band responded to the recent orchestral activities of Harvest label-mates Deep Purple by inviting Ron Geesin into the studio to help them tease melody into megalith.

Their instincts were correct. While "Atom Heart Mother" is archetypal Floyd, it is also utterly unlike anything else they had ever recorded (or would, for that matter), while Ron Geesin threw himself into the project with the same wild abandon as Bob Ezrin would demand a decade later, on *The Wall*. Mindless of the musicians' personal feelings or preferences, Geesin gleefully rewrote and rearranged entire sequences of the pudding. He introduced harmonies and melodies where their initial vision had lacked them, and he envisioned the nature of the extracurricular musicianship that would give the piece its ultimate flavor.

Then, still only halfway through his intentions for the piece, he announced that he was completely exhausted and asked that he be replaced.

Classically-trained orchestrator John Alldis took over, completing the piece of music and introducing his own visions and notions to the piece, and what could have been a nightmarish clash of ideals instead developed even further, into a musical creation that veers from hot jazz to soporific richness without a second thought, a piece that *Frendz* magazine promptly labeled "huge, timeless, sweeping, universal. . . ."

Geesin, on the other hand, listened to the playback of the final mix and announced, "Okay, that's a good demo. Can we do it for real now?"

Working, he recalled, "with the absolute minimum of creative suggestions from [the band] . . . , it was a month's work stripped to the underpants in a hot padded studio in Ladbroke Grove." Hot and very often bothered.

Gerald Scarfe's terrifying portrait of motherhood: Nassau Coliseum, February 1980. (Al Munson/Frank White Photo Agency)

Bob Geldof, *The Wall*'s punky Pink. (MGM/Photofest)

After the split: Richard Wright, David Gilmour, and Nick Mason. (Michael Putland/Getty Images)

Waters on tour, August 1987. (Frank White)

One small candle: onstage at the PNC Bank Arts Center, Holmdel, New Jersey, September 6, 2006. (Eleanor Reiche/Frank White Photo Agency)

A drink, a good book, and an audience of several thousand. Waters relaxes at Madison Square Garden, September 13, 2006. (Eleanor Reiche/Frank White Photo Agency)

Fear builds walls: onstage at Madison Square Garden, September 13, 2006. (Eleanor Reiche/Frank White Photo Agency)

Mason and Waters reunited, September 13, 2006. (Eleanor Reiche/Frank White Agency)

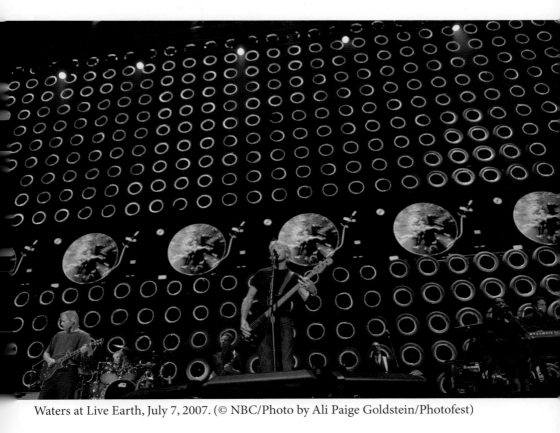

Waters at Live Earth, July 7, 2007. (© NBC/Photo by Ali Paige Goldstein/Photofest)

Pay attention to the pig! The Theatre at Continental Airlines Arena, East Rutherford, New Jersey, May 24, 2007. (Eleanor Reiche/Frank White Photo Agency)

All four together again: Live 8 at Hyde Park, London. (Dave M. Benett/Getty Images)

The nightmare reborn: the Wall in Kansas City, Missouri, October 2010. (GabeMc/ Wikimedia Commons)

Waters in Barcelona, 2011. (Alterna2/Wikimedia Commons)

I was about to hit one of the horn players. They were hard EMI-type session brass players. That was uncomfortable and I was exhausted from doing the work. I obviously cared a lot about it and I cracked up. I had to hand over to the choirmaster fellow [John Alldis] who conducted the rest of the sessions. But because he was a classical man, he didn't know about pushing the beat, or hot rhythm, and so it's a bit spongy. If I had more experience at the time and got the brass players to give it out, it would be a little edgier, tighter.

The members of Pink Floyd, although they would bite their tongues for the moment, were also less than happy with the way the final piece came out—Waters went so far as to suggest that the whole thing be "thrown into the dustbin and never listened to by anyone, ever again." And a quarter of a century later, interviewed by Radio One's Richard Skinner, he snarled, "If somebody said to me now: 'Right . . . here's a million pounds, go out and play "Atom Heart Mother,"' I'd say: 'You must be fucking joking . . . I'm not playing that rubbish!'"

Impressive though it undoubtedly sounded, the musicians nevertheless believed that that was all it was, an impressive wall of sound, but lacking in substance or any real sense of creativity.

It's an argument that a lot of other fans have since come to agree with, particularly when *Atom Heart Mother* is compared to what the band would go on to achieve, beginning with their next full LP, *Meddle*. As a construct, it is unimpeachable, but it does feel less than complete, and it certainly lacks the warmth and imagination that would so soon become an integral part of Pink Floyd's musical approach. Elements of the title piece feel grating today, particularly when the horns kick in with their bludgeoning fanfares; it is not a piece of music that you can comfortably relax into.

But was it ever intended to be? Progressive rock, the musical form that Pink Floyd did so much to pioneer but which, at the time, was still very much in its infancy, was as much a learning experience for the musicians as it was a listening experience for the audience. It was by its very nature experimental, and it is a rare discipline indeed wherein every experiment is a success.

Compared to its immediate predecessor, *Ummagumma*, and the *More* soundtrack before that, *Atom Heart Mother* was a massive step forward for both the band and for their audience's expectations of the band. And lined up alongside the albums that the other proclaimed giants of the prog field were delivering around the same time—edifices that range from Deep Purple's *Concerto for Group and Orchestra* to Emerson Lake & Palmer's debut, from period productions by Barclay James Harvest, Gentle Giant, and the Moody Blues to the veritable plethora of meanderings that emerged further down the food chain—*Atom Heart Mother* was indeed a magnificent achievement, one that deserves praise not for how it sounds today but for what it permitted other records (Floyd's included) to sound like in the future.

"My own sense was that Floyd were still finding their own rhythm," Malcolm Jones said in an interview some twenty years later.

> They were the biggest band on the label, and that allowed them a certain latitude. Harvest's attitude at that time was to let the musicians get on with their music, and for us to interfere as little as possible, whether or not we thought what they were doing actually "worked," because we believed that it was only by doing something that they'd learn how to do it better next time. Which Pink Floyd proved.
>
> But we also knew that the band was still basically rudderless at the time. Roger was certainly stepping into the foreground as the group's musical leader, but his speciality was vision, not music— he knew where he wanted the band to go, but he also relied on

[Gilmour and Wright] to make that vision work, by making the sounds that matched his ideas.

Right now, as they recorded then toured *Atom Heart Mother*, the two teams were still pushing to make that particular connection. But it was close, and it was growing closer.

13

More of Those Days

Bryan Morrison had been the band's manager for the past two years, the relationship operating, apparently, on the strength of trust and a handshake, and with everybody doing well from so casual an arrangement. Tony Baws explains, "The booking team at Bryan Morrison Agency saw to it that bands worked as much as possible. For the smaller bands there were always the clubs to fall back on. For the bigger names, and Pink Floyd rapidly became the main act on the roster, there were venues far and wide and the band were on the road for much of the time."

The musicians themselves were rarely sighted around the office, but with their requirements now being channeled through "the quietly persuasive personality of Steve O'Rourke," they scarcely needed to be. O'Rourke ensured that whatever they needed was supplied.

"Steve O'Rourke quickly became Pink Floyd's man in charge on foreign gigs, while Tony Howard took care of business back home. Steve would sidle up to me in his quiet way, to produce expense vouchers for trips abroad and to tutor me in the arcane workings of the French carnet, a system used to keep track of instruments moving in and out of France. The band were obviously relieved to have someone looking after all of this for them and forged close relations with Steve and Tony."

One night, however, Morrison called up the four musicians and explained that he was encountering difficulties booking Pink Floyd's next

US tour and was legally bound to produce a signed management company before the necessary authorities would approve it.

They signed, and the following day, Morrison sold his agency to NEMS, the management company founded by Beatles manager Brian Epstein back in the heyday of that band's fame, but which since his death had transformed into just another rapacious business.

"One lives and learns," Waters sighed a decade later. The NEMS deal not only took the Morrison Agency's bands. The staff, too, was included in the deal, as Pretty Things front man Phil May recalls. "NEMS bought the agency out. Bryan got a grace and favor free office and telephones in Hill Street, but it left everybody else completely up the swanee. Tony Howard rang me up after the deal was done. 'Your fucking manager, he's only signed Steve [O'Rourke] and I up to keep working for the next year to keep continuity.' So they were all nailed, the bookers were nailed, they were sold as part of the package. . . ."

The Pretty Things were lucky; they got out early. May continues, "The guy who ran it, he had these very posh offices and we all went there after this has happened, we were all sitting in the lobby downstairs, and he came in and apparently turned to the secretary and said, 'Who's that bunch of tossers in the waiting room?' She says, 'I think you own them,' and he said, 'Well, give them their contracts back and get rid of them.' We were cluttering up the place."

Pink Floyd, however, would remain on NEMS's books for some time longer — until, as Waters continued, "we left NEMS [and] we took Steve with us."

It was a wise move, one of the smartest Pink Floyd ever made. O'Rourke knew the four band members as well as they knew one another and was also fully versed in the conflicts that the four endured, musical and personal. He understood the petty resentments that Gilmour and Wright sometimes nursed toward Waters, recognized, too, the social divide that separated the two musicians in the band from what even the musicians jokingly referred to as the two architects. But he also knew what needed to be done to bridge that divide. It was time, he told them, to stop farting around.

Bluntly and brutally, he laid it on the line. Three years had elapsed since the last real Pink Floyd album. A movie soundtrack (*More*), a disc's worth of solo meanderings, a live album (*Ummagumma*), and an only partially successful collaboration (*Atom Heart Mother*) had all done well enough commercially. And every time he spoke, it sometimes appeared, Waters was outlining another possible project.

> We're writing a ballet for Roland Petit which will be on Paris next June, and the sky's the limit for that. They're spending so much money on that that they'd be quite willing to pay for an orchestra. But it might take it out of our hands to a certain extent if the stuff had to all be written down, because we can't write it down ourselves, and there's always a communication gap involved between what you can sing or play on a piano and what gets written down as music. And then you never hear it until you've got the orchestra there at the first rehearsal, and you probably only get two rehearsals anyway, so by the time you hear it, it's too late to change it; whereas our stuff is all based on doing something and then throwing it out and using something else.

But still Pink Floyd remained a mystery to their audience, and not necessarily in a good way. Every band with which they could be compared, on a commercial basis if not musically, had made its definitive statement by now: Black Sabbath's *Paranoid*, Deep Purple's *In Rock*, ELP's *Tarkus*, and so forth. How did Floyd compare with any of those? It was a dilemma with which Waters did not especially want to wrestle.

Stung by accusations that the socialist principles that seemed to dictate most of his interviews were scarcely supported by the E-Type Jag in which he raced around town, he had recently replaced it with a Mini. But that spoke only to those people who judge an artist by his political status, and after the firestorms of radicalism that consumed the late 1960s, that was a dying breed.

"I'd like to help the revolution when it comes," Waters mused in 1971, but he could not resist adding, "It would be nice if somebody could visualize the revolution, so we could have a slight idea of what to do."

Too many theories, too much idealism, too many half-baked notions masquerading as brilliant political theory—the underground of the late 1960s and early 1970s, both musical and political, may have been a melting pot, but it was one within which the ingredients had yet to coalesce. "The double bind is that people who tend to involve themselves in politics do it for strong personal motives. Some have a social context, but it's largely an ego thing and the people who should be running the country are just pottering about in their gardens and reading the *Guardian*"—two pursuits, it might wryly be noted, that Waters acknowledged devoured much of his time. "Altruism and power politics just don't go together."

And Harvest already had one band on its books that made similar statements in its music, in the form of the Edgar Broughton Band. The idea of Floyd even considering throwing themselves onto the free concert circuit that helped sustain the Broughtons' reputation was one that few observers could ever countenance.

Make an album that sounds like Pink Floyd, O'Rourke insisted. Whatever that may be. And Waters hit a creative wall. He was still looking toward experimental film for impetus, still pipe-dreaming the kind of theatrical crossovers that dated back to the days of the ballet idea, still seeing the band as a playground for ambition over art (or art over amusement, for he remained a very serious young man), and the songs he and his comrades were sketching for the band's next album were just that. Sketches.

There was a novelty song about Humble Pie singer Steve Marriott's dog Seamus, whom Gilmour was looking after at the time. A reflection on the band's recent visit to Saint-Tropez (the only wholly Waters-penned composition targeted toward the new record). "Fearless," a Waters lyric that was applied to a driving Gilmour melody, then given a working class twist by the addition of a taped performance of "You'll Never Walk Alone," courtesy of the Liverpool soccer club's crowd. Filler, in other words. Novelty songs. Ditties.

But Gilmour, whose own melodic sensibilities had lain dormant for far too long, was no longer in the mood to allow Waters to ride roughshod over the sessions once again, and it was he who would be responsible for ushering in O'Rourke's dream: a Pink Floyd album that sounded like Pink Floyd, that was bookended, via five minutes at the start of side one, and the entirety of the second side, by two of the most powerful, and the two most perfectly realized, pieces of music the band had yet created.

"One of These Days" was a single-note bass riff that Waters fed through the same echo box he'd been relying on since Barrett was in the band, a trusty old Binson. Foreboding and fearsome, it was mantric moodiness, a firm base upon which the rest of the band could build. Scything Gilmour guitars. Growling Wright organs. Manic Mason percussion. A howling wind and a brief Mason vocal, a distorted but damaging snarl of the song's original title, "One of these days I'm going to cut you into little pieces." Initially, that imprecation washed over the song's intro (the babblings of a disc jockey taped off the radio), and then fed through the remainder of the performance, as though an especially laryngitic psychopath was seated in his living room, cursing the radio DJ.

It was only later, at least a couple of studio demos further on, that the DJ was dropped and Mason's mutterings were picked up, isolated, and dropped a few minutes further in, as the curtain raiser to the song's mid-riff rage, a wise decision that transformed a "typical" piece of Floydian over-cleverness into a work of concise and sense-shattering genius. For the first time since *Piper*, Floyd had created an album opener that actually sounded like it was opening an album.

The other end of the process was a series of experiments that the band called "Nothings," which in turn gave way to a series more that were sensibly titled "Son of Nothings" and on again to "The Return of the Son of Nothing," a patchwork of some thirty-six different pieces of music that the band improvised in Abbey Road one day in January 1971, and which was to demonstrate just why Floyd worked so well when they wanted to.

A true group composition, the sundry Nothings had their roots in the very dichotomy that had divided the band for so long, the endless tug of war between the two musicians in the group, Gilmour and Wright, and the two architecture students, Mason and Waters. It was Wright and Gilmour who created the music, it was Waters and Mason who knitted it together, and who did it so effectively that it is impossible now to even imagine a time when "Echoes," as the piece was ultimately titled, was anything but a seamless whole.

Those two songs define the album that the band had now titled *The Return of the Son of Nothing* in the same way that "Baba O'Reilly" and "Won't Get Fooled Again" define the Who's *Who's Next* album, still relatively warm on the shelves as Floyd began work on the new album, and still a source of amazement and astonishment for anyone who heard it.

It did not matter that the journey between those two peaks—the opening and closing numbers—is, to borrow one of that other band's own most self-deprecating titles, "the Who by numbers." Two songs nevertheless crystallize *Who's Next* and its attentions, reestablishing the Who's credentials following the bloated diversion of *Tommy*, and Pink Floyd's adhesion to that same template was neither accidental nor coincidental. "Pete and Roger Waters were already friends by then," Who bassist John Entwistle explained in the mid-1990s, "and our bands spent a fair bit of time together back then, just talking about the way things were. . . ."

The members of Floyd were not renowned social animals, were not the kind of band that was forever hanging out, partying, and generally being groovy with their contemporaries, or even acting especially socially toward them. One night in 1970 at the Fillmore East in New York City, they peremptorily demanded security throw a bunch of scruffy looking characters out of the backstage area, and only later did they discover they had just ejected members of the Band.

Even at home, among bands that could be considered their contemporaries, Pink Floyd was regarded as standoffish. Hawkwind manager Douglas Smith remembered, "They were so stuck up they wouldn't talk to the likes of Hawkwind. They thought of them as a bunch of dirty hippies. We did a gig with the Floyd in Paris. They were there in their smart new outfits, 'cos they'd had a couple of hit records and we were poor little nobodies. They just ignored us."

The Who, however, was different. Waters's friendship with Pete Townshend was the crystallizing factor, of course, although it was a surprising friendship given the totally different sonic ends that the pair appeared to be striving toward.

Like was attracted to like, nevertheless. The Who's Pete Townshend had been a Pink Floyd fan since the early days at UFO. "I fell in love with the band. Syd Barrett was wonderful and so were the rest of them."

He had been especially struck by Waters at that time. "I found him a little scary. It was evident that he was going to be the principle driving force behind Pink Floyd. . . . A towering and formidable presence." Much as Townshend was the Who. What he didn't realize at those earliest encounters was just how alike the two were.

Like Townshend, Waters was consumed with the notion of rock as an art form capable of raising itself high above the "three chords and a prayer" impressions that its opponents (and, for that matter, many of its exponents) were convinced were all it required.

Townshend had already taken one major step toward realizing that with *Tommy* and was now embarking upon an even more extravagant concept, *Lighthouse*. He nursed, too, a becoming fascination with the proletariat, evidenced in his lyric writing but also in the personas that the

Who had strived to put across since the band's inception six years earlier. That was a luxury in which Pink Floyd could never indulge; their roots in architectural studies were so well known that even the non-architects were tarred with them.

But striking out on a lifelong friendship, Waters and Townshend could philosophize regardless, with the latter adding his voice to those others insisting that Waters was capable of creating something far more meaningful, musically and culturally, than he had allowed himself in the past. All he needed do was apply the same intellect to his lyrics as he applied to every other idea he spoke of.

"Fearless" may or may not have been the first lyric Waters wrote under the influence of Townshend, a triumphantly acoustically based rhythm into which sundry scholars and observers have planted his first, perhaps subconscious, ruminations on the decline of Syd Barrett—not in the oft-quoted line about the idiot "fearlessly . . . facing the crowd," but in the challenge that Barrett laid down to him in the band's earliest days, not quite questioning his commitment, but certainly suggesting that the pair of them were cut from a very different cloth of ambition.

Or perhaps it was Townshend again, wondering aloud whether Waters had the energy to climb that hill, "chiding" him for his uncertainties. Remember, too, that Townshend's most personal lyrics were rarely sung by him; Roger Daltrey was the mouthpiece he wrapped around his confessionals. The lyrics to "Fearless" were written by Waters, but they are voiced by Gilmour.

Recording took the band through the first half of 1971, beginning at Abbey Road, then shifting to AIR and Morgan after it became apparent that the original studio's eight-track machines simply weren't up to the task of completing "Echoes"; that required sixteen tracks at least.

There were breaks, too, for live shows, much to Waters's discomfort: a string of UK dates in May and a handful of European engagements the following month, which were highlighted by an appearance at the Crystal Palace Garden Party festival in London in May.

For the most part, though, *The Return of the Son of Nothing* was Pink Floyd's overriding preoccupation. Having been tasked to create a definitive album, the band was largely left unmolested in the studio; friends dropped by, of course, but management's main concern was allegedly to provide recreation in the form of enthusiastic words and the occasional joint. And so *The Return of the Son of Nothing* came together, its title shifting to the more concise *Meddle*, and Hipgnosis serving up a sleeve that Storm Thorgerson still shudderingly describes as the least favorite of all his Floydian artwork, but which was certainly a hit among the fans of the day.

It depicts a human ear picking up waves of sound (Thorgerson's original suggestion, approved by the band but this time defiantly nixed by Harvest, was of a baboon's bum), but even with that knowledge in hand, it is difficult to actually see the picture. Rather, the shapeless, formless color collage hung like a freeze-frame of an angry lava lamp, and given Floyd's continued reputation as a band tailor-made for getting stoned to, what could have been more appropriate?

The band hit the road. *Meddle* was poised for a late October 1971 release, and having toured Australia and Japan in August, and a couple of nights in Montreaux, Switzerland, in September, Floyd finally unveiled *Meddle*, at least in part, with a concert at the BBC Paris Theatre, for broadcast on DJ John Peel's evening show.

Gilmour's "Fat Old Sun" opened the proceedings, one of just four numbers crammed into the hour of airtime, and immediately the disciplines of *Meddle* layered themselves across a piece that few fans had ever considered much more than one of *Atom Heart Mother's* more palatable entrées. Tighter and tauter than past performances, with a confident vocal that seemed to be doing more than simply reading off the cue sheet, it was nevertheless a deceptive introduction, fifteen minutes of stately pastorals that floated and faded toward their conclusion, and into what Waters told the evening's host, Peel, was a "poignant appraisal of the contemporary social situation."

Wind gusted. A bass line reverberated, silence echoing even louder in the gaps between the thumps. And then the riff kicked in and the organ swooped, and for seven long minutes, the Paris Theatre (and the listening millions at home) sat spellbound as "One of These Days" crashed resolutely, ragingly, raucously—the Floyd's most rocking remark since "The Nile Song," their most ferocious ever. The audience is initially silent when it ends, and the applause sounds more stunned than appreciative, but Floyd had only just started.

"Embryo," an incomplete *Ummagumma*-era outtake that Harvest popped onto the *Picnic* sampler album was next, revised so far from its original form that if Peel had not introduced it (and reminded the audience of the band's unhappiness about the compilation LP), it might not even have been recognized until the vocal line kicked in.

And then it was time for "Echoes." "The last one takes up the whole of the second side of the LP and the group's roadies Pete and Scott say it's an extraordinarily good number," explained Peel. Then the submarine pings reverberated through the audience's sepulchral silence, and the next twenty-seven minutes of prime BBC radio time were devoured by a song that started life as "Nothing." Which is as good a description of the creative process as any.

The show was broadcast on October 3, the same night Floyd played a show in Naples. Home, they were in Birmingham on October 11, and then it was away to America for a month-plus tour that would bring *Meddle* to the masses. What nobody expected, as the band returned home and prepared for their next British outing—set to kick off in Brighton on January 20—was that *Meddle* had already been left behind. The first half of their live show would round up songs that they already considered to be oldies, "Careful with That Axe, Eugene," "Set the Controls for the Heart of the Sun," and "Echoes." The rest would be devoted to a brand-new piece of music, the foundation not for the next album, but for the album after that. It was called *The Dark Side of the Moon*.

Waters had started writing for the set, without actually knowing what the set was, during the *Meddle* sessions, starting with a song that was indeed called "The Dark Side of the Moon." Later revised as "Brain Damage," it was in line for inclusion on *Meddle* for a short time, only to be dropped again as Waters considered the themes that it voiced and considered too Pete Townshend's advice.

The heart of *The Dark Side of the Moon* (or *Eclipse* as it was then known), incredibly, took less than six months to sketch; recording it would take just as long, as the band worked the material into shape on the road and in the studio, and then took an utterly unscheduled break to answer a fresh call from Barbet Schroeder, who had directed *More*. A new movie required a new soundtrack, and so the band came off the road in March, following another Japanese tour, and moved straight into the Château d'Hérouville studios outside Paris to record an entire album in less than a week.

Obscured by Clouds is neither a follow-up to *Meddle* nor the precursor to *The Dark Side of the Moon*. Its contents return Floyd to the troughs and valleys of their earlier soundtrack and singles work, a gathering of simple songs that were given no more polish and sheen than they needed. Rather, the band just went in and kicked out, turning in an album that Mason later described as "sensational," and Richard Wright more thoughtfully reckoned was a snapshot of the direction "we might have taken if *Meddle* had failed and *Dark Side* had gone the way of some of Roger's other ideas."

That is not necessarily an alluring description, but *Obscured by Clouds* remains the sound of Pink Floyd playing as a band, rocking out with no regard for the niceties and (not always attainable) perfections that hallmarked their previous two albums and were now being pushed into their next.

Guitars sliced through everything. Gilmour would certainly play more memorable solos and passages in the future, but he would never play so many in one place, abandoning any claims on, or search for, his own instantly identifiable sound by simply allowing each song, each lyric, its own mood. And, in so doing, allowing the band's own musical influences to raise their heads, not least of all in the supremely Kinks-ish "The Gold It's in the . . . ," the Deep Purple-esque "Burning Bridges," and Waters's raucously knockabout "Free Four," a somewhat maudlin deathbed reflection that disguised the debt it would be owed by "Time" by strumming along like a Boy Scout's campfire sing-along. Certainly no cheerier-sounding song has ever included the lyric "you are the angel of death."

Reflective, too, is Gilmour's "Childhood's End," a song written around his love of the Arthur C. Clarke novel of the same name, but hamstrung by his inability to come up with the final verse that it required. Waters wrote one instead, and the balance of power shifted just a little as Waters seized upon that as a reason to write all of the band's lyrics himself in future.

That this song, too, could have slipped into *Dark Side* as a substitute for "Time" has been acknowledged by most listeners. Less remarked upon, but equally potent, are the echoes of King Crimson that point to another of Floyd's collective interests. Never critical favorites, Crimson was nevertheless poised as one of those bands that can be described as musicians' musicians, with the occasionally dictatorial reign of front man Robert Fripp additionally offering Waters a glimpse into his own future. He, Waters, would never follow Fripp's example so far as the random hiring and firing of bandmates that scarred much of Crimson's future . . . not yet, anyway. But it was also increasingly apparent that only one person could be calling the shots in Pink Floyd. And Waters knew who it was to be.

Another US tour in April, a few dates around Europe in May, and the band was back in the studio by June, to welcome director Adrian Maben into the room to film them as they continued working on a new album that was, for now, titled *Eclipse: A Piece for Assorted Lunatics*. This somewhat bland footage, spliced into a more extravagant vision of the band performing in the vast amphitheater of Pompeii, Italy, was destined to become a movie in its own right, *Pink Floyd Live in Pompeii*. Half concert performance, half home movie, the band filmed wandering around the summit of Mount Vesuvius, the end result often feels little more than an afterthought—the group marking time while their minds were firmly on another project entirely. And there are moments scattered throughout the film where hindsight, at least, proves the wisdom of that attitude. The excerpts from *Eclipse* that make it into the movie are little more than that, mere excerpts, moods, suggestions. But pieced together at the end of the day, they would change Pink Floyd—and the world's perception of Pink Floyd—forever.

14

Forward, He Cried

The statistics are astonishing. In the forty years that have elapsed since its March 1973 release, *The Dark Side of the Moon* has sold in excess of forty million copies worldwide. Recent figures insist that one household in four in the UK owns a copy of either the LP, CD, eight-track, or cassette; in the US, one person in fourteen either owns, or has owned, a copy.

In a poll of the world's biggest-selling albums of all time, the album more or less ties the soundtracks to *Saturday Night Fever* and *The Bodyguard* for second place (Michael Jackson's *Thriller*, of course, occupies the top spot), and while *The Dark Side of the Moon* only ever spent seven days at the top of the *Billboard* album charts, still it remained on those listings for a staggering 741 weeks before a change in the way the charts were compiled, in April 1988, shifted it to the Pop Catalog chart, and its dominance continued there. In May 2006, *The Dark Side of the Moon* achieved a combined total of 1,500 weeks on the *Billboard* 200 and Pop Catalog charts, with the *Wall Street Journal* reporting that it continues to sell close to ten thousand copies every week.

Why? What was so special . . . spectacular . . . about this album that it should so explode beyond the confines not only of Pink Floyd's career, but of the rock music audience in general?

Prior to the album release, Floyd had ticked along relatively smoothly, of course, topping the UK LP charts with their annual new releases, and naturally selling out their concert performances. But they were never a big band, in the way that Led Zeppelin, Deep Purple, Black Sabbath, or Jethro Tull were big; somebody once described Pink Floyd as the best-loved cult band in the world, and that summed them up very nicely. A lot of people liked them, but they did so from at least one step away from unmitigated fandom, and if you put on one of the band's earlier albums, *Atom Heart Mother* or *Meddle* or *Obscured by Clouds*, it was more likely to be as the soundtrack to some other (possibly illegal) activity than because you really wanted to get down and boogie to the Floyd.

Then *The Dark Side of the Moon* came along, and all predictions were off.

All four band members have admitted, at different times over the years, that they cannot understand why the album just keeps on selling. Nick Mason has cited the songwriting, but that can surely be only a part of the equation. So can the musicianship, and the fact that the band, for the first time, had the luxury of being able to live with their endeavors before pushing them out onto the market. But those things only explain why the record sounds so good. Why so many people keep on buying it is one of those great imponderables.

Certainly there had never been anything quite like it in the past—rock historians note that the title, *The Dark Side of the Moon*, had already seen service once, courtesy of the last Medicine Head album. But that band, hit makers in 1970, and destined to be so again in 1973, were in something of a trough—vocalist John Fiddler still smiles away the irony of how the title of an LP that his band could scarcely give away became the byword for multiplatinum success just a few short months later.

The Dark Side of the Moon made its own way to glory, created its own momentum. Of course, once the ball started rolling, and the first few million people acknowledged the sheer brilliance of the record, others had to pick up their own copy, simply to find out what the fuss was all about. And that became a self-perpetuating process, all the more so as successive advances in sound reproduction—from quadraphonic sound to CD to Mobile Fidelity gold to SACD—made it appear somehow imperative that one keep one's copy up to date. The fact that almost every one of us could name at least two other Floyd albums (the earlier *Piper at the Gates of Dawn*, the subsequent *Animals*, for example) that they prefer to the leviathan is irrelevant. The average consumer has probably purchased no more than one copy of either of them. Various formats of *Dark Side*, on the other hand, now have their own bookcase.

Pink Floyd knew that *The Dark Side of the Moon* represented a major step forward for them, even before recording commenced, at a time when they still referred to it as *Eclipse: A Piece for Assorted Lunatics*. As Gilmour put it, their earlier music was intended to "spark off people's imagination," a feat that it accomplished admirably, across sidelong soundscapes and vast feats of atmospheric derring-do. The new music, however, was aimed at making individual points and ideas without allowing anything else to get in the way, ideas like the innocence of childhood ("Breathe"), growing old ("Time"), the power of consumerism ("Money"), the nature of religion ("The Great Gig in the Sky"), personal conflict ("Us and Them"), the importance of free will ("Eclipse"), and, most famously of all, madness ("Brain Damage").

The popular belief that *The Dark Side of the Moon* is consumed by the latter theme is an easy mistake to make—among the muttered voices that percolate through the stereophonic experience, such murmurings as "I've always been mad . . ." and "There is no dark side of the moon, as a matter of fact it's all dark" do allow the listener to create conceptual bookends that dovetail exquisitely into the band's own history.

But when *The Dark Side of the Moon* appeared, just five years had elapsed since founder-member Syd Barrett had exited the band, and no more than two since his last solo album, the stark acoustics of *Barrett*. Another year or more needed to elapse before the first whispers about the nature of his malaise went screaming into the public consciousness. But once they did, once Barrett became as renowned for his post-psychedelic insanity as for the marvelous songs that he spread across three LPs (Floyd's debut and his own self-powered pair), and those songs themselves became clinical casebooks for any would-be pop psychologist looking to gain cheap Brownie points with the rock intelligentsia, *The Dark Side of the Moon* was seized upon as Pink Floyd's own exorcism of Barrett's haunted, haunting influence.

But Barrett was not the only albatross with which *The Dark Side of the Moon* was to be saddled, as Roger Waters complained later in 1973. The other was the media's continued insistence that Pink Floyd played "space rock."

It was a tag with which the band had lived since the days of "Astronomy Domine" and "Interstellar Overdrive," and which persisted no matter how often Waters, in particular, pointed out that the latter was simply titled that because they liked the sound of the words together—while conveniently ignoring the somewhat less ambiguous lyrical claims laid by "Let There Be More Light" and "Set the Controls for the Heart of the Sun."

Add the spatial expanses of "Echoes" and "Cirrus Minor," and for those people who do allow music to conjure images in their mind, whether through the power of suggestion or not, great swaths of the band's most impressive material did convey a certain science-fiction inclination (Arthur C. Clarke, author of the book that inspired "Childhood's End" would have been shocked to be described as anything but a sci-fi author). And while Waters was right to seethe at the new album's incorporation into that bag just because it had the word "moon" in its title, he was certainly being a little disingenuous in his attempts to distance the band from an imagery that they had never balked at courting.

Space rock, after all, does not have to revolve around songs about space. Borne aloft by the music of bands as far afield as Hawkwind and the Grateful Dead, Gong and Tangerine Dream, even Jefferson Airplane when the mood hit them ("Have You Seen the Saucers?"), space rock is a frame of mind, and—if one divorces it from its most literal connotations—one that the group should have been proud of exemplifying. It meant that their music was vast and expansive, psychedelia beyond the realms of mere psychedelics, and utterly untethered to earthly concerns, no matter how mundane the subject matter might be.

At the same time, of course, Waters conceded that the album was open to a degree of interpretation, which of course was another reason for its universal appeal. Shortly after the album's release, he told *ZigZag*, "The way our music impinges on your mind makes it very easy to conjure up some vision, very easy to imagine some scene. If you're listening to John Cage or Stockhausen, it's very difficult because the music is all squeaks and bubbles. It's more like hard edge, real abstract painting. There are definite things in it like triangles and squares . . . that you respond to in an intellectual way. Our music is non-intellectual, it is straight emotional response gear."

His starting points were certainly fundamental. He cited "the sun and the moon, the light and the dark, the good and the bad, the life force as opposed to the death force" as motivating themes behind the album. "The line 'I'll see you on the dark side of the moon' is me speaking to the listener, saying, I know you have these bad feelings and impulses, because I do too, and one of the ways I can make contact with you is to share the fact that I feel bad sometimes."

It was Waters who wrote the lyrics to the album, stepping wholeheartedly into a role that both Gilmour and keyboard player Richard Wright had previously helped him fill, albeit with less enthusiasm than Waters would have liked to see them exhibit. Past albums had nevertheless allowed both to shine if they felt like it; this time around, the onus fell firmly upon Waters, and he rose enthusiastically to the challenge.

"I was getting strong urges to make extended pieces with segues between tracks and also to develop pieces where the songs have relationships. 'Echoes,' which was one side of *Meddle*, was very much the father and mother of *Dark Side of the Moon* in that it had a lot of similar techniques. We had already started improvising around some pieces . . . and, after I had written a couple of the lyrics for the songs I suddenly thought, I know what would be good: to make a whole record about the different pressures that apply in modern life."

At the time, the process seemed natural: Waters had the concept; Waters would carry it through. Had one of his bandmates stepped forward with a lyric that both fit the concept and plugged a gap within it, doubtless it would have been incorporated into the overall scheme. But they let him get on with it, referring to the project as Roger's baby, and acknowledging also that the new project was very much Waters's way of discovering himself as a lyricist.

Many observers have remarked upon the almost stellar leap in lyrical delivery that Waters made in just the few short months between *Meddle* and the earliest sketches of *Dark Side*, the realization (and once again, one can look toward Pete Townshend's example here) that a simple pop song could simultaneously convey a very complicated message. Very early on in the process, in fact, Waters said as much to Gilmour, telling him that this time around, he wanted to get away from the "psychedelic warblings" that had hitherto been his lyrical default and actually say what he wanted to.

Obscured by Clouds was the rough sketch for that resolution, but so, in many ways, was the failed experiment of *Atom Heart Mother*. There, Waters had remained hung up on the idea of conveying his messages in musical terms, without resorting to what seemed the lazy alternative of spelling them out in words. His old architectural training was a hard beast to shake off. But now he had discovered language, the power of language and the beauty of it too. For the first time in his songwriting career, words were not simply another layer of sound. They were the engine that drove the song.

Besides, it was only the lyrics that were Waters's preserve. The actual music—which, if we are to be honest, is what truly powers the album from start to finish — was written by all four musicians. Indeed, many of its ultimate elements were already knocking around the band's archive years before the record was even considered, and a large part of the album's preparation was spent poring through old tapes to see if there was anything there that they could utilize this time around.

Shards of "The Labyrinths of Auximenes," from the abandoned *Massed Gadgets* project, were incorporated into "Money"; "Breathe" was derived from the movie soundtrack *The Body*; Wright introduced a slow, breathy outtake from another of the band's soundtrack efforts, *Zabriskie Point*, that would ultimately become "Us and Them," and then remembered a piano chord sequence he had once worked out, but which the band had previously not had any use for, "The Great Gig in the Sky."

If the creation of *The Dark Side of the Moon* was a democratic process, it was also a remarkably relaxed one. Unlike past albums, where the band members would really only meet up to work, and where the best ideas were conceived either onstage or with the studio clock ticking, most of the band meetings for *Dark Side* took place at Nick Mason's home in Saint Augustine's Road, Camden, seated around his kitchen table.

In the past, the band had always relied on group dinners as the place where they cleared the air, usually without any regard for who might be witnessing the ensuing fireworks. Rumors that Pink Floyd was on the verge of splitting up were a regular whisper on the grapevine during the early 1970s, and Nick Mason later admitted that many of them were born out of one especially fiery meal or another, usually paid for by the record company, and the more expensive the wine on the menu, the more combustible the conversation. "I now feel deeply sorry for some of the unfortunate promoters and record company people who took us out," Mason reflected. "We frequently behaved appallingly."

The decision to conduct such business in private felt strange at first, especially on those afternoons when all four knew that as soon as the meeting ended, they would be seeing one another again at the studio, or on their way to the next gig—sometimes, in fact, the roadies would pick them up from Mason's house, to make their way to the show. But the moment they left the kitchen table, the meeting itself was at an end.

Compared to the sporadic and bitty method Pink Floyd had employed in the past, where pieces of music were as likely to emerge from jamming and improvisation as they were from concerted songwriting sessions, and any shortfall in the playing time would be filled with last-minute doodles, all four found themselves with downtime in which to pursue their own thoughts about the album. Thoughts which could then be brought, with any accompanying arguments, to Saint Augustine's Road. Occasionally one or other might signal his weariness by playing with a teaspoon or looking around the room while someone else labored a point a little too long, but the lack of other distractions (an idle guitar, a nearby drum kit, an audience of drinking buddies) forced them all to focus on the job at hand.

The formulation of a definite theme for the album, based around the lyrics that Waters had all but completed, added to the sense of cohesion; so did the decision to take the new music out on the road in the new year, to be further refined onstage.

This was not an altogether painless process. The bootleggers were out in force when Floyd toured the UK in early 1972, and the prospect of an entire album's worth of unreleased material being unveiled every night was not one that they were willing to miss. Long before Pink Floyd had completed the recording of *The Dark Side of the Moon*, bootleg versions of the performance were on the streets, and it is incredible to discover that the band itself did not learn what should have been a very obvious lesson. Or perhaps they didn't want to, because they knew that the benefits outweighed the disadvantages. No arena on earth can replace the live environment as the best place in which to work through new material, to iron out the bugs and see what works best, and the ultimate cohesion of the completed *Dark Side* proved that beyond any doubt whatsoever.

So, when they toured again in 1974, as they worked toward what became *Wish You Were Here*, once again the new music was being unveiled onstage, and, once again, the bootleggers were able to thrill the streets with an all-new Floyd album months before the band's own finished opus was due for release.

The opening night's concert in Brighton, England, on January 20, 1972, remains the most familiar to most listeners, both from bootlegs and from its inclusion in the band's anniversary box set edition of the finished album. The second, in Portsmouth, is harder to find but just as rewarding. Both are unquestionably historic recordings. Unfortunately, Pink Floyd really wasn't a compelling live band at this particular juncture.

Jamming, spreading out, spacing out, they could be amazing, locking into moods and moments with Teutonic precision and simply flying. But tied to the short, sharp discipline of songs (and lest we forget, *Dark Side* was the Floyd's first truly song-based cycle since the *More* soundtrack) they were equally capable of falling apart. Waters's vocals, in particular, were dreadful—weedy, thin, and sounding so utterly uninvolved in the music that he might have been at home sketching demos. Or painting the bathroom.

Harmonies didn't help either; now, instead of one person sounding bored, there'd be two or three. *The Dark Side of the Moon* became a masterpiece in the studio. But there's a reason why the band didn't release an official, concert-length live album until 1988, and every one of the vocal performances here spells it out.

Which is a shame, because the actual mood of the piece, the atmosphere that even a bootlegger's handheld microphone detected, is rife with a curiosity and a passion that later, post-release renditions simply couldn't muster. Compare a tape of Portsmouth with, say, the Tampa, Florida, show of eighteen months later, the final night of the now painstakingly regulated *Dark Side* tour. In terms of energy and intensity, they are polar opposites.

What these first sightings reveal, then, for all their faults and flaws, is the sound of a band still working out the material, inserting passages and touches which would never be heard again—and, contrarily, lacking a few which would soon become de rigueur. Add some genuinely heartfelt audience responses (the Brighton bootleg has an all but running commentary from one awestruck onlooker), and you truly get a very real impression of what it was like to see Floyd at this particular juncture.

Too many post-*Moon* live Floyd recordings ultimately come across as sterile and as (again that word) bored as the band themselves sound. The Brighton recording, shot through with palpable surprise and infuriating gremlins, is one of the most human performances the band ever gave; Portsmouth, where everything went right, one of the most triumphant. Just don't expect them to compare with the studio album.

—

Sessions with engineer Alan Parsons were held at Abbey Road Studios in north London between May 1972 and January 1973, with the band purposefully calling up the most advanced recording equipment and techniques that they could lay their hands on. Most famously, this included a quadraphonic mix, but the band was also experimenting with one of the first analog sequencers ever developed, the EMS Synthi-A, a device that took English designer Peter Zinovieff's VCS3 (Voltage Controlled Studio) and added a keyboard to it.

The machine's wild oscillations and effects dominate "On the Run," the band reveling in the possibilities of the synths and sequencers that Abbey Road placed at their disposal, and a lot of other toys as well. The EMI sound effects library, too, proved an invaluable source. Famously, the Beatles always kept a close eye on its contents and employed them gleefully across their later recordings. The members of Pink Floyd too became regular visitors to the archive, and their only regret was that many of the best noises they discovered were ones they never could find a use for. The sound of an overstuffed cupboard being opened, followed quickly by the sound of a mountain of junk falling out, was one that Mason never lost affection for.

It is scarcely missed. For, elsewhere, the conscientious listener (play it on the headphones, man!) can hear one of Parsons's assistant engineers running around inside an echo chamber (again during "On the Run"), a specially treated bass drum emulating the sound of a human heartbeat ("Speak to Me" and "Eclipse"), and, of course, the sound of a roomful of antique clocks chiming simultaneously ("Time"), a piece that Parsons had created a few months earlier while preparing a quadraphonic demonstration disc for EMI.

Then there's "Money," which opens with the clatter of cash registers and adding machines, the rattle of coins, and the tearing of paper, to create one of the most distinctive intros that any song could boast.

Another key element in the album's overall sound was the aforementioned snatches of spoken word that filter through the piece. These were obtained using a series of printed flash cards, devised by the band members and all relating to the central themes of the album. Interviewees would be called in from every corner of the Abbey Road studio complex, placed in front of a microphone, and told simply to give the most honest answer they could to the questions as they appeared. These included roadies Chris Adamson, who opens the album with the insistence that "I've been mad for fucking years, absolutely years, over the edge for yonks," and Roger "The Hat" Manifold, whose contributions included the insistence that somebody or other be given "a quick, short, sharp shock."

Road manager Peter Watts was responsible for the laughter that echoes so evocatively through "Brain Damage," while his wife, Puddie, speaks of "geezers . . . cruisin' for a bruisin'" and "I never said I was frightened of dying." Wings guitarist Henry McCullough confesses, "I don't know, I was really drunk at the time," but contributions from bandmates Paul and

Linda McCartney (who were recording their *Red Rose Speedway* album at the studio at the same time) ultimately went unused. Their responses, all agreed, were too guardedly self-conscious.

Nine months after they started work on the project, with the recording finally completed, cross-faded, and mixed, Pink Floyd sat back to await the album's release. Gilmour reflected upon the last day in the studio. "There was a moment when it all came together. We'd finished mixing all the tracks, but until the very last day we'd never heard them as the continuous piece we'd been imagining for more than a year. We had to literally snip bits of tape, cut in the linking passages, and stick the ends back together. Finally you sit back and listen all the way through at enormous volume. I can remember it. It was absolutely . . . it was really exciting."

The album was not without its critics, of course—no record is ever received with unanimous joy from every listener. As journalist Ian Mac-Donald wrote a year later, when the album marked up its forty-seventh week on the UK chart,

> If you'd played this to an average record-company executive at the beginning of '73 and told him it would become the year's best-selling rock LP . . . he'd have laughed in your face. For one thing, it's far too serious. For another, it's hopelessly slow—not a single rocker among its six songs (unless you count "Money," which is actually no faster than the rest, but feels raunchier). And for the capper, this exec would have explained, *Dark Side* wouldn't be a hit because the same slow seriousness had been preempted by *More* and *Ummagumma*—and the relative commercial disappointment of *Atom Heart Mother* and *Obscured by Clouds* only emphasised the fact.

But dissenting voices, both in the media and among Pink Floyd's own audience, weren't just simply in the minority, they were crushed beneath the roar of the album's multimillion-selling success. The group that Richard Thompson, with both good humor and droll irreverence, once condemned as "a blues band with alarm clocks," had transformed itself into the biggest-selling recording artists of the year, while the accompanying tour pushed Pink Floyd toward heights in attendance, box office, and reach they had never imagined possible.

"*The Dark Side of the Moon* is a fine album with a textural and conceptual richness that not only invites, but demands involvement. There is a certain grandeur here that exceeds mere musical melodramatics and is rarely attempted in rock. *The Dark Side of the Moon* has flash—the true flash that comes from the excellence of a superb performance," raved *Rolling Stone*, in a review that mystifyingly painted "Time" as "a country-tinged rocker."

And where *Rolling Stone* went, the rest of the media followed, and still follow to this day.

Not for *The Dark Side of the Moon* the hollow crown worn by *Sgt. Pepper*, declared the greatest album ever made because nobody ever dares say otherwise.

Not for *The Dark Side of the Moon* the superficial supremacy of *Thriller*, which might remain the bestselling album of all time, but when was the last time you heard someone play it without forwarding through half the songs?

And not for *The Dark Side of the Moon* the flash-in-the-pan notoriety of whatever other fashionable accessory the industry has thrown at us, convinced that, if the hypesters only shout loud enough, we might actually believe what they're saying.

The Dark Side of the Moon lives on because, from start to finish and from dawn to dusk, it is a bloody marvelous record, quite possibly the most perfectly realized rock record ever conceived, and undoubtedly the most deserving success story in rock 'n' roll history.

15

Shining On Crazily

We may never know the genuine truth about Syd Barrett's departure from the Floyd: Did he jump, was he pushed, did he turn into a platypus and pour paint down Nick Mason's periscope? Or did he just fall silent? Because that was all he'd done—fallen silent. There were rumors that he'd resumed his old love of painting. Floyd's growing immensity, and sales of their back catalog certainly ensured he could afford that luxury, while David Bowie's decision to cover "See Emily Play" on *Pin Ups* would keep the wolf from the door even longer. No-one was saying he was in orbit; nobody thought he was strange. He was, simply, a recluse, and it wasn't as if pop had never seen one of those before.

When *ZigZag* magazine ran journalist Barry Miles's account of the Floyd's early years in August 1972, the worst accounts of Barrett's state of mind were a few wistful regrets about his dislike of the circus into which Floyd's pop-star fame had suddenly plunged him, and the occasional night when the acid got the better of him.

A year later, Floyd themselves followed up with their own account of those heady days for the same magazine, and the only mention of Barrett's madness was in conjunction with his genius—that tragically unrecorded day on which he tried to teach the band a new song and kept changing it subtly on every run-through.

And then the *New Musical Express* published Nick Kent's masterful deconstruction of the disintegrating Barrett mind (April 13, 1974), and everything fell into place: for EMI, who suddenly discovered an entire generation hankering for a couple of albums that hadn't sold a sausage since 1970 (the Syd Barrett twofer was released just three months later); for the Floyd, who'd been struggling to follow up *Dark Side of the Moon* for two long years, then wrote the elegiac "Shine On You Crazy Diamond" practically overnight. And for Barrett, who was heartily sick of being asked about a comeback, and now had the perfect excuse to postpone it forever: "Sorry, but haven't you heard? I'm mad."

It is a fascinating piece of writing. Six months earlier, Kent composed a dry run of the Barrett story for *Creem* (October 1973) in which he ruminated on the possibility of Barrett's return: "A few months back . . . a friend told me he'd seen Syd Barrett drifting down Charing Cross Road, looking in guitar shops. His hair was long again, and he was back to wearing his old snakeskin boots."

The Barrett who emerged from that article was "a genuine eccentric, one of those people that people just love to wonder about. He joins in that category the likes of Brian Wilson, Bob Dylan (vintage 1966), Lou Reed and Iggy Pop (before their respective resurrections) and Brian Jones."

What changed over the next six months? How did Barrett slide from being a simple "acid casualty" prone to bouts of "general weirdness" to become rock's favorite madman?

Barrett himself had something to do with it. He knew what people were saying about him, and he also knew that, if he really wanted to be left alone, the best thing was to let them keep saying it. He had his own life away from music, and, again, he had enough money coming in to keep it that way. If he truly had redirected his muse away from music and back to his art, why on earth would he need to try recreating it?

So he didn't. In August 1974, with the *NME* article still resonating, what history records as "a mysterious benefactor" booked Barrett into Abbey

Road to see if there was any way of shaking a third solo album out of the newly re-illuminated star.

Both David Bowie and Brian Eno have been credited with this act of great, but supremely misguided, kindness. So have some of Pink Floyd; so have Kevin Ayers and Bryan Ferry; and so has Jack Bruce, with whom an unrecognized Barrett shared an informal jam at a small hall in Cambridge sometime during the summer of 1973. Pete Brown, Bruce's lyricist, remembered seeing an "odd-looking guitarist" playing acoustic jazz during a break in the sound check that afternoon; it was only later that evening, during the actual gig, that Brown realized who it was. He had just dedicated a poem, "Goodnight Eliza Doolittle: The Death of Flower Power," to Barrett, describing him as the person responsible for setting that ball rolling in England. At which point, to Brown's astonishment, that "odd-looking guitarist" stood up from the audience and announced, "No I didn't."

In fact, it was manager Bryan Morrison who lay behind Barrett's latest studio sojourn, and he was swiftly disavowed of his dream. For starters, Barrett apparently turned up for only two days of the four-day session, during which he debuted a few loose chord sequences, a few blues riffs, and just one song title, "If You Go." None of which was usable, none of which even seemed to have any kind of formulated structure from which to alchemize anything approaching a song.

No vocals were attempted, and listening to the inconsequential crackles of guitar playing that were recorded, Barrett's lack of interest in the proceedings is deafening. He was only in the studio because someone somehow persuaded him to do it (the promise of a room full of brand new guitars probably helped as well), and the fragments themselves could have been played by anyone. It was Barrett's last ever attempt at recording.

Rock legend likes to treat the Syd Barrett story like some kind of vast romantic tragedy and draws on the events of a few months in his very early twenties as evidence. "Syd is now being glorified in a manner that is almost Arthurian," Mick Farren wrote in 2011. "He is the golden psychedelic boy-king, admired and desired, fashionably tortured in a poet's ruffled shirt, and with dark hair falling into already haunted eyes. His power peaks and he is sacrificed to drugs, a troubled mind or splendid madness. He retreats into an exile of isolation."

Whether he dictated, demanded, or even deserved such deification is not the issue. Society takes its heroes from wherever it can, and Barrett in the early twenty-first century occupies the role that Brian Jones took in the late twentieth, the god who died so that lesser mortals could prosper. Barrett, Farren concluded, "has graduated to a role in our popular culture that is more symbolic than actual."

As legends go, it was all very lucrative, too.

There is no suggestion whatsoever that anybody connected with either Floyd, Barrett, or their respective record companies ever woke up one morning and said, "Wouldn't it be great if Pink Floyd had a tragic legend hanging over their head, a spirit that could be invoked whenever Roger writes another of his depressing songs about irrevocable loss, that would keep the back catalog ticking over while maintaining interest in the band as a whole."

Nobody ever sat down with Barrett and told him, "Keep your head down, sonny, and we'll see you all right . . . stick the occasional song on our compilations, dig them out when we're playing live, and talk up your own records for the next wave of romance-starved teenagers." And, given the weight of evidence that Barrett certainly did suffer from mental problems later in his life, if not in the early 1970s, it is laughable to perceive a commercial interest in formulating or perpetuating such a ridiculous plot.

But . . . it is interesting to note that, for all the hours of outtakes from both *Madcap* and *Barrett* that have flooded out over the last two decades of reissues, not one unreleased note of Syd's time with the Floyd has ever been given the green light. The official line, first rolled out for "Scream Thy Last Scream," but patiently reiterated on occasion since then, is that it was to keep Syd from being embarrassed. But what really showed him in the best light? The CD's worth of pristine Pink Floyd BBC sessions recorded at the peak of his powers, whose release the band has (so far) pointedly refused to countenance? Those completed studio masters from the end of his tenure with the band that rate among his most glittering highlights? Or the sound of him falling off his chair and dropping his guitar, as presented in living stereo across the bonus tracks on the official reissues of his two solo albums?

Hindsight rushes to rescue the situation, scholars delve deep into the band's songwriting, and Waters's in particular (*Dark Side*'s somewhat egalitarian songwriting credits disguise the fact that Waters later claimed that he "gave away" half of them to nonwriting bandmates), to pull out traces of his own awareness of Barrett's state of mind. But while there can be no doubt that *The Dark Side of the Moon* was at least partially concerned with madness, it was troubled by other themes as well—old age, sickness, death, hatred, paranoia.

Kent's *NME* story on Syd had the effect of a genie coming out of the bottle—opportunity shrouded in mystery—and Waters knew exactly what to do with it. In June, two months after the article appeared, Waters unveiled a new song during Pink Floyd's French tour, a lengthy guitar-led piece titled "Shine On," its subject matter reinforced by the incorporation of Barrett's "Dark Globe" into the opening sequence of the twenty-minute opus.

That Waters was already hard at work writing toward a new Pink Floyd album came as no surprise to those who knew him, nor that he was impatient to bring the music out into the public gaze before a single note had been consigned to tape. Had things gone to plan, however, a whole different LP might have been on display as the band toured through 1974, drawn from the sessions that the group convened the previous autumn, for a project prosaically titled *Household Objects*.

A legend in Floyd circles until the appearance of two of the three completed tracks within the Immersion editions of *Dark Side of the Moon* and

Wish You Were Here in 2011 and 2012, *Household Objects* was to feature no conventional musical instruments whatsoever. Rather, it would be created by utilizing, indeed, household objects—a wine bottle tapped across the top of the neck, rubber bands stretched between tables and twanged, rolls of adhesive tape loudly unpeeled.

It was a process that would, less than a decade later, be adapted by a plethora of experimental electronic and industrial bands; the difference was, they were working with samplers, computers, and the wealth of other gadgets that technology offered to the aspiring musician as the 1970s moved into the 1980s. Pink Floyd was working with the real thing, in real time, and while the experiments were undoubtedly fascinating (and the resultant tracks barely gave away their origins), it was also apparent that they were working so hard to replicate the sound of actual instruments that they might as well have been using the instruments to begin with.

Besides, they had just inked a million-dollar deal with Columbia Records in the United States, at a time when such figures were practically unheard of in the music industry. One can scarcely imagine the New York bigwigs being overwhelmed by an album recorded using furniture and aerosol cans. *Household Objects* was dropped, and the band members separated for a time, taking the opportunity instead to recharge their batteries away from the demands of their career.

Gilmour was the busiest, gigging with his friends Sutherland Brothers and Quiver after their regular guitarist, Tim Renwick, was taken ill, and spending time with the full band, too. Renwick recalls, "There was a fair bit of socially 'hanging out' with him—he did jam with us from time to time and we recorded some tunes at his home studio.

"David . . . also produced a Sutherland Brothers and Quiver B-side, 'We Get Along.' For a while [we] were managed by Steve O'Rourke and represented by their agents (NEMS Enterprises). This led to us playing on the same bill with them (notably the Crystal Palace Bowl concert when they featured a massive inflatable 'monster' in the lake) on various occasions."

Gilmour guested alongside their old Blackhill Enterprises stablemate Roy Harper at the annual Hyde Park Festival, and took a new band, Unicorn, under his wing to produce the first of three albums they cut together. He also, although nobody foresaw the significance, recorded a clutch of demos with an unknown fifteen-year-old singer-songwriter named Katie Bush, inviting her to his farm to record with Unicorn as her backing musicians.

Mason, too, launched what would become a patchy, but always fascinating, sideline as a record producer, working with former Soft Machine drummer Robert Wyatt on his *Rock Bottom* solo album, and enjoying an utterly unexpected hit when Wyatt's rendition of the Monkees' "I'm a Believer" hit the UK chart. Wyatt was still slowly recovering from a horrific accident just months earlier, when he fell from a window and broke his back; now he was wheelchair bound, and on November 4, 1973, the full Floyd lineup was among the guests at the London Rainbow for a benefit gig for Wyatt.

Waters had less time in which to relax. After five years of marriage, he and Judy were heading inexorably toward divorce, a sad state that Waters later said was precipitated during a holiday in Greece in 1974 but crystallized the night when Waters called home from the latest halt on the band's American tour, and the phone was answered by a stranger. A male stranger.

There had been flash points long before that—the couple's apparent inability to have children, and Waters's own apparent drive to fertilize every willing woman he met. Nick Mason recalls one particular evening, sitting around with Roger and Judy, and his own wife, Lindy, discussing "Roger's infidelity on the road"—a conversation that grew increasingly heated, the drummer admitted, when he joined in with "the girls' censorious tutting at [Roger's] behavior mainly because I had been no better."

Manager O'Rourke, too, spoke in later years of Waters's sexual proclivity, although he couched it with a smile that could easily have been construed as ironic. In the annals of rock fantasy, after all, the individual members of Pink Floyd have rarely figured high on the totem of dreams. Their naughty parts were never immortalized by the Plaster Casters. No epic of confessional groupiedom has ever discussed a night of passion with Floyd and his pink thing, although author Jenny Fabian came close; her novel *Groupie* features an only barely disguised Floyd cavorting beneath the name Satin Odyssey, although it is "Ben" (Barrett) alone who strides through their appearance, a relic of the afternoon Fabian interviewed him for *Harpers & Queen*.

But the opportunities were there regardless. Despite their public image as serious musicians rising far above traditional rock 'n' roll hijinks, they were, after all, millionaire rock stars, and that came with all of the attendant perquisites, as a swift listen to Wright's "Summer '68" will demonstrate.

Sparking, too, were the ideologies that Judy, still fervently left-wing, felt were lacking in her husband's attitudes and behavior—Waters was not simply a champagne socialist but also one who quaffed the most expensive bubbly that money could buy. It was not, as so many other people in his position have discovered, an easy reputation to shake off, a consequence of the post-Orwellian notion that a person can only truly empathize with the struggles of the "proletariat" by living the life of one too. (Famously, the author of 1984 spent time living as a vagabond in order to write his *Down and Out in Paris and London*).

The idea that a surfeit of money is not conducive to a surfeit of sympathy remains—for those who would characterize the entire world in terms of black and white alone—an extraordinarily adhesive one. As if the complaints of the poor are somehow more valid than the rhetoric of the rich—which in itself may be true. But it's the rich who are heard the loudest.

Six months away from the band went by so quickly, and in June 1974, the band undertook a short French tour. The fall then brought their first British outing since the release of *Dark Side of the Moon*, and it was clear that the machine was back in action—an observation that an already weary Waters promptly wrote into a new song, "Welcome to the Machine."

Three songs from the gestating next album were in the set list now: "Shine On," under its full title of "Shine On You Crazy Diamond," with its sorrowful reflections on Syd Barrett, and two more that lashed out at the evils of society in general, twelve minutes of the wonderfully titled "Raving and Drooling" and eighteen minutes of "You've Got to Be Crazy." Over fifty minutes into their first British concerts in so long, and Pink Floyd had played just three songs, not a single moment of which anyone in the stadium would have recognized. In an industry where audience recognition and participation were regarded as the most sacrosanct of all an artist's responsibilities, one of the biggest bands in the world had turned the equation on its head and forced their audience to sit through what amounted to an entire album's worth of new material. Again!

It would be the last time they did so.

Nobody could deny the quality of the material. "Shine On You Crazy Diamond" was especially powerful, and almost heartbreakingly evocative. Ron Howden, whose band Nektar headlined at Syd Barrett's last ever concert, in Cambridge in 1972, recalls, "I do remember sitting in the dressing room with Syd, and being very excited to meet him. It was a really tiny room especially for all the bands (Henry Cow were also on the bill). He was very approachable, but also very distant at the same time. A very nice person. [But] when I hear 'Shine On You Crazy Diamond,' I immediately think of the moment I caught his eyes."

The British tour was just concluding when the nation's Christmas stockings were treated to what both looked and felt like a brand new Floyd album, a live set from the Stoke-on-Trent show on November 19, its contents split across the three new songs. It was, of course, a bootleg, albeit a remarkably well-presented one, and *Winter Tour 74* would become one of the fastest-selling records of the season, without its performers seeing a penny from the proceeds.

It also effectively stymied Waters's own intentions for the group's new studio album, itself germinating in his mind as a three song offering, with "Shine On You Crazy Diamond" devouring side one, the other pair on side two. Past rehearsals and discussions as to the actual album were suddenly scrapped; "Shine On You Crazy Diamond" would remain in the repertoire, but the remainder of the album, the whole of side two as it were, needed to be started from scratch.

Tempers flared; moods grew ugly. Gilmour had never fully come over to those songs—"Raving and Drooling," he felt, sounded "a bit recycled," and "Gotta Be Crazy" still needed a lot of rearranging before he would be happy. "Roger wrote the words to fit over a certain part and I'm not sure that we did it quite the right way."

Brian Humphries, the band's long-standing sound engineer, explained, "There were changes in the studio. . . . They weren't exactly sure whether they should record the three new tracks they do live all in one album. There was some pressure because the fans had heard them all onstage, and in fact some bootlegs were selling very, very well in Europe."

But the idea of having to start all over again was even worse.

Conversations between the band members grew fraught, all the more so as Mason began wrestling with the breakdown of his marriage to Lindy and sank into a depressive state that Waters would have recognized but was nonetheless unsympathetic toward. His own divorce had run its course, and now he was rebuilding; he forgot, perhaps, that his own darkest days had taken place privately, away from the pressures of the band. For Mason, they were still fresh, and the group's (or, rather, Waters's) demands were simply one straw too many. He clung on, but he was scarcely happy, a mood that Waters was swift to pick up on.

"Wish You Were Here," one of the songs with which he intended plugging the side-length hole in the new album, was directed wholly at his bandmates in general, but maybe Mason in particular, commenting sadly upon their apparent distance from the proceedings. It could, he later joked, as easily have been called "Wish We Were Here," but perhaps he had already realized that a little mild retitling would allow (and ultimately guarantee) the song's adoption by every listener who has ever suffered loss or separation. The song remained as affecting (and well chosen) close to forty years on, at the November 2012 Stand Up for Heroes benefit in New York, as it had been the first time he strummed it to his bandmates.

Still fuming over the *Winter Tour 74* debacle, Waters devoted the rest of the album to two songs that effectively savaged both the personal and the creative pressures that the band's sudden elevation to superstardom had unleashed — "Welcome to the Machine" and "Have a Cigar."

Still there were difficulties. Even as recording continued, arguments raged over a set of music that was split between Waters's ruminations of insanity on the one hand and his loathing of the music business on the other. What, he was asked, was the average listener to make of a song (make that two songs) that were effectively nothing more than Waters complaining about the demands of his day job? His response included a pointed reminder that if his bandmates were prepared to put as much into the lyrics as he did, then maybe they could sing about something else. The resentment over "Childhood's End" was still alive and well.

Waters, for his part, saw the nature of Pink Floyd as an encumbrance on his own wish to make his musical points clearly and cogently: the extended instrumental passages that Gilmour and Wright layered around his words were a distraction from the message, and the fact that Floyd's audience demanded such symphonic gestures did not, in his mind, justify them.

For the moment, the four agreed to compromise. There could be no doubt, after all, that what became the *Wish You Were Here* album was a remarkable achievement, as solid a piece of work (if not concept) at its lauded predecessor, and as vital a component in the ongoing legend of Pink Floyd as well. The days of scrapping around the experimental pastures that fed *Atom Heart Mother* were over, the days too of simply knocking off a song as a few minutes of filler at the end of side one of *Meddle*.

Like it or not, Pink Floyd was firmly established as the king of the extended meandering, and if the band members had any awareness at all of a growing grassroots movement that rejected such a crown, alive in the pubs of London and the bars of New York, they gave no sign of it.

Or did they?

It would be another six months before a teenage Johnny Rotten was recruited to the Sex Pistols on the strength, initially, of the T-shirt upon which he had inked the words "I HATE" above the name "Pink Floyd," another year before the Pistols began making their first loud noises in the pages of the British music press.

But Waters's growing impatience with Pink Floyd's proclivity for the extended solo, and his own need to lash out at every target that offended him, societal or industrial, was not that different from the demands of the first wave of punk rockers, with the lyrics to the two songs slashed from the new album's lineup, "You've Got to Be Crazy" and "Raving and Drooling," themselves standing as standard-bearers for the new moods that were percolating into rock.

The notion that Roger Waters was, emotionally and intellectually at least, as attuned with the musical furnaces in which punk was cast is, in terms of received history, absurd; if anything, he had one of the biggest targets of all painted in neon across his backside. But if his so orderly mind perceived anything about life in the rock 'n' roll gutter, he had already arranged for it to be spoken aloud on *The Dark Side of the Moon*. Rock music needed "a short sharp shock." And only Pink Floyd's need to be "Pink Floyd" prevented him from administering it.

———

By the end of 1974, Waters had moved out of the Islington home he had refurbished himself and into a new dwelling on the other side of the city, Broxash Road near Clapham Common. He would not remain there long;

soon, he would follow Richard Wright in purchasing his own country seat, a Georgian mansion on the banks of the River Test in Kimbridge, Hampshire. But still it was at Broxash Road that he wrote some of the loveliest laments of his career.

"Wish You Were Here," which actually started life as a poem, was exquisitely melded to a folksy Gilmour melody, and then bolstered by the presence of master violinist Stéphane Grappelli — whose contribution vanished into the mix before being restored among the bonus tracks to the album's 2011 reissue. Another folk legend, Roy Harper, was called in to sing "Have a Cigar," a song that neither Waters nor Gilmour had truly come to grips with, but which Harper's long-suffering tones of whimsical weariness were ideally suited to. And "Shine On You Crazy Diamond" was slashed in half, one segment opening the album, the other closing it. Those bookends offer *Wish You Were Here* a complexity and thematic completeness that remain as spellbinding as any intended concept album.

Venturing back out onto the road proved to be as fraught as the recording sessions. Twice, the band's studio endeavors were interrupted by the need to tour America — the need, of course, being something that the band failed to comprehend, but which they were contractually obliged to accede to regardless. Waters was especially outraged; no less than the actual music the group was making, he saw the concert itself as something that was growing increasingly artificial the further up the superstar ladder the band climbed.

He was becoming thinner skinned, too. Particularly after a review of the November 1974 Wembley show, published in the English *New Musical Express*. Apparently tired of critiquing the band's music, the writer lashed out instead at David Gilmour's split ends, as though fame alone could afford a rock star the very best in hair-care treatment. The barriers between musician and audience, player and played-to, had always been pronounced. But never had they felt so insurmountable as they did now, with audiences so distanced from the performers that there might as well have been a physical wall erected between them. A wall that Pink Floyd, with the armies of security and crew that were essential before they could even set foot on a stage, was never going to demolish.

Or could they? Musing to himself one night on the road, back in the United States in June 1975, Waters imagined a stage that was literally cut off from the audience by a huge black polystyrene wall, one which was being built as the concert played on, and which would be completed just in time to block the group from view as the performance ended. And then demolished for the encore.

Again, that was a concept that the punks of a year or so later would take to heart, describing their own concerts as the seamless communion of musicians and audience, with all the trappings of actually being in a band subsumed by a new egalitarianism.

Of course that was a hopelessly idealistic theory, and it did not take long for the first young utopians to realize that the barrier between audience and stage, whether physical or not, was there for the musicians' own protection as much as it was a sign of the performer's untouchability. Every audience holds its fair share of weirdos, every crowd comprises a handful (at least) of would-be stage invaders, and inside every arch fan there is an attention-seeking lunatic who would think nothing of grabbing his own moment in the spotlight by interrupting the performance, assaulting the performer . . . or shooting a Beatle.

Waters was well aware of these practicalities, knew perfectly well why the barriers existed. His protest, then, was symbolic, but even symbolism can have a practical purpose. Now, with the machine already welcoming Pink Floyd back into its grasp, was not the time to make such a gesture. But as with so many other of his ideas, the wall was filed away for future reference, and the tour marched on.

The American dates were a success, despite the musicians' own impatience and, occasionally, boredom. But their one British show of 1975, headlining the massive Knebworth Festival in the depths of the Hertford-shire countryside, teetered on the brink of disaster.

Timing arrangements for the concert were set in stone, opening with a flyby by two vintage World War II–era Spitfire fighter planes. Events and delays elsewhere in the day seriously cut into the band's sound-check time, however, and when they finally took the stage, it was to discover Wright's keyboards were horribly out of tune. It is unlikely that too many fans noticed, being overwhelmed by the sheer spectacle of the event and the revolutionary quadraphonic sound that pumped out of the band's massive PA, but journalists—already smarting from having been banned from the backstage area—were to be less forgiving. The show continued and concluded with a perfect rendering of *The Dark Side of the Moon*. But the following week's reviews sniped and snarled, and none too surprisingly, either.

"The first part was poor," mused *Melody Maker*'s Chris Charlesworth. "Tuning problems hampered the early songs and Roger Waters hit many a bum note in his vocals as the group laboured along with what appeared to be little enthusiasm for the event." And while he acknowledged that things picked up later, it was only a fleeting gesture. "The closing two songs, unfortunately, suffered again through Waters' vocals and it limped, rather than romped, to its usually stunning climax."

Other reviews echoed Charlesworth's observations, and Pink Floyd fell silent. It would be two years before they released a new album, two years before they played another concert.

They returned to the studio, struggling through the final weeks of re-cording and mixing, exhausted by the tours and haunted by the need to get out of one another's presence for a few weeks. Neither was the process ended by the completion of the album, and its release—to their biggest initial sales yet—in mid-September. A quadraphonic mix still needed to be completed, ten days of further debate and argument as knobs were turned, sliders were slid, phasers were phased.

With more time in which to work — or, rather, more time since the last time they had worked together — they might have turned in an album that itself could have reversed the failing fortunes of the quadraphonic format. But half a decade after quad was ushered in as the future of recorded sound, and hyped to the skies by an industry that thought it would be as easy to sell as stereo a few years earlier, it became clear that the music-buying public was not so gullible. Buying a new record player was not such a big deal. But the tangled confusion between competing formats saw four different manufacturers pushing four different systems into the marketplace, and the various record companies apparently choosing the one they would utilize at random.

The result was chaos. If you bought a system, then you could play only records that were recorded with that system in mind. Which was great if you only wanted to listen to one band — Pink Floyd quad was produced on the SQ system. But what happened if you also wanted Eric Clapton's *461 Ocean Boulevard* (which required a CD-4 setup) and Steely Dan's *Pretzel Logic* (QS)? Three different albums, three different quad setups. It was asinine, and at the back of the band's mind as they remixed *Wish You Were Here*, the knowledge that they were effectively creating an instant museum piece was never far from view.

They turned their attention instead to equipping and improving the three-story converted chapel on Britannia Row, Islington, that they originally purchased as a storage facility, but which they now envisioned transforming into a state-of-the-art studio. It was a costly venture, and one whose expenses they intended defraying by renting the studio out to other artists, unlocking some of their own technical secrets in the process.

TV Smith, whose band TV Smith's Explorers cut their debut album at Britannia Row with house engineer Nick Griffiths in early 1981, recalls, "The room where we recorded the drums was huge with a massively high ceiling and there were microphones set up throughout the whole room to capture the natural reverb. We couldn't believe what a massive drum sound we got when we put down the first recordings for the album, sounded like Pink Floyd and Led Zeppelin rolled into one."

Against that, however, was the urge to keep the studio free for Pink Floyd's own purposes, a hole-in–the-wall that would be available to them day or night, whenever the urge struck.

16

Bleating and Babbling

Animals is Pink Floyd's masterpiece. And, at the same time, it was their swan song. Factoring in the continued development of the Britannia Row studios, recording the album consumed close to ten months of 1976, yet of all their albums to date, *Animals* was closer in spirit to the garage band, gang mentality that created *Obscured by Clouds* than either of the behemoths that preceded it. No lengthy, dreamy passages, no gentle lures into the land of nod, nothing (to reawaken the hoary old cliché) to lie back and get stoned to.

Graham Parker, one of the new wave of young Turks who were tearing down prog's playhouse during 1976 and 1977, once condemned Pink Floyd as music for people who wanted to "lie down in the dark listening to *Dark Side of the Moon*, and they all jump when the alarm bell goes off and they all roll a joint." *Animals* was alarm clocks from start to finish.

Waters was driven, and he drove his bandmates accordingly. Richard Wright later acknowledged that he had no hand in the writing of *Animals*, that Waters had taken over completely, with even Gilmour's invention sidelined by the bass player's original blueprint. "Dogs" did boast a Gilmour cowriting credit, with the guitarist responsible for the driving melody that pushes the track inexorably onward, but it was also an old song, the pre–*Wish You Were Here* "You've Got to Be Crazy" revisited and revised. "Sheep," the second of the three major pieces on the album too was drawn from that same luckless era, the 1974 concert staple "Raving and Drooling," and the gestation had done them both a world of good.

Animals is aggressive; it is assaultive; it is abusive, Waters's lyrics verging on a stream of belligerent consciousness as he hits out at his biggest target yet—humanity: the sheep who play follow-the-leader behind whoever is fronting the herd this week; the dogs, snarling and backstabbing their way toward what they consider to be the top of the heap; and the pigs, who believe they have already reached it and now expect everyone else to do as they say.

"Hey you, Whitehouse," snarls Waters on "Pigs," and depending upon which side of the Atlantic you live on, he could be singing about the British moral crusader Mary Whitehouse, whose blinkered vision of Victorian values was responsible for her making well-publicized assaults on any media (generally television and movies) that offended her. Or he could be singing about the White House, suppressing free speech and free thought in the name of American foreign policy. Either way, the blade sank home, and now Waters was asking the sheep if they might ever rise up in revolt, raving and drooling, bleating and babbling. Or had centuries of suppression already knocked all the fight out of them?

And was it deliberate? Or just a joyous accident? Ironically, while no one raised an eyebrow as Waters highlighted Pink Floyd's own ranking among the pigs of this world by co-opting the words of the Twenty-Third Psalm for a mid-"Sheep" muse on the reality of the slaughterhouse, New York punk poetess Patti Smith was feeling the first lashes of disapproval when she adapted the same sacred verse for her rendition of the old Paul Jones hit single "Privilege." One rule for the pigs, one rule for the dogs.

The thrusting of the pigs to the forefront of the dystopian society that *Animals* portrays did not necessarily work to its conceptual advantage. George Orwell's *Animal Farm* made the same observation, and those listeners who had grown to expect every new Pink Floyd album to be somehow conceptual would be swift to leap upon the comparison and regard the album as a musical interpretation of the book.

Wrong. In fact, *Animals* is closer to Orwell's 1984, both in spirit and in delivery; the easiest assumption about the Orwell book, after all, was that he was visualizing the future, when he believed he was commenting upon the present (the title 1984 simply reversed the final two digits of the year in which the book was written, 1948). The futurist angle was a smoke screen. And so the true intentions of *Animals* too were obscured by clouds, a subterfuge that rendered it all the more powerful once you did finally see through the obfuscation. A revelation that was revealed not through the self-confessed scream of rage that devoured the bulk of the album, but in the couple of minutes of introspection and calm that frame the animals themselves.

"Pigs on the Wing" was a stately ballad that Waters recorded with guitarist Snowy White on hand, dedicated (in thought if not words) to his girlfriend, Carolyne Christie—a niece of the Marquis of Zetland, and therefore as blue-blooded in ancestry as ex-wife Judy was politically red. She had been working as producer Bob Ezrin's assistant when they met, and was married then, too, to Grateful Dead associate Rock Scully. Now pregnant with Waters's first son, Harry, it was Carolyne to whom Waters addressed perhaps the most tender love song he has ever written.

Shedding White's solo and being bisected as bookends, parts one and two of "Pigs on the Wing" portray the lovers standing, looking out at a world that has spiraled out of control, and wondering who is the most to blame for it—the pigs, with their militant morality; the dogs, with their careless ambition; or the sheep, who just happily wander around the pasture, indifferent to the unfolding carnage even at the moment of their own brutal deaths.

Musically, the animals matched the lyrics word for note. There are no moments of calm, just foreboding; no passages of pleasantry, just power chords. All the way back to *Atom Heart Mother*, American FM radio programmers had relied on Pink Floyd to offer them those ten-, fifteen-, twenty-minute diversions during which a DJ could take a break from the microphone, and if you looked at the timing strip splashed over the front cover of *Animals,* you could believe that they'd done it again.

But there was nothing radio friendly about this album, no stand-out radio favorites like "Money" and "Time," "Wish You Were Here," or even "One of These Days." The disc jockey who programmed "Dogs" into his show was preparing to subject his audience to seventeen minutes of unrelenting bludgeoning. "Pigs" arrived bearing an undeleted expletive, and "Sheep" was just so savage that even the echo of "One of These Days" that percolates through the opening keyboard melody cannot prepare the listener for the explosion to come.

———

Punk rockers heard that *Animals* was coming and dismissed it unheard and unconcernedly; Johnny Rotten's old T-shirt was too well-known now to permit anything else. The old dog ensured that the sheep would sniff disdainfully at even the prospect of a new Pink Floyd album.

How we laughed, then, when the evening news one night in December 1976 carried reports of the launch of the bloated dinosaurs' new record — what should have been a happy day of backslapping bonhomie suddenly became a public relations disaster. The giant inflatable pig that the band had tethered to one of the chimneys of Battersea Power Station to promote *Animals* broke its bonds and sailed off into the wide blue yonder, a hazard for air traffic and, presumably, for any cocktail-hour imbibers who happened to look up at the sky in time to see forty feet of fat pink piggy drifting over their heads.

Or was it a disaster after all? Without the escape, the event would probably not have received more than a few seconds of TV as newscasters chuckled at the pictures of the porcine pose. Instead, the escape and the ensuing hunt for the beast consumed as much prime-time attention as an airing of the album itself, and when piggy turned up in a farmer's field some twenty miles southeast of its point of origin, that was worth a hit single in its own right.

You couldn't do any of that with a prism.

———

Not everybody bitten by the punk virus that swept the UK of 1976 to 1977 was immune to the charms of *Animals*. Disc jockey John Peel, the only British radio DJ at that time who would give the new music airtime, broadcast *Animals* in its entirety on the night of January 20, and he had no qualms in doing so. For him, the music was always more important than the fashions that surrounded it, which is why he won the UK's "best DJ" award year after year after year. (Twelve months later, in 1978, he gave almost equal airtime to David Gilmour's self-titled solo debut album, in a show otherwise packed to the rafters with reggae and punk.)

Elsewhere, journalist Angus McKinnon, writing in the ferociously punk-partisan *New Musical Express*, described *Animals* as "one of the most extreme, relentless, harrowing and downright iconoclastic hunks of music to have been made available for public perusal this side of the sun"—sentiments which his readers were better accustomed to hearing applied to the works of punk's prehistoric progenitors, the Velvet Underground, the Stooges, and the MC5.

But expectation and reality are very different creatures, and just as the punk bands themselves generally proved less than capable of matching their media rhetoric with music (the aforementioned holy trinity notwithstanding), so the notion of Pink Floyd not only equaling, but chronologically preempting, punk's own societal firestorm was one step too far for even the most enlightened listener.

December 1976 was still early days in punk's recorded lifespan; the Damned and the Pistols had released one single apiece, the Vibrators and the Buzzcocks likewise. The New York contingent was a little further ahead, with the Ramones and Patti Smith either marching toward, or already celebrating, their second LPs, but punk rock as it has come down in history was still a newborn baby, photographed by everybody who could get inside the maternity ward, but not yet either walking or talking. Just babbling noisily to itself and letting out foul noises and smells from either end.

Still, Pink Floyd saw what was happening around them, and prepared the *Animals* launch accordingly. The London birth of the flying pig aside, their attentions were focused immediately on Europe and America, where the pigs and dogs of the music press had less sway over the sheep who read their words. A tour titled Pink Floyd in the Flesh kicked off in Dortmund, Germany, on January 23, trailed around the continent for a month, and barely even looked at the band's homeland: four nights at the megastadium Wembley Pool in mid-March, three nights at the slightly more intimate Bingley Hall in Stafford a couple of weeks later, and that was it. Then it was off to America for a tour that began in Miami on April 22 and wouldn't stop until it reached Montreal in early July.

But what a tour it was. Past Pink Floyd outings had been described as spectacles, and they merited that term, a visual cornucopia of lights and lasers, film shows and slides, and of course those two gorgeous Spitfires that overflew the Knebworth Festival. This time, however, the flying pig would be the centerpiece of the performance (Waters's original idea would have added flying dogs and sheep to the menagerie), and not just any old flying pig. With headlights for eyes, it hovered to menace every corner of the auditorium, a gargantuan grunter that rose out of the smoke that choked the building to fix the audience with its piggy-eyed glare and nail them to their seats. While all around, the band—augmented by guitarist Snowy White and saxophonist Dick Parry—spat Waters's bile in all directions. Even the barnyard noises were in quadraphonic sound.

As usual, the set was divided into two halves but this time, there was no room for unheard songs or unreleased material; the specter of *Winter Tour 74* still hung heavy over the band. Instead, an adrenalized *Animals* would consume the first half of the show, a ragged and often similarly raging *Wish You Were Here* the second, before the encore pulled either "Money" or "Us and Them" from the archive. (Except once, when they lurched into "Careful with That Axe, Eugene" instead.)

With an attention to detail that certainly provoked a fresh wave of reminders that he had trained as an architect, Waters choreographed the music to the nth degree, introducing a click track to make sure that the musicians were never out of sync with the films, and placing the effects crew on a knife-edge of discipline by pinpointing the precise moment when the smoke could be released, and the exact volume of smoke as well.

Not every night went according to plan. Nothing was left to chance, which meant that chance became the band's most potent foe—the night in Frankfurt when the smoke was so thick that the audience started hurling bottles at the stage . . . if they could even figure out where the stage was; the evenings when either musicians or click track would fall out of sync (Waters wore headphones onstage for many of the shows to ensure that he alone would not lose his place); and most damaging of all, the occasions when Waters would gaze out at an audience lost in rapt contemplation and privately beg for them to react in a manner that was not as coldly mechanical as the stage show itself.

It was a study in contrasts.

He hated the vast, soulless, stadia that the Floyd's live ambitions demanded they play, at the same time as it was he who conceived those ambitions in the first place.

He loathed the unquestioning adoration that radiated from the eyes of the first few rows of the seated audience, at the same time as he resented the knowledge that in a building this huge, probably half of the crowd was only there because they wanted to be a part of an event, because their friends were going and they just tagged along, or for the beer and the chance to wave pretzels in the air.

And he still couldn't reconcile his distaste for the sheer size of the moneymaking machine in which he was cast with his love for all that machine allowed him. He even rode a helicopter to every venue (the rest of the band traveled by limo), while the budget for every pre- and post-concert celebration that hallmarked the tour's progress probably consumed most people's household budget for a year.

The tour grew uglier. The band had been joined on the road by Gilmour's wife, Ginger, and Roger's new wife, Carolyne, and Wright murmured darkly that nobody wanted to be in the room "when that pair [the Waters] got started." To the Gilmours in particular, Carolyne seemed completely out of place, an aristocrat slumming it with the dirty rock 'n' rollers. Around the same time as the Floyd were touring, the *Rolling Stones* were garnering disapproving headlines in Canada when Margaret Trudeau, wife of politician Pierre, became a regular visitor to their hotel. At least one Floyd insider recalls the private in-joke that rechristened Carolyne "Margaret."

The tour hit Philadelphia, and Waters fell ill, suffering unbearable stomach cramps that the doctor insisted were the fruits of food poisoning. He was handed three tranquilizers and expected to get on with the show; it was only later that he learned that he had, in fact, contracted hepatitis.

He fell into a peculiar ritual. Every night, during "Pigs," he would call out a number . . . "twenty-one" tonight, "twenty-two" tomorrow, "twenty-three" the night after that. He was counting the number of shows he had played on the tour. And each night, he seemed to bark it out with more frustration and rage.

Thirty-three, thirty-four, thirty-five . . . One night, Waters tried to talk to Steve O'Rourke, tell him how unhappy he was. O'Rourke heard him out, then reminded him of the latest concert's gross takings.

Thirty-nine, forty, forty-one . . . Another night, in New York, Waters grew so furious with the constant explosion of fireworks (the following day was July 4, with all the pyrotechnic jollity that it demands) that he finally demanded the audience either "shut up or fuck off." They did neither and the remainder of the concert was rendered a brittle stand-off, the band playing doggedly on, the audience unconcernedly making its own amusement around the music.

Fifty, and finally fifty-one, the last night in Montreal, and the end of Waters's tether. One kid in the audience, a teenager who had committed no crime greater than demonstrating how much he was enjoying the show and calling out for "Careful with That Axe Eugene," caught Waters's attention, and the more he watched him, the more his loathing grew.

Waters started playing for the boy alone, catching his eye and acting the rock star, and the kid picked up on this miraculous dance and began acting back to his hero. Until finally it was time for consummation. Waters leaned forward, his eyes never leaving the fan's, then spat in his face.

That was the night that Gilmour left the stage at the end of the set, and failed to return for the encore. That was the night the band wrapped up with a slow blues encore that continued on even as the crew began dismantling the equipment, and the band members started to drift offstage, and ended only when there was nobody left to keep playing. And that was the night, too, when Waters came to a decision that would shape his, and Pink Floyd's, career for evermore.

Backstage, he and O'Rourke were horsing about, just a playful fight, but one that ended with Waters being driven to the hospital after he kicked out at his manager and connected with something else. With blood pouring from the ensuing foot wound, he hopped into his limo, Carolyne on one side, her employer, Bob Ezrin, on the other. And as they drove away from the Olympic Stadium, Waters let his companions know exactly what he was thinking.

Pink Floyd, as their audience knew them, as the kid with superstar spit dripping off his face remembered them, was no more. It was time to leave the machine; it was time to stub out the cigar.

Nine years before, nine years and three months to be precise, Syd Barrett had walked out of Pink Floyd and built a wall around himself. Now it was time for Waters to do much the same thing, and no matter how opposed to his plans his bandmates might be (and there was no doubt in his mind that they would be), he knew what he was doing.

The Wall was to be Roger Waters's first solo album.

He just hadn't told the band yet.

Epilogue

Roger Waters's long-gestating (if not necessarily long-awaited) opera, *Ça Ira*, was finally delivered in September 2006. It was four years since its overture alone had been heard at the Royal Albert Hall, during a benefit concert for the Countryside Alliance, two years since a fifteen-minute excerpt of the now-completed recording of the opera was heard when Malta was granted entry into the European Union on May 1, 2004, and two years since its cocomposer Étienne Roda-Gil passed away at the end of that same month. And that was the cue for Waters to plunge into overdrive, hustling in every direction to assure a release for the opera.

He personally would not play any active role in the recording beyond coproducing it with movie-score composer Paul Wentworth (the pair also collaborated on the choral and orchestral arrangements). But a cast that included soprano Ying Huang, tenor Paul Groves, and baritone Bryn Terfel was gathered; the proceedings were gleefully, and protractedly, documented by *Live at Pompeii* director Adrian Maben; and on November 17, *Ça Ira* received its official premier in Rome, before a capacity crowd.

It was a dramatic night, one that was widely praised by the critics and applauded just as heavily the following evening, when the production was staged again. Other rock musicians had ventured into the turbulent oceans of opera in the past, most notably Beatle Paul McCartney, and they had been roundly whipped by the critics for their hubris. Waters escaped such chastisement, and why? Because *Ça Ira* was actually very good.

There was just one minor cloud hanging over the evening.

The premiere of the opera coincided, with ghastly bad timing, with Pink Floyd's induction into the UK Music Hall of Fame in London. Obviously there would be no question as to where Waters would be spending the evening, but he was present at the ceremony via video link, and anybody looking for signs that Live 8 had not wholly healed all the old wounds would have been gratified by Waters's response to Gilmour's onstage dedication to Roger, Syd, and "all the passengers on this fabulous ride we've been on."

"I confess I never felt like a passenger," Waters replied.

Neither, one hopes, did Syd Barrett, but on Friday, July 7, 2006, he finally got off the carousel. Poor health had dogged him for several years, and he had recently admitted himself to the Cambridge hospital where his own father once worked. His death surprised many but shocked few and ignited a whole new industry in Barrett-shaped memoirs, biographies, tributes, and, perhaps, misconceptions. One hopes that the madcap continues to laugh.

Pink Floyd was further apart than ever before, a point that David Gilmour's next solo album, 2006's *On an Island*, brought home when Richard Wright was the only one of his bandmates invited to perform. The pair would tour together, too, alongside Dick Parry, Jon Carin, and Roxy Music's Phil Manzanera, and a live set loaded down with scarcely heard Floyd epics, stretching back to "Fat Old Sun" and "Wot's . . . uh the Deal," a marathon "Echoes," and so forth. Nick Mason would be among the onstage guests when the outing arrived in London, but with David Bowie, David Crosby, and Graham Nash having already graced the stage, only hardened Pink Floyd addicts were especially thrilled by the brief, two-song reunion for the *Division Bell* band.

Roger Waters, meanwhile, had relocated both physically and emotionally. Growing increasingly uneasy in a Britain that had slipped so far beneath the glove of what the acclaimed TV spy drama *Spooks* was calling the government of "velvet Fascism," a land where CCTV policed the smoking ban (which would also drive Mike Oldfield from those shores, loudly bemoaning "prep school Britain"), juvenile offenders were rewarded with acronymic Anti-Social Behavioral Orders —ASBOs—that promptly became a badge of honor among their recipients, and the nation's cities had become grotesque showcases for showboating architects and rapacious chain-store operators, Waters finally cracked when the incumbent Labour government of Tony Blair passed an anti-hunting bill.

Not because he, Waters, supported hunting (he had in fact been vocal in his support of animal welfare for many years), but because the bill itself divided the nation with, again, a fascist disregard for opinion and lifestyle; at the same time, it was shot through with so many loopholes and caveats that its sole purpose could only have been to broaden the class divides that the facade of past democracy had done so much in recent years to close.

In the eyes of the media, the Countryside Alliance, the new bill's most vociferous opponent, made strange bedfellows with the Comrade Waters of earlier days, being top-heavy with country squires and lords of the manor, and horsey-faced debutantes who couldn't understand why they were no longer permitted to tear foxes to pieces with dogs.

But there were deeper forces at work than simply another go round for the old class warfare, heavier forces that compelled Waters to walk out on the land he had always loved: the fact that Britain no longer felt like Britain, the fact that history, culture, and tradition were no longer worth anything beyond what a rapacious businessman could extract from them. When a musician couldn't even autograph a record for a fan without it turning up on eBay the following day, you knew the rules of the game had changed forever—which is why Waters no longer signs his autograph for fans. There are enough little pieces of him for sale already without him adding to the pile.

He left the UK, moving with his new partner, Laurie Durning, to her home in the Hamptons, on Long Island, and promptly proceeded to rile up great swaths of his newly adopted countrymen with a song called "Leaving Beirut," slipped into the set as the In the Flesh tour went back on the road (revolving this time around a full performance of *The Dark Side of the Moon*) and pointedly condemning what the statesmen called "justifiable war" at a time, of course, when American politicians were doing their damnedest to prove that that was exactly what they were fighting in Iraq.

A new guitarist stepped into the show. Dave Kilminster was fresh from Keith Emerson's reformed Nice (replacing original guitar player David O'List in the lineup that had toured Britain with Pink Floyd in 1967), and jokingly admits that he was among that vast legion of music fans who knew what Floyd's music sounded like but had no clue who the musicians actually were.

"I didn't know who Roger was! But once my manager explained, I contacted Andy Fairweather and was asked to submit a recording of myself playing some Floyd numbers. I guess I didn't feel too intimidated at the audition, as it wasn't really music that I grew up listening to . . . and also it was very early in the morning. But I slowly began to realize the enormity of the situation, and thought, 'This could actually be pretty huge.'"

It could. But he needed to circumvent an absolutely disastrous audition first.

> Firstly my acoustic guitar wasn't working. The tech managed to fix it, and we began to play "Wish You Were Here." I'd worked out all the bottleneck solo bits, but stupidly left my bottleneck in my bag!! Ha-ha . . . what an idiot!! Next up was "Money" . . . and I'm feeling a little more confident about this one, because I've worked out all three rhythm-guitar parts, and all the solos. [And then] Roger says to me, "Are you OK with the lyrics?" I didn't realize they wanted me to sing it too!!! So I stumbled my way through

> that, trying to read the lyrics, sing, and play this syncopated guitar
> part at the same time . . . what a nightmare. . . .

He returned home convinced that the moment was over, only to receive a call telling him that he'd passed the audition. Rehearsals were set, and there, further surprises awaited. "I was assuming that Andy and Snowy [White] would be taking most (if not all) of the solos, but they just kept trying to give them all to me!! Which of course I didn't mind . . . until I realized that there's actually loads of pressure in playing those parts, as everyone knows how they're supposed to sound, so it's really very obvious if you make a mistake!"

Clearly he succeeded, not only impressing Waters but also satisfying audiences that he knows are expecting perfection every night.

> I just approach the material (and the band) with reverence and
> respect, and try to play the parts on the record as well as possible.
> I never get bored, because I'm constantly trying to improve my
> performance every night . . . not just the guitar tone and effects,
> but also the subtleties like vibrato, timing, etc.
>
> It's the same for Roger, he's constantly trying to improve the
> show. Post gig, he'll watch back a video of the night's performance,
> and then during sound check for the next gig he'll come in with
> a list of things he wants to work on. He's a perfectionist.

Even with Waters's tour still underway, and doing great business, rumors that Pink Floyd was on the verge of a fresh reunion were never far away. Their reality, however, proved as elusive as Waters's own occasional references to his next rock album, a concept piece revolving around the increasingly intoxicated conversation of a Balkan-born New York cabdriver. His sole new release of the late 2000s, *Ça Ira* notwithstanding, was a download-only single, "Hello (I Love You)," recorded for the soundtrack to the sci-fi movie *The Last Mimzy* and, like the movie, scarcely something one would return to all that often.

Reunion fever picked up again in the run-up to the planet-spanning Live Earth concerts in June 2008, seven concerts staged on seven continents to help raise awareness of the perils of global warming. No number of denials would quell the chatter, especially after it was revealed that Waters would be performing at the North American show, at Giants Stadium, New Jersey. But the gig passed by with no sign of his bandmates, and suddenly, just three months later, the world awoke to learn that there would never be another opportunity. Richard Wright passed away on September 14, 2008, following a short struggle with cancer.

It was, and it remains, a shattering loss.

For all his differences with Waters during the final years of Pink Floyd, Wright's keyboard talents were solidly instrumental in driving Floyd's music toward the peaks it ultimately hit. "Summer '68" from *Atom Heart Mother* remains a favorite Wright composition, although his best-known piece is surely "The Great Gig in the Sky," that most evocative moment in the whole of *The Dark Side of the Moon*. He also cowrote (with Waters) that album's "Us and Them," although opportunities for further such collaborations sadly fell away as Waters strengthened his grip on the group's creative output, a stranglehold that could not help but spark tension with his bandmates.

Having launched his solo career in 1978 with the release of the oddly underrated *Wet Dream* album, Wright then launched a new band, Zee, with ex-Fashion mainstay Dave Harris. Zee cut one album, *Identity*, before Wright was invited to rejoin Mason and Gilmour in Pink Floyd, following Waters's departure in 1985. Wright also cut a second solo album, 1996's *Broken China* — comprised, says Tim Renwick, of "just a series of very enjoyable sessions. Rick was always an easygoing character (if a little confused at times) who endured a hard time from Roger and was eventually fired from the band for not coming up with his share of ideas. I think he enjoyed the good life a little too much!"

A decade later, in the aftermath of Live 8, Wright's reunion with the solo Gilmour not only produced the *On an Island* album, but also two subsequent DVD releases, *Remember That Night* and *Live in Gdansk*. Both capture phenomenal live shows, but more than that, they exemplify the remarkable presence that this consummate musician brought to the stage. And so the perpetual speculation that Pink Floyd itself might someday reform to tour again receded into the history books, and, with Wright's death, one of the most monumental chapters in the history of rock was finally ended.

The passage of time was no longer an abstract concept, no longer a thoughtful lyric in an old, old song. Wright was sixty-five when he died, the same age as Waters. Nick Mason was sixty-four; David Gilmour was sixty-two, ages which had once seemed impossible for a functioning rock 'n' roller to attain, but which all too many had now reached or even surpassed. How people smiled when Paul McCartney discovered how it would really feel "when I'm sixty-four." How they chuckled as Mick Jagger reached retirement age, and looked back at the magazine articles that once had voted Keith Richards the rock star most likely to die next, some thirty years before a fall from a coconut tree may or may not have come close to fulfilling that prophesy.

Bob Dylan would be seventy in 2010, the same year that Pete Townshend hit sixty-five. David Bowie suffered a near-fatal heart attack before he even got out of his fifties, and in performing and recording terms, spent the next decade in silence. An entire generation of sixties and seventies icons was now entering its sixties and seventies, and their original audience was marching into twilight alongside them, living out the lyrics to *Dark Side of the Moon*'s "Time" and hoping only that they might live to see the album itself attain an equally venerable age, "hanging on in quiet desperation" for the umpteenth reissue of an album that has been the soundtrack, both figuratively and literally, for more lives than any comparable piece of art of the last hundred years.

That was the thought process behind Roger Waters's own exhumation of the song cycle for the 2006 tour; that might, knowing Waters's eye for irony, be why he chose his own son Harry to replace keyboard player Jon Carin in his backing band—as a permanent onstage reminder of the aging process. And that—as audiences filed home and filed the experience away in their memory banks—was the impression that many of them were left with. In the arena, in their several-hundred-dollar seats, the performance of the entire album by the man who conceived and largely wrote it was a cause for celebration, a night of wonder, amazement, and awe.

But afterward, once the crowds had gone home and real life resumed around the credit card bills, who could not reflect back to the first time they heard the album? Or the first time they saw Pink Floyd, and paid just a couple of bucks for the right to do so? Or, in one man's case, to the first time he realized that somewhere within the couple of songs that he'd written in the studio as the band completed *Meddle* there lay the seeds of the next Pink Floyd album?

The archive door yawned wide. New editions of *The Dark Side of the Moon*, *Wish You Were Here*, and *The Wall* were prepared, each one restating the original album in best-ever sound quality, and then ladening it down with as much bonus material as you could possibly dream of—a regular single-disc edition for the regular listeners, an Experience double-disc package for the somewhat more curious, and a phone directory–sized Immersion edition for fans who wanted the demos, the outtakes, the first mixes, and the live shows.

All three were magnificently packaged; all three were accompanied by booklets and trinkets. One might wonder until the end of time precisely what purpose is served by the individually bagged marbles that accompanied each Immersion edition, or when would be the correct occasion upon which to wear the silken scarves therein. But there is reading matter galore to pound through, and so much music and video content to absorb that hearing each of the albums in their newly packaged form is akin to experiencing their original release over again: An unused mix of *Dark Side of the Moon.* The *Wish You Were Here*–era concert performances that ultimately formed the heart of *Animals.* Relics of the abandoned *Household Objects* production, and the Stéphane Grappelli–fired outtake of "Wish You Were Here." The first ever live performance of *Dark Side of the Moon,* and one of the final live renditions of *The Wall.* The in-concert films that bedecked so many shows, and largely unspoken but rumored all the same, the possibility that choice other chunks of the catalog will be next.

A Syd Barrett–years collection that will finally rescue from bootleg oblivion the outtakes that we have already heard, and those that are only rumored to exist. A deluxe repackaging for *Meddle,* perhaps, with a demo of "Seamus" given pride of place. A full recounting of the *Animals* sessions, a complete forensic dissection of *Atom Heart Mother.* Pink Floyd's own early sketches of *The Pros and Cons of Hitch Hiking,* boxed up with a breakdown of what they became.

So many gems, so many promises, and so much magnificent music. And in the meantime, there is more being made.

After so many years of speculation and false beginnings, a new Roger Waters album was finally in the pipeline. Talking at the end of 2012, he had tentatively titled it *Heartland,* but he insisted that a lot could change between then and whenever it was completed. "I'm not sure what it will be called. I'll tell you what the first line is . . . the first line is, 'If I had been God. . . .'"

The idea behind the set (another conceptual effort, of course) came from "another song I wrote maybe fifteen years ago, or longer even . . . for a . . . really, really bad movie called *Michael* that was about an angel. I'm absolutely determined to make another album. And I think this new song may give me the chance to do that. It provides a cornerstone and a core idea for me to write a new album about. You know, it's just one of my obsessions, which is, I'm sort of obsessed with the idea that religious extremism is a maligned factor in most of our lives."

Waters made his acting debut, too, playing the role of Gary Gauger across a five-day run of the documentary play *The Exonerated* in New

York City at the end of November, and he guested at both the Homes for Heroes concerts for disabled servicemen.

He was onboard, too, for the Robin Hood Foundation's 121212 Hurricane Sandy benefit on December 12, 2012—just weeks after one of the most violent storms in living memory ripped the northeastern seaboard and beyond to shreds.

There, like almost everyone else on the bill (the Stones, the Who, Eric Clapton, Bruce Springsteen, et al), his presence was completely overshadowed by the faintly ludicrous sight of a Nirvana "reunion" that allowed Paul McCartney to replace Kurt Cobain, and a member of the Germs to be in a band with a Beatle. But "Another Brick in the Wall," "Money," and "Us and Them" lit Madison Square Garden with memories, and "Comfortably Numb" survived the addition of Eddie Vedder to round out the short set.

Dave Kilminster speaks for all who performed.

> What an amazing evening!!! And an incredible lineup!!! It was such an honor to be a part of such an historic event, and I was obviously very happy to be able to help the victims a little too.
>
> The pressure was pretty intense though. Viewing figures on the website were estimated at two billion, and I knew that they were already taking presales on iTunes for the performance, so I really didn't want to mess up or let anyone down. Fortunately I think it went pretty well though, and I was relatively happy with my performance. Actually, everyone I saw that evening played great!!! And we raised over thirty-six million dollars too!

Later, reviewers would gripe that Waters's set was no more than the same abbreviated hits performance that he rolled out at every such event (the revised title "Another Brick in the Atlantic Wall" didn't fool them, then), that, whereas several other acts (Springsteen, Billy Joel) drew on songs that could be construed as being "relevant" to the event, Waters was simply sticking to his usual script. Forgetting, perhaps, that the best songs for the night would each have lasted longer than his entire set. And presumably ignoring the presence of Pearl Jam vocalist Eddie Vedder caterwauling across "Comfortably Numb." But if Paul McCartney was replacing Kurt Cobain in Nirvana, one wonders who Vedder was meant to be.

This burst of year-end activity was a surprise, nonetheless. Waters had also just completed the latest leg of another tour, restaging *The Wall* in all its glory, at the same time reinventing its central message away from the autobiography of old, and into a wider universe, one in which the current events of a world ripped asunder by recession, resentment, and political demagoguery are the bricks that must be torn down.

It was the success of the *Dark Side of the Moon* re-creation that inspired the new show, that and the realization that modern technology would permit him to stage it even more effectively than ever before. The original crew—Scarfe, of course, stage designer Mark Fisher, and tour director Andrew Zweck—was recalled; but the old storyline had been completely re-envisioned.

"When I wrote it, it was mainly about me, a little bit about Syd Barrett, but by and large it's about fear. Fear makes you defensive and when you're defensive, you start building defenses and that could be seen as a wall." Fear was still the central premise. But the nature of the things we fear had dramatically shifted. "We are controlled by the powers that be who tell us we need to guard against the evil ones who are over there and different from us, and who we must be frightened of."

Three years on the road, with shows scheduled through the summer and fall of 2013, and costing an estimated $50 million to mount, this latest staging of Waters's most grandiose conceit has rightfully been proclaimed the most complex and expensive stage production ever mounted, and one of the most viewed as well.

No matter that his voice is barely a shadow of even the less-than-perfect tone that hallmarked his earlier excursions, nor that age, and the associated hearing problems, has taken its toll on what he is able to do. At sixty-nine years of age, with touring scheduled to extend beyond his seventieth birthday, Roger Waters remains a spectacle to behold, and close to 1.5 million pairs of eyes had beheld him by the time the tour reached Latin America in spring 2012.

And among the highlights that have illuminated the outing, there is one that just perhaps suggests that time is not only a thief, it is also a healer.

On May 12, 2011, during the tour's visit to that ignominious, carbuncle-shaped tent that Londoners now call the O2 Arena, an extra figure appeared onstage as the set rolled around to "Comfortably Numb." David Gilmour had not even been introduced before the entire canvas erupted into a spontaneous celebration, and the evening was not even over. For later, for "Outside the Wall," a second figure made his way across the stage and settled at a drum kit that had been miraculously vacated while the stage lights were elsewhere. Nick Mason.

Pink Floyd will never reform; the mere passage of time has ensured that. But like the Who on the road without Keith Moon and John Entwistle, or the Sensational Alex Harvey Band without Alex around to tell them they're great, or even Pink Floyd with both Syd Barrett and Roger Waters off in their private corners, sometimes it is not the presence of all the right players that matters. It is the existence of the right frame of mind.

The three surviving Floydians may or may not come together again. Theirs is already a fast-diminishing family, as the deaths of Bryan Morrison in September 2008 and Storm Thorgerson in April 2013 tore further heart from their historical circle. But in their reunion in London that night, the years rolled back regardless, back to a time when Floyd was four, with an unforgotten fifth, when the division bell had yet to sound and no one had suffered a loss of reason, when flying pigs soared and the crazy diamond still shone.

And Roger Waters had not yet started work on his first solo album.

Tear down the wall!

Discography

PINK FLOYD

The Piper at the Gates of Dawn
August 5, 1967
"Astronomy Domine" / "Lucifer Sam" / "Matilda Mother" / "Flaming" / "Pow R Toc H" / "Take Up Thy Stethoscope and Walk" / "Interstellar Overdrive" / "The Gnome" / "Chapter 24" / "Scarecrow" / "Bike"

A Saucerful of Secrets
June 29, 1968
"Let There Be More Light" / "Remember a Day" / "Set the Controls for the Heart of the Sun" / "Corporal Clegg" / "A Saucerful of Secrets (Something Else / Syncopated Pandemonium / Storm Signal / Celestial Voices)" / "See Saw" / "Jugband Blues"

More
June 13, 1969
"Cirrus Minor" / "The Nile Song" / "Crying Song" / "Up the Khyber" / "Green Is the Colour" / "Cymbaline" / "Party Sequence" / "Main Theme" / "Ibiza Bar" / "More Blues" / "Quicksilver" / "A Spanish Piece" / "Dramatic Theme"

Ummagumma
October 25, 1969
"Astronomy Domine" / "Careful with That Axe, Eugene" / "Set the Controls for the Heart of the Sun" / "A Saucerful of Secrets" / Richard Wright: "Sysyphus (Parts 1-4)" / Roger Waters: "Grantchester Meadows" / "Several Species of Small Furry Animals Gathered Together in a Cave and Grooving with a Pict" / David Gilmour: "The Narrow Way (Parts 1-3)" / Nick Mason: "The Grand Vizier's Garden Party (Entrance / Entertainment / Exit)"

Zabriskie Point soundtrack
May 30, 1970

Reissued in 1997 as a double CD album with a number of previously unissued outtakes
"Heart Beat, Pig Meat" (Pink Floyd) / "Brother Mary" (David Lindley) / "Dark Star" (Jerry Garcia) / "Crumbling Land" (Pink Floyd) / "Tennessee Waltz" (Pee Wee King) / "Sugar Babe" (Jesse Colin Young) / "Love Scene" (Jerry Garcia) / "I Wish I Was a Single Girl Again" / "Mickey's Tune" (David Lindley) / "Dance of Death" (John Fahey) / "Come in Number 51, Your Time Is Up" (Pink Floyd) / "Love Scene Improvisations" (Jerry Garcia) / "Country Song" (Pink Floyd) / "Unknown Song" (Pink Floyd) / "Love Scene" (Pink Floyd) / "Love Scene" (Pink Floyd)

Atom Heart Mother
October 10, 1970
 "Atom Heart Mother (Father's Shout / Breast Milky / Mother Fore / Funky Dung / Mind Your Throats Please / Remergence)" / "If" / "Summer '68" / "Fat Old Sun" / "Alan's Psychedelic Breakfast (Rise and Shine / Sunny Side Up / Morning Glory)"

ROGER WATERS AND RON GEESIN

Music from The Body
November 28, 1970
"Our Song" / "Sea Shell and Stone" / "Red Stuff Writhe" / "A Gentle Breeze Blew Through Life" / "Lick Your Partners" / "Bridge Passage for Three Plastic Teeth" / "Chain of Life" / "The Womb Bit" / "Embryo Thought" / "March Past of the Embryos" / "More Than Seven Dwarfs in Penis-Land" / "Dance of the Red Corpuscles" / "Body Transport" / "Hand Dance—Full Evening Dress" / "Breathe" / "Old Folks Ascension" / "Bedtime-Dream-Chine" / "Piddle in Perspex" / "Embryonic Womb-Walk" / "Mrs. Throat Goes Walking" / "Sea Shell and Soft Stone" / "Give Birth to a Smile"

PINK FLOYD

Relics
May 14, 1971
"Arnold Layne" / "Interstellar Overdrive" / "See Emily Play" / "Remember a Day" / "Paintbox" / "Julia Dream" / "Careful with That Axe, Eugene" / "Cirrus Minor" / "The Nile Song" / "Biding My Time" / "Bike"

Meddle
November 13, 1971
"One of These Days" / "A Pillow of Winds" / "Fearless" / "San Tropez" / "Seamus" / "Echoes"

Obscured by Clouds
June 3, 1972

"Obscured by Clouds" / "When You're In" / "Burning Bridges" / "The Gold It's in the . . ." / "Wot's . . .uh the Deal" / "Mudmen" / "Childhood's End" / "Free Four" / "Stay" / "Absolutely Curtains"

The Dark Side of the Moon
March 24, 1973
"Speak to Me" / "Breathe (In the Air)" / "On the Run" / "Time" / "The Great Gig in the Sky" / "Money" / "Us Them" / "Any Colour You Like" / "Brain Damage" / "Eclipse"

Wish You Were Here
September 15, 1975
"Shine On You Crazy Diamond (Parts 1-5)" / "Welcome to the Machine" / "Have a Cigar" / "Wish You Were Here" / "Shine On You Crazy Diamond (Parts 6-9)"

Animals
January 23, 1977
"Pigs on the Wing (Part 1)" / "Dogs" / "Pigs (Three Different Ones)" / "Sheep" / "Pigs on the Wing (Part 2)"

The Wall
November 30, 1979
"In the Flesh?" / "The Thin Ice" / "Another Brick in the Wall (Part 1)" / "The Happiest Days of Our Lives" / "Another Brick in the Wall (Part 2)" / "Mother" / "Goodbye Blue Sky" / "Empty Spaces" / "Young Lust" / "One of My Turns" / "Don't Leave Me Now" / "Another Brick in the Wall (Part 3)" / "Goodbye Cruel World" / "Hey You" / "Is There Anybody Out There?" / "Nobody Home" / "Vera" / "Bring the Boys Back Home" / "Comfortably Numb" / "The Show Must Go On" / "In the Flesh" / "Run Like Hell" / "Waiting for the Worms" / "Stop" / "The Trial" / "Outside the Wall"

A Collection of Great Dance Songs
November 23, 1981
"One of These Days" / "Money" / "Sheep" / "Shine On You Crazy Diamond" / "Wish You Were Here" / "Another Brick in the Wall (Part 2)"

The Final Cut
March 21, 1983
March 29, 2004 (remaster)
"The Post War Dream" / "Your Possible Pasts" / "One of the Few" / "When the Tigers Broke Free" [added into remastered edition] / "The Hero's Return" / "The Gunners Dream" / "Paranoid Eyes" / "Get Your Filthy Hands Off My Desert" / "The Fletcher Memorial Home" / "Southampton Dock" / "The Final Cut" / "Not Now John" / "Two Suns in the Sunset"

Works
June, 1983
"One of These Days" / "Arnold Layne" / "Fearless" / "Brain Damage" / "Eclipse" / "Set the Controls for the Heart of the Sun" / "See Emily Play" / "Several Species of Small Furry Animals Gathered Together in a Cave and Grooving with A Pict" / "Free Four" / "Embryo"

ROGER WATERS

The Pros and Cons of Hitch Hiking
May 8, 1984
"4.30 AM (Apparently They Were Travelling Abroad)" / "4.33 AM (Running Shoes)" / "4.37 AM (Arabs with Knives and West German Skies)" / "4.39 AM (For the First Time Today Part 2)" / "4.41 AM (Sexual Revolution)" / "4.47 AM (The Remains of Our Love)" / "4.50 AM (Go Fishing)" / "4.56 AM (For the First Time Today Part 1)" / "4.58 AM (Dunroamin', Duncarin', Dunlivin')" / "5.01 AM (The Pros and Cons of Hitch Hiking Part 10)" / "5.06 AM (Every Stranger's Eyes)" / "5.11 AM (The Moment of Clarity)"

When the Wind Blows soundtrack
October 30, 1986
"The Russian Missile" / "Towers of Faith" / "Hilda's Dream" / "The American Bomber" / "The Anderson Shelter" / "The British Submarine" / "The Attack" / "The Fall Out" / "Hilda's Hair" / "Folded Flags"

Radio K.A.O.S.
June 15, 1987
"Radio Waves" / "Who Needs Information" / "Me or Him" / "The Powers That Be" / "Sunset Strip" / "Home" / "Four Minutes" / "The Tide Is Turning (After Live Aid)"

The Wall—Live in Berlin
September 17, 1990
"In the Flesh?" / "The Thin Ice" / "Another Brick in the Wall (Part 1)" / "The Happiest Days of Our Lives" / "Another Brick in the Wall (Part 2)" / "Mother" / "Goodbye Blue Sky" / "Empty Spaces" / "Young Lust" / "One of My Turns" / "Don't Leave Me Now" / "Another Brick in the Wall (Part 3)" / "Goodbye Cruel World" / "Hey You" / "Is There Anybody Out There?" / "Nobody Home" / "Vera" / "Bring the Boys Back Home" / "Comfortably Numb" / "In the Flesh" / "Run Like Hell" / "Waiting for the Worms" / "Stop" / "The Trial" / "The Tide Is Turning"

Amused to Death
September 1, 1992
"The Ballad of Bill Hubbard" / "What God Wants (Part 1)" / "Perfect Sense (Parts 1-2)" / "The Bravery of Being Out of Range" / "Late Home Tonight (Parts 1-2)" / "Too

Much Rope" / "What God Wants (Part 3)" / "Watching TV" / "Three Wishes" / "It's a Miracle" / "Amused to Death"

PINK FLOYD

Shine On box set
November 9, 1992
Comprises: *A Saucerful of Secrets, Meddle, The Dark Side of the Moon, Wish You Were Here, Animals, The Wall, A Momentary Lapse of Reason* (all remastered) plus *The Early Singles* EP
"Arnold Layne" / "Candy and a Currant Bun" / "See Emily Play" / "Scarecrow" / "Apples and Oranges" / "Paint Box" / "It Would Be So Nice" / "Julia Dream" / "Point Me at the Sky" / "Careful with That Axe, Eugene"

The Wall Live—Is There Anybody Out There?
April 10, 2000
MC: Atmos / "In the Flesh?" / "The Thin Ice" / "Another Brick in the Wall (Part 1)" / "The Happiest Days of Our Lives" / "Another Brick in the Wall (Part 2)" / "Mother" / "Goodbye Blue Sky" / "Empty Spaces" / "What Shall We Do Now?" / "Young Lust" / "One of My Turns" / "Don't Leave Me Now" / "Another Brick in the Wall (Part 3)" / "The Last Few Bricks" / "Goodbye Cruel World" / "Hey You" / "Is There Anybody Out There?" / "Nobody Home" / "Vera" / "Bring the Boys Back Home" / "Comfortably Numb" / "The Show Must Go On" / MC: Atmos / "In the Flesh" / "Run Like Hell" / "Waiting for the Worms" / "Stop" / "The Trial" / "Outside the Wall"

ROGER WATERS

In the Flesh
December 5, 2000
"In the Flesh" / "The Happiest Days of Our Lives" / "Another Brick in the Wall (Part 2)" / "Mother" / "Get Your Filthy Hands Off My Desert" / "Southampton Dock" / "Pigs on the Wing (Part 1)" / "Dogs" / "Welcome to the Machine" / "Wish You Were Here" / "Shine On You Crazy Diamond (Parts 1-8)" / "Set the Controls for the Heart of the Sun" / "Breathe (In the Air)" / "Time" / "Money" / "The Pros and Cons of Hitch Hiking Part 11 (aka 5:06 a.m.—Every Stranger's Eyes)" / "Perfect Sense (Parts I and II)" / "The Bravery of Being Out of Range" / "It's a Miracle" / "Amused to Death" / "Brain Damage" / "Eclipse" / "Each Small Candle"

PINK FLOYD

Echoes—The Best Of
November 6, 2001

"Astronomy Domine" / "See Emily Play" / "The Happiest Days of Our Lives" / "Another Brick in the Wall (Part 2)" / "Echoes" / "Hey You" / "Marooned" / "The Great Gig in the Sky" / "Set the Controls for the Heart of the Sun" / "Money" / "Keep Talking" / "Sheep" / "Sorrow" / "Shine On You Crazy Diamond (Parts 1-7)" / "Time" / "The Fletcher Memorial Home" / "Comfortably Numb" / "When the Tigers Broke Free" / "One of These Days" / "Us and Them" / "Learning to Fly" / "Arnold Layne" / "Wish You Were Here" / "Jugband Blues" / "High Hopes" / "Bike"

ROGER WATERS

Flickering Flame — The Solo Years Volume 1
May 6, 2002
"Knockin' On Heaven's Door" / "Too Much Rope" / "The Tide Is Turning" / "Perfect Sense (Parts 1 & 2)" / "Three Wishes" / "Every Stranger's Eyes" / "Who Needs Information" / "Each Small Candle" / "Flickering Flame" (demo) / "Towers of Faith" / "Radio Waves" / "Lost Boys Calling" (original demo)

PINK FLOYD

The Dark Side of the Moon — 30th anniversary SACD
March 31, 2003
"Speak to Me" / "Breathe (In the Air)" / "On the Run" / "Time" / "The Great Gig in the Sky" / "Money" / "Us and Them" / "Any Colour You Like" / "Brain Damage" / "Eclipse"

ROGER WATERS

To Kill the Child/Leaving Beirut
January 3, 2005
"To Kill the Child" / "Leaving Beirut"

Ça Ira
September 27, 2005
"The Gathering Storm" / "Overture" / "A Garden in Vienna 1765" / "Madame Antoine, Madame Antoine" / "Kings, Sticks and Birds" / "Honest bird, simple bird" / "I want to be King" / "Let us break all the shields" / "The Grievances of the People" / "France in Disarray" / "To laugh is to know how to live" / "Slavers, Landlords, Bigots at your door" / "The Fall of the Bastille" / "To freeze in the dead of night" / "So to the streets in the pouring rain" / "Dances and Marches" / "Now Hear Ye!" / "Flushed with wine" / "The Letter" / "My dear Cousin Bourbon of Spain" / "The ship of state is all at sea" / "Silver, Sugar and Indigo" / "To the Windward Isles" / "The Papal Edict" / "In Paris there's a rumble under the ground" / "The Fugitive King" / "But the Marquis of Boulli has a trump card up his sleeve" / "To take your hat off" / "The echoes never fade from that

fusillade" / "The Commune de Paris" / "Vive la Commune de Paris" / "The National Assembly is confused" / "The Execution of Louis Capet" / "Adieu Louis for you it's over" / "Marie Antoinette—The Last Night on Earth" / "Adieu my good and tender sister" / "Liberty" / "And in the bushes where they survive"

PINK FLOYD

Oh by the Way—mini vinyl album replicas studio album box set
December 10, 2007
Comprises: *The Piper at the Gates of Dawn, A Saucerful of Secrets, More, Umma-gumma, Atom Heart Mother, Meddle, Obscured by Clouds, The Dark Side of the Moon, Wish You Were Here, Animals, The Wall, The Final Cut, A Momentary Lapse of Reason, The Division Bell*, with all reproduced original inserts (posters, stickers, etc.), a pair of coasters, and a fortieth anniversary poster

Discovery box set
September 26, 2011
Comprises 2011 remasters: *The Piper at the Gates of Dawn, A Saucerful of Secrets, More, Ummagumma, Atom Heart Mother, Meddle, Obscured by Clouds, Dark Side of the Moon, Wish You Were Here, Animals, The Wall, The Final Cut, A Momentary Lapse of Reason, The Division Bell*. Each album also available individually as a Discovery edition with new packaging alongside its 2012 remaster.

The Dark Side of the Moon—Experience edition
September 26, 2011
Disc one: *The Dark Side of the Moon* (remaster). Disc two: *The Dark Side of the Moon* live 1974 Wembley.

The Dark Side of the Moon—Immersion edition
September 26, 2011
The Dark Side of the Moon (remaster) / *The Dark Side of the Moon* live 1974 Wembley / *The Dark Side of the Moon*, James Guthrie 2003 5.1 Surround Mix in standard resolution audio at 448 kbps / *The Dark Side of the Moon*, James Guthrie 2003 5.1 Surround Mix in high resolution audio at 640 kbps / *The Dark Side of the Moon*, Alan Parsons Quad Mix in standard resolution audio at 448 kbps / *The Dark Side of the Moon*, Alan Parsons Quad Mix in high resolution audio at 640 kbps / *Live in Brighton 1972* / *The Dark Side of the Moon*, 2003 documentary / Concert Screen Films (60 min. total): *British Tour 1974, French Tour 1974, North American Tour 1975* / *The Dark Side of the Moon*, 1972 Early Album Mix engineered by Alan Parsons (previously unreleased) / "The Hard Way" (from *Household Objects*) / "Us and Them," Richard Wright Demo (previously unreleased) / "The Travel Sequence," live June 1972 Brighton (previously unreleased) / "The Mortality Sequence," live June 1972 Brighton (previously unreleased) / "Any Colour You Like," live June 1972 Brighton (previously unreleased) /

"The Travel Sequence," studio recording 1972 (previously unreleased) / "Money," Roger Waters's Demo (previously unreleased)

Six discs plus booklet designed by Storm Thorgerson (less than two years before his death on April 18, 2013), exclusive photo book by Jill Furmanovsky, Storm Thorgerson Art Print, five collectors' cards featuring art and comments by Storm Thorgerson, replica of *The Dark Side of the Moon* tour ticket, replica backstage pass, scarf, three black marbles, nine coasters featuring early Storm Thorgerson design sketches, and a twelve-page credits booklet.

A Foot in the Door—The Best Of
November 7, 2011
"Hey You" / "See Emily Play" / "The Happiest Days of Our Lives" / "Another Brick in the Wall part 2" / "Have a Cigar" / "Wish You Were Here" / "Time" / "The Great Gig in the Sky" / "Money" / "Comfortably Numb" / "High Hopes" / "Learning to Fly" / "The Fletcher Memorial Home" / "Shine On You Crazy Diamond" (edit) / "Brain Damage" / "Eclipse"

Wish You Were Here—Experience edition
November 7, 2011
Disc one: *Wish You Were Here* (remaster). Disc two: "Shine On You Crazy Diamond (Parts 1-6)" live at Wembley / "You've Got To Be Crazy" live at Wembley / "Raving and Drooling" live at Wembley / "Wine Glasses" (from *Household Objects*) / "Have a Cigar" alternative version / "Wish You were Here" featuring Stéphane Grappelli

Wish You Were Here—Immersion edition
November 7, 2011
Wish You Were Here (remaster) / "Shine On You Crazy Diamond (Parts 1-6)" live at Wembley / "You've Got to Be Crazy" live at Wembley / "Raving and Drooling" live at Wembley / "Wine Glasses" (from *Household Objects*) / "Have a Cigar" alternative version / "Wish You Were Here" featuring Stéphane Grappelli / "Wish You Were Here," James Guthrie 2009 5.1 Surround Mix in standard resolution audio at 448 kbps / "Wish You Were Here," James Guthrie 2009 5.1 Surround Mix in high resolution audio at 640 kbps / "Wish You Were Here," Original Mix / "Wish You Were Here," Quad Mix in standard resolution audio at 448 kbps / "Wish You Were Here," Quad Mix in high resolution audio at 640 kbps / Concert Screen Films: *Shine On You Crazy Diamond Intro, Shine On You Crazy Diamond, Welcome to the Machine* animated clip, Storm Thorgerson short film

Five discs plus booklet designed by Storm Thorgerson, photo book edited by Jill Furmanovsky, an exclusive Storm Thorgerson Art Print, five collectors' cards featuring art and comments by Storm Thorgerson, replica of *Wish You Were Here* tour ticket, replica backstage pass, scarf, three clear marbles, nine coasters, and a twelve-page credits booklet.

The Wall—Experience edition
February 27, 2012
The Wall (remaster) / Program 1—Roger Waters Original Demo and Band Demos:
"Prelude (Vera Lynn)"—Roger's Original Demo / "Another Brick in the Wall (Part
1)"—Band Demo / "Thin Ice"—Band Demo / "Goodbye Blue Sky"—Band Demo /
"Teacher, Teacher"—Band Demo / "Another Brick in the Wall (Part 2)"—Band
Demo / "Empty Spaces"—Band Demo / "Young Lust"—Band Demo / "Mother"—
Band Demo / "Don't Leave Me Now"—Band Demo / "Sexual Revolution"—Band
Demo / "Another Brick in the Wall (Part 3)"—Band Demo / "Goodbye Cruel World"—
Band Demo // Program 2—Band Demos: "In the Flesh?" / "Thin Ice" / "Another Brick
in the Wall (Part 1)" / "The Happiest Days of Our Lives" / "Another Brick in the Wall
(Part 2)" / "Mother" // Program 3—Band Demos: "One of My Turns" / "Don't Leave
Me Now" / "Empty Spaces" / "Backs to the Wall" / "Another Brick in the Wall (Part
3)" / "Goodbye Cruel World" / "The Doctor (Comfortably Numb)" / "Run Like Hell"

The Wall—Immersion edition
February 27, 2012
The Wall (remaster) / *Is There Anybody Out There: The Wall Live 1980–81* (remaster) /
The Wall Work in Progress Part 1, 1979: Program 1—Excerpts from Roger Waters Origi-
nal Demo: "Prelude (Vera Lynn)" / "Another Brick in the Wall (Part 2)" / "Mother" /
"Young Lust" / "Another Brick in the Wall (Part 2)" / "Empty Spaces" / "Mother" /
"Backs to the Wall" / "Don't Leave Me Now" / "Goodbye Blue Sky" / "Don't Leave Me
Now" / "Another Brick in the Wall (Part 3)" / "Goodbye Cruel World" / "Hey You" /
"Is There Anybody Out There?" / "Vera" / "Bring the Boys Back Home" / "The Show
Must Go On" / "Waiting for the Worms" / "Run Like Hell" / "The Trial" / "Outside the
Wall" // Program 2—Roger Waters Original Demo and Band Demos: "Prelude (Vera
Lynn)"—Roger Waters Original Demo" / "Another Brick in the Wall (Part 1)"—Band
Demo / "The Thin Ice"—Band Demo / "Goodbye Blue Sky"—Band Demo / "Teacher,
Teacher"—Band Demo / "Another Brick in the Wall (Part 2)"—Band Demo / "Empty
Spaces"—Band Demo / "Young Lust"—Band Demo / "Mother"—Band Demo / "Don't
Leave Me Now"—Band Demo / "Sexual Revolution"—Band Demo / "Another Brick
in the Wall (Part 3)"—Band Demo / "Goodbye Cruel World"—Band Demo // Pro-
gram 3—Band Demos: "In the Flesh?" / "The Thin Ice" / "Another Brick in the Wall
(Part 1)" / "The Happiest Days of Our Lives" / "Another Brick in the Wall (Part 2)" /
"Mother" / *The Wall Work In Progress Part 2, 1979*: Program 1—Roger Waters Original
Demos and Band Demos: "Is There Anybody Out There?"—Roger Waters Original
Demo / "Vera"—Roger Waters Original Demo / "Bring the Boys Back Home"—
Roger Waters Original Demo / "Hey You"—Band Demo / "The Doctor (Comfortably
Numb)"—Band Demo / "In the Flesh"—Band Demo / "Run Like Hell"—Band
Demo / "Waiting for the Worms"—Band Demo / "The Trial"—Band Demo / "The
Show Must Go On"—Band Demo / "Outside the Wall"—Band Demo / "The Thin

Ice Reprise"—Band Demo // Program 2—Band Demos: "Outside the Wall" / "It's Never Too Late" / "The Doctor (Comfortably Numb)" // Program 3—Band Demos: "One of My Turns" / "Don't Leave Me Now" / "Empty Spaces" / "Backs to the Wall" / "Another Brick in the Wall (Part 3) / "Goodbye Cruel World" // Program 4—David Gilmour Original Demos: "Comfortably Numb" / "Run Like Hell" / *The Happiest Days of Our Lives—Pink Floyd The Wall—Earls Court, 1980* (film) / *Another Brick in The Wall (Part 2)* promotional video restored in 2011 / *Behind the Wall Documentary* / Gerald Scarfe interview

Six discs plus booklet designed by Storm Thorgerson, photo book, Gerald Scarfe art print, four collectors' cards, replica tour ticket, replica backstage pass, scarf, prints/cards of Mark Fisher's stage drawings, three white marbles with a brick design, nine coasters, an eight-page credits booklet, and a handwritten lyric booklet.

ROGER WATERS

12-12-12: The Concert for Sandy Relief to Benefit the Robin Hood Relief Fund, Madison Square Garden
January 2013
"Another Brick in the Atlantic Wall Parts I, II & III" / "Us and Them" / "Comfortably Numb (featuring Eddie Vedder)"

Notes

Unless otherwise noted, all quoted material is drawn from my own interviews and conversations.

Chapter 1: Learning to Fly
5   "I've got nothing against the people . . ."—interview with Chris Welch, *Melody Maker*, August 5, 1967.
6   "We all had the opportunity . . ."—interview with Carol Clerk, *Uncut*, June 2004.

Chapter 2: Raving and Drooling
21   "strikingly handsome"—Pete Townshend, *Who I Am: A Memoir* (Harper, 2012).

Chapter 3: Let There Be More Light
37   "something Pete Townshend might have written . . ."—"Blind Date," *Melody Maker*, 1970.

Chapter 5: The Great Gig in the Sky
57   "*The Final Cut* was about how, with the introduction of the Welfare State . . ."—quoted in Mark Blake, *Comfortably Numb: The Inside Story of Pink Floyd* (Da Capo Press, 2008).

Chapter 6: Charade You Are
74   "Steve is an effective hustler . . ."—"Over the Wall: An interview with Roger Waters," Chris Salewicz, *Q*, August 1987.
76   "They forced me to resign . . ."—interview with Carol Clerk, *Uncut*, June 2004.

Chapter 7: Reset the Controls for the Heart of the Sun
84   "My [lawyer] told me over a year ago . . ."—"Roger Waters: Out of Troubled Waters," Mark Cooper, *The Guardian*, November 20, 1987.

89   "I'm completely different . . ."—"How Roger Waters rebuilt *The Wall*," Hugh Fielder, *Classic Rock*, June 2011.

95   "We're both passionate about the idea . . ."—"Roger Waters," Steve Turner, *Radio Times*, May 25, 1990.

96   "When I came to listen to the album again . . ."—"Roger Waters: The Wall in Berlin," Phil Sutcliffe, *Q*, September 1990.

Chapter 8: Wot's . . . uh the Deal?

105   "The line they give you is . . ."—interview with Richard Cromelin, *Los Angeles Times*, 1992.

Chapter 9: Emily, Playing

124   "I pinched the line . . ."— interview with Nick Jones, *Melody Maker*, April 1, 1967.

Chapter 10: The Death of Amusement

137   "When I look back . . ."—quoted in Karl Dallas, *Bricks in the Wall* (Sure Sellers, 1987).

137   "Trying to talk to him was like talking to a brick wall . . ."—quoted in "Wish You Were Here," *Mojo*, September 1996.

142   "The Cheetah Club was the occasion . . ."—Nick Mason, *Inside Out: A Personal History of Pink Floyd* (Chronicle Books, 2005).

Chapter 11: The Near Side of the Moon

162   "Syd had maintained fairly . . ." Malcolm Jones, *The Making of the Madcap Laughs* (private publication, 1982).

Chapter 12: A Slice of My Pie

176   "with the absolute minimum of creative . . ."—Ron Geesin quoted by Mike Barnes, *The Wire*, September 2003.

Chapter 13: More of Those Days

182   "One lives and learns . . ."—"Over the Wall: An interview with Roger Waters," Chris Salewicz, *Q*, August 1987.

183   "We're writing a ballet . . ."—"An Interview with Pink Floyd," Mike Quigley, *The Georgia Straight*, October 14, 1970.

184   "I'd like to help the revolution . . ."—interview with Chris Welch, *Melody Maker*, October 9, 1971.

184   "Altruism and power politics . . ."—interview with Chris Welch, *Melody Maker*, October 9, 1971.

187 "They were so stuck up . . ."—Douglas Smith quoted by Carol Clerk, *The Saga of Hawkwind* (Omnibus, 2004).

187 "I fell in love . . ."—Pete Townshend, *Who I Am: A Memoir* (Harper, 2012).

Chapter 14: Forward, He Cried

199 "The way our music . . ."—*ZigZag*, 1973.

199 "the sun and the moon . . ."—quoted in Karl Dallas, *Bricks in the Wall* (Sure Sellers, 1987).

199 "I was getting strong urges . . ."—"The True Story of The Dark Side of the Moon," Phil Sutcliffe and Pete Henderson, *Mojo*, March 1988.

206 "There was a moment . . ."—"The True Story of The Dark Side of the Moon," Phil Sutcliffe and Pete Henderson, *Mojo*, March 1988.

206 "If you'd played this to an average record-company executive . . ."—"Pink Floyd: Dark Side of the Moon," Ian MacDonald, *New Musical Express*, February 23, 1974.

Chapter 15: Shining On Crazily

211 "Syd is now being glorified . . ."—"Barrett: The Definitive Visual Companion," Mick Farren, *Classic Rock*, June 2011.

215 "Roger's infidelity . . ."—Nick Mason, *Inside Out: A Personal History of Pink Floyd*, (Chronicle Books, 2005).

218 "Roger wrote the words . . ."—interview with Pete Erskine, *NME*, November 23, 1974.

218 "there were changes . . ."—"Pink Floyd: More Gritty, Less Giddy," Alan Betrock, *Circus*, October 1975.

Epilogue

245 "I'm not sure what it will be called . . ."—televised interview with Eric Ripert, *On the Table*, November 2011.

247 "When I wrote it, it was mainly . . ."—"How Roger Waters Rebuilt The Wall," Hugh Fielder, *Classic Rock*, June 2011.

Bibliography

Blake, Mark. *Pigs Might Fly: The Inside Story of Pink Floyd*. Aurum Press Limited, 2007.

Chapman, Rob. *Syd Barrett: A Very Irregular Head*. Faber & Faber, 2010.

Dallas, Karl. *Pink Floyd: Bricks in the Wall*. Spi Books, 1987.

Fitch, Vernon. *A Collectors Guide to Pink Floyd Video Recordings*. Pink Floyd Archives, 1998.

Fitch, Vernon. *A Collectors Guide to Pink Floyd Audio Recordings 1966–1983 and Solo Tours*. Pink Floyd Archives, 1998.

Harris, John. *The Dark Side of the Moon: The Making of the Pink Floyd Masterpiece*. Da Capo Press, 2005.

Hodges, Rick and Ian Priston. *Embryo: A Pink Floyd Chronology 1966–1971*. Cherry Red Books, 1998.

Jones, Cliff. *Echoes: The Stories Behind Every Pink Floyd Song*. Omnibus Press, 1996.

Jones, Malcolm. *The Making of the Madcap Laughs*. Private publication, 1982.

Mabbett, Andy. *The Complete Guide to the Music of Pink Floyd*. Omnibus Press, 1995.

MacDonald, Bruno, ed. *Pink Floyd: Through the Eyes of the Band, its Fans, Friends, and Foes*. Sidgwick and Jackson, 1996.

Mason, Nick. *Inside Out: A Personal History of Pink Floyd*. Weidenfeld & Nicolson Books, 200.

Miles, Barry and Andy Mabbett. *Pink Floyd: The Visual Documentary, Twenty-Fifth Anniversary Edition*. Omnibus Press, 1994.

Miles, Barry. *Pink Floyd: The Early Years*. Omnibus Press, 2006.

Miles, Barry. *Pink Floyd: The Illustrated Discography*. Omnibus Press, 1981.

Palacios, Julian. *Lost in the Woods: Syd Barrett and the Pink Floyd*. Boxtree Books, 1998.

Parker, David. *Random Precision: Recording the Music of Syd Barrett 1965–1974*. Cherry Red Books, 2001.

Povey, Glenn and Ian Russell. *Pink Floyd: In the Flesh — The Complete Performance History*. Bloomsbury Publishing, 1997.

Povey, Glenn. *Echoes: The Complete History of Pink Floyd*. Mind Head Publishing, 2007.

Sanders, Rick. *Pink Floyd*. Futura Publications, 1976.

Scarfe, Gerald. *The Making of Pink Floyd The Wall*. Weidenfeld & Nicholson, 2010.

Schaffner, Nicholas. *Saucerful of Secrets: The Pink Floyd Odyssey*. Harmony Books, 1991.

Shea, Stuart. *Pink Floyd FAQ: Everything Left to Know . . . and More!* Backbeat Books, 2009.

Taylor, Phil. Pink Floyd: *The Black Strat—A History of David Gilmour's Black Fender Stratocaster, Third Edition*. Hal Leonard Books, 2010.

Thorgerson, Storm and Peter Curzon. *Mind Over Matter: The Images of Pink Floyd, Fourth Edition*. Omnibus Press, 2007.

Watkinson, Mike and Pete Anderson. *Crazy Diamond: Syd Barrett and the Dawn of Pink Floyd*. Omnibus Press, 2006.

Welch, Chris. *Pink Floyd: Learning to Fly*. Castle Communications, 1994.

Acknowledgments

This is not the first time I have written about Roger Waters and/or Pink Floyd. A band that I have been listening to for forty years has raised its head in my writings on innumerable occasions, frequently in a form and fashion that I still consider applicable today. In particular, the chapters concerning *Atom Heart Mother* and *The Dark Side of the Moon*, which here are based upon shorter pieces written for *Goldmine* magazine, and my discussions of the group's earliest days, which grew from chapters within my now out-of-print publication *Space Daze* (Cleopatra Books, 1994). Finally, certain ruminations on the life and times of Syd Barrett were likewise first raised in *Pandemonium*, a free monthly newspaper that circulated around Seattle/Tacoma during the early to mid-1990s.

I would also like to acknowledge the contributions to this book made by a long list of past interviewees and acquaintances, often discussing Pink Floyd within interviews that were nominally concerned with other matters entirely: Richard Wright, Steve O'Rourke, Tony Secunda, Tony Baws, Bryan Morrison, Larry Fast, Nik Turner, John Alder, Tim Renwick, Phil May, Dick Taylor, Ron Howden, June Child, Dave Kilminster, Roye Albrighton, Michael Bruce, Dave Brock, Mick Farren, Malcolm Jones, John Peel, Joe Boyd, Peter Wood, Norman Smith, Richard Thompson, Graham Parker, Tim Cross, David O'List, Brian Perera, and anyone else I've forgotten. Thank you!

Also to Amy Hanson, for her tireless championing of *Animals* and enduring love for *The Final Cut*; Mike Edison, for commissioning this book; Brian Luster, for copyediting; and to Bernadette Malavarca at Backbeat Books, for bringing it to life.

And finally, thanks to all the people who threw ingredients of their own into the stew. Rita and Eric (but especially Rita, who made *The Wall* sound so good!), Karen and Todd, Linda and Larry, Jo-Ann Greene, Jen, Dave and Sue, Gaye and Tim, Oliver, Trevor, Toby, Barb East, Bateerz and family, the gremlins who live in the heat pump, and to John the Superstar, the demon of the dry well.

Index